Introduction to Industrial Relations

Introduction to Industrial Relations

Mike Vincent

Senior Lecturer in Social Science and Curriculum Development
Brunel Technical College

HEINEMANN: LONDON

This book is dedicated to my wife,
Eileen, who taught me a great deal
about negotiation and 'free'
collective bargaining!

William Heinemann Ltd
10 Upper Grosvenor Street, London W1X 9PA
LONDON   MELBOURNE   TORONTO
JOHANNESBURG   AUCKLAND

© Mike Vincent 1983
First published 1983

434 92200 5

Filmset by Deltatype, Ellesmere Port
Printed by Redwood Burn Limited,
Trowbridge, Wiltshire

Preface

This book has been written for BEC students studying industrial relations. It is essentially geared for National Level students but there are topics and themes covered within the book that will almost certainly be of use to both General and Higher National students as well. In addition, other students who could well find this text useful include those on introductory management and trade union courses, TEC students on general and communication studies modules and students in colleges of further and higher education on social, industrial and general studies courses who want some basic insights into the world of industrial relations. In all, it is an introductory text to what is a complicated, but fascinating area of study.

First of all, it is important to stress that the book is a very basic introduction. It has been deliberately designed to be just that. It reflects BEC philosophy in that it attempts to be truly inter- and multi-disciplinary. The four BEC themes are woven in throughout the book. It tries to involve the reader actively through assignment work. It has been produced to be useful and stimulating and it can be used by one individual, or by a group of individuals, to explore the complexities of industrial relations. It tries to explain matters in a simple way, yet, at the same time, gives the reader a real understanding of a very wide, and important, area of human behaviour.

There are very many people to whom I owe a great deal for their help in preparing this book. My sincerest thanks go to John Pursaill and Wendy Stafford at BEC for their genuine support through many difficult initial drafts. I would like to thank generally all those individuals who have contributed in some way, and, in particular, especial thanks must go to those people who very kindly allowed me some of their valuable time to interview them. Special mention must be made of my wife for her patient help in the typing and retyping of the manuscript and of family, friends and colleagues who tolerated my continuous ramblings about the project. I would like to thank the staff of Heinemann for their support and guidance, and, lastly, but by no means least, I want to thank all my students for their interest and questions that first made me think of writing this book.

Mike Vincent

Contents

This book is made up of the following three parts:

These three sections are further split into fourteen chapters, four in Section One, four in Section Two and six in the Third and final Section.

Section One

Chapter 1
Today's subject for discussion is industrial relations . . .

Objectives

At the end of this chapter you should be able to:

1 understand some of the events taking place in the industrial relations field;
2 realize how complex industrial relations are;
3 list the main 'players' on the industrial relations 'stage'.

THIS CHAPTER COVERS the following subjects:

1 an introduction to the field of industrial relations;
2 the major groups of people who have a part to play in industrial relations.

Three major groups will be covered:

(a) workers/unions
(b) employers
(c) government.

In this, the first chapter of the book, I want to introduce you to the vast, complex and fascinating world of industrial relations. Quite often when I talk to students about industrial relations they say things like 'Oh, I'm not interested in subjects like industrial relations and politics, they're boring'. In my view, nothing could be further from the truth. Industrial relations is all about people, money, work and communication. It's an area of study that's of interest and value to all of us. Let me give you an example to push home that fact.

In our modern, industrial life, work (whether we like it or not) has an importance for all of us. Although I shall say more about this in Chapter 5 ('You've got to work at it . . .') it's an important point to make right from the word 'go'. Whether we work in factories or offices, in the home or outside it, whether we think that work is more important than leisure or that leisure is the reason for working, whether we have a job (in the accepted sense of the word) or not, there can be no doubt that the idea of and the activities related to work all have an effect and an influence on our everyday lives.

Having said that it follows very logically that if work is important to people then the place of work is also going to have an impact on our lives.

'Industrial relations: everybody's an expert; everybody has a view. There have been some real 'rousers' in recent years, for example, the great 'industrial democracy' debate seen in many different ways by different kinds of people. . . . They are big public issues and everybody is interested. . . .'

Source: courtesy Alan Swinden, CBI

Work and Politics: Who Cares?

'In their rating of the values of life, most British people put their health first. A slightly selfish response, perhaps, but closely followed by an attachment to family life.

'The community at large is a matter of importance to most of the population, but they see its value not so much in terms of a welfare state as in a stable, ordered environment. 'Law and Order' figures in third place in the Birds Eye Barometer of Life's Values, 1982.

'Other aspects of community life get short shrift. Most people would seem to be quite happy if all politicians lost their deposits, while religion tolls no more than a passing bell for fewer than half of them.

'Love, friendship, the home, money and personal appearance all find a high place in most people's rating of the value of life. 'A Gallup Survey specially commissioned for the Birds Eye Report established as the ten most important values of life, in order:

1 Health; 2 Family life; 3 Law and order; 4 Friendship; 5 House or flat; 6 Love; 7 Personal appearance; 8 Money; 9 Steady employment; 10 Job satisfaction'

'Travel, sport, religion and politics fall well behind, with fewer than half the population rating them 'important.''

Source: The Quest for Values Birds Eye Food Ltd/Gallup, 1982

We earn money there. We make friends there. What happens there affects us in many ways. As we shall see later in the book the workplace brings together those four BEC themes that we mentioned earlier that are important in all our lives; the themes of work, money, spoken and written communication. All of these are highlighted at the workplace. If that's the case then it's very easy and very clear to see how important industrial relations has to be for all of us. Talking about money and working conditions, job security and relationships with people at work, all these matters bring us straight into the field of industrial relations so let's make a start and see what it's all about.

Having emphasized the importance of industrial relations in our everyday work (and leisure and non-work lives) we now need to examine in a little more depth the exact meaning of a phrase so often used yet so often used with very little meaning on the part of those hearing it, industrial relations. Here you immediately bump against a problem in that it's rather a vague term. It covers such a wide range of human activities.

At its most basic we can say that when we talk about industrial relations we are talking about the complex web of relationships and discussions that are continually going on between employers, trade unionists and workers. It's as simple and complicated as that all in one go! This book will try to show you some of the issues, problems and solutions that come up as these relationships have developed and as they continue to develop and grow. Hopefully, by the

end of the book you will have a basic, but fundamentally, realistic picture of this important area of study.

However, there is one thing about which most people actively involved in industrial relations will agree. It's not an easy life! Negotiations, whether they are at factory level with the workers, or at national level with the government, can be very tough going indeed. If the negotiations break down (and the mass media have a field day when this happens) the consequences, perhaps in the form of a strike if all else fails, can be very, very serious indeed. It is not difficult to see how, when a strike occurs, lives can be disrupted. What is often forgotten and taken for granted is that the majority of the time industrial life in many firms is free of open industrial conflict. This state of affairs we accept without question.

To summarize, then, we can say that this chapter will examine those groups involved in industrial relations who, generally speaking, are able to keep the wheels of industry moving, even though there are often real conflicts of interest between the groups concerned.

Your final view of industrial relations may very well differ from that of other readers which in turn may well differ from that of various 'experts' in the field (shop stewards, full-time trade union officers, managers, workers and individuals in government and teachers of the subject). There is absolutely no harm in this since observers of industrial relations have many different views. (See the newspaper extract on p. 11 for some examples and quickly glance through the index to see some of the individuals and groups whose names you may well recognize as an everyday part of industrial life in Britain today.) Once you have done this you may find it useful to do the assignment on p. 11 which enables you to 'capture' some of the different viewpoints encountered.

Incidentally, it is often the case when talking about industrial relations that many people will say that certain facts and ideas are 'common sense'. Beware of this idea! I think it's very important to point out immediately that what is 'common sense' to one person (or one group) may not be seen to be 'common sense' to another individual or group. For example, it may seem 'senseless' to a member of the general public when workers in a contracting industry (such as the steel industry) go out on strike. After all, it seems 'sensible' to think that any strike in that industry would be suicide for the future of the firm. However, the situation could appear very different when seen from the side of the workforce. They know that they are in a contracting industry. They may also believe or know that the plant in which they are working will be closed in the near future. 'Common sense' may tell these men that it is worth having a good pay rise *before* the plant closes because they know very well that once the plant and their jobs go there will be no more pay, let alone pay rises. The '(wo)man in the street' may think that the most important aspect of the whole affair is the 'economic state of the country' or the industry. There's a slightly different 'common sense' at work in this viewpoint.

So keep in mind as you read the book that what is 'common sense' to one group may not be seen as such by another. It's not that the worker or the manager are being awkward or bloodyminded when there is a conflict of interest. It is simply that they want different things from the industrial relationship.

Assignment 1.1

I want you to think about the term 'INDUSTRIAL RELATIONS'. Try to list some of the relationships within industry and commerce by picking out some of the *groups* involved:

    WORKERS–MANAGERS
and some of the *jobs* they do
    WORKERS WORK – what kinds of work?
    MANAGERS MANAGE – what do they manage?
    SHOP STEWARDS NEGOTIATE – with whom and for whom?

Once you have done this go on and try writing your *own* definition of '*industrial relations*'. If possible, ask friends, colleagues, relatives, etc., etc., to do the same tasks and compare and contrast your ideas and statements with theirs.

Ideally, the very best things you can do is to contact an industrial relations' practitioner (that is somebody actually involved in industrial relations, for example, a trade unionist or a manager) and talk to them. Contact local firms and unions wherever possible and discover in what ways the 'experts' ' view is the same as, or differs from, your own and that of your friends, etc.

Sense and Nonsense

Parliamentary Picket

Civil servant strikers in the 1981 dispute with their employer, the government, made use of the above slogan in a protest outside the House of Commons. By all accounts only one Downing Street worker stopped.

The key question always to bear in mind whenever discussing industrial relations is that, when a plea is made for a return to 'common sense', we need to ask ourselves 'with whose common sense are we interested and concerned'?

Is it the workers', the unions', the managements' or the governments' 'common sense'? They may be very different.

Hold down price of workers' wages	Push up level of workers' wages
Try to get more work from the workers	Try to get less work for the workers (for example, a shorter working week)
Keep and gain more control over its own developments	Try to gain (perhaps) more control over the management of work

We've talked a little about the importance of industrial relations and we have been introduced to the term. I now want to look at the various groups of 'actors' on the 'stage' of industrial relations. Like any theatre we must remember that the production, in order to be successful, relies a good deal on people out of the public eye. They are the men and women who rarely make the headlines but who do a large amount of work, quietly and effectively, throughout the year. When a crisis occurs, as it obviously will from time to time, we all see and hear politicians, trade union leaders and managers of large firms being interviewed on the television. What is all too often forgotten are the large numbers of managers and trade unionists (paid and unpaid) who ensure that small problems and issues at 'shop floor' level do not escalate into a major dispute. Industrial relations work is not glamourous work by any means! There is much unremitting toil by all those involved often with very little praise and reward other than a good job well done.

In looking then at who is actually involved in industrial relations I want to take a somewhat simplified picture and look at:

WHO the 'actors' are
WHAT THEY DO and what
their parts are in the industrial
relations 'production'
WHAT THE RELATIONSHIPS
ARE between the main players

If we take each of these points in turn we can

look much more closely at the whole process of industrial relations.

I have divided these 'actors' up into *three* main groups (although there are other important agencies involved: *see* p. 6).

1 **Workers** and the people who represent them (i.e. **trade unions** and the Trades Union Congress or TUC)

2 The **management** and the people who represent them (i.e. employers' associations and the Confederation of British Industry or CBI)

3 The **government**: that is the officials and the individuals who represent the government (such as the civil service, local government, etc.).

The first of these groups, the trade unions, were set up to represent their members, namely the workers in a firm, office, factory, shop, school, etc. It is important to remember this basic fact because it means that unions are responsible to workers first and foremost and not to management or government. Unions and their officials do not manage the members. They represent the members' views. Unions are owned by the members, who regularly pay contributions to it. Some of this money is used to pay for the running of the union for example, the salaries of full-time officials and to provide workers with benefits of certain kinds (for sickness, strike, etc.) and also, if the union is affiliated* to the

---

* **Affiliate** (here) the attachment of trade unions to the TUC: (generally) the attachment of organized bodies to a larger body or organization.

'Solve Problems before they become Problems'

Often management and unions are seen as 'them' and 'us'. The following passage emphasizes the importance of working together in industrial relations.

'*The industrial dispute we aim to prevent is one that would take place in five or ten years' time. To prevent it, we begin talking now – not about wage differentials but about other things, horses, fishing, music or football.*'
'*We have first to establish that we (the managers) are men with names, personalities, interests and, possibly, weaknesses. We are not 'they' but Tom, Dick and Harry. We have next to show that the men on the shop floor are not mere personnel but are characters known to us by name and personality. They are Bill, Sam and Bob. . . .*

'*It should be possible to create a man-to-man relationship but it will take time and effort. When you are known as a man among men you can set out to prove that you are also a man to be trusted. When you promise to keep quiet about something, you keep quiet about it. You prove over the years that what you say is the truth, that what you promise you will do.*
Then, at long last, a crisis comes and you realize that an industrial dispute is possible. Knowing your men as you do, you hear of the trouble long before it starts. The probable result is that it never starts at all. You are there first and you are a man they will believe. It may seem, and it is, a laborious process, but there is no other way.'

Source: Communicate, *C. Northcote Parkinson and Nigel Rowe, Pan, 1979*

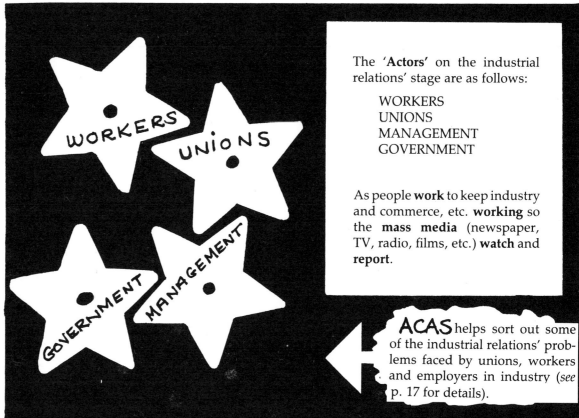

'*The people who are involved in industrial relations in an industry should have an in-depth knowledge of the industry. There are far too many people, particularly on the management side, who become involved in industrial relations and who really are square pegs in round holes because they:*

(a) don't have an in-depth knowledge of the industry and;

(b) have very little, if any, understanding of the emotions of people and industrial relations is all about people; it's all about individuals either on a single or collective basis.

So these are two prerequisites.'

Source: courtesy Alex Ferry, Confederation of Shipbuilding and Engineering Unions (CSEU)

The '**Actors**' on the industrial relations' stage are as follows:

WORKERS
UNIONS
MANAGEMENT
GOVERNMENT

As people **work** to keep industry and commerce, etc. **working** so the **mass media** (newspaper, TV, radio, films, etc.) **watch** and **report**.

ACAS helps sort out some of the industrial relations' problems faced by unions, workers and employers in industry (*see* p. 17 for details).

TUC, to pay the affiliation fee. On top of the union subscription there is what is known as a **levy** (or 'tax') which union members can pay if they wish. This levy is used for political purposes, namely that of providing funds for the Labour Party. (*See* Chapter 9 for further information on the relationships between the unions and politics.) Any money remaining is invested.

I want now to go on to take a general look at the ways in which trade unions are organized. However, I think that before doing that I have to issue a word of warning. Trade unions are like houses, they come in all shapes and sizes. Some are small and compact, others are large and well spread out. Some are to be found all over the country while others are found only in specific

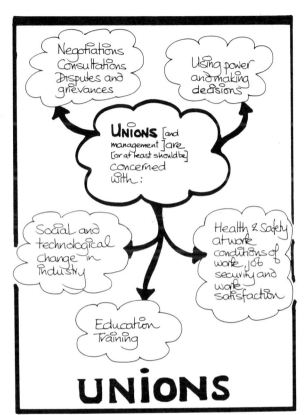

UNIONS

areas serving specific industries, perhaps.

It's very important to remember, therefore, that unions vary a good deal in the ways in which they are structured and organized. An example might help here, I think. Contrast the life and problems of a union official in a small union, working from a poky office and with no clerical help with that of an official from a large union, working as a member of a team from a modern, regional office and working, not on his own, but

with the back-up of research and administrative staff. So, remember that, although I'm now going to describe a *'typical'* union set-up, there are very real differences *between* unions. They are definitely not all the same even though they do have features in common.

Unions are organized in the following ways. At the 'grass-roots' of the union (factory floor, office, shop, railway or dock yard, etc.) union members elect their own spokesperson. (S)he is generally known as the 'Shop Steward' or 'Representative'. Shop stewards are not paid for the work that they do on behalf of the union. They do, however, get time off from their work for union activities.

The shop steward speaks to management on behalf of the members on questions that need handling on the spot. It may have to do with pay rates for a particularly difficult or dirty job. It may have to do with safety at work. (S)he is the person who can keep the 'wheels oiled' to help the workplace run smoothly. The shop steward is an important person in getting the views of the employees across to management and in negotiating with the company concerned.

'*Full-time officers are often elected or appointed after they have given service as voluntary officers of the union. During this time they not only become widely known to local members but also develop those qualities and characteristics which are necessary in full-time officers. Experience, knowledge of their union and of the employers, negotiating skills, the ability to communicate, and the ability to identify with their membership usually outweigh their lack of formal qualifications, administrative expertise and even youthful vigour.*'

Source: Understanding Industrial Relations, *D. Farnham and J. Pimlott, Cassell Ltd, 1979*

Local Union Branch

What is it?

It's a local group of unionists usually based on a town or factory or a small group of factories

Who runs it?

The members.
They elect a branch:
  secretary
  chairperson
  committee
  delegates to the union's national conference

What does it do?

Besides dealing with local problems, it can send **resolutions** to the union's national conference which in turn determines union policy

Shop stewards belong to a local union branch. Above are a few questions and answers about the branch.

Tying the local and national levels together are the full-time union officials (who are paid by the union). They give help and advice to the local branches and represent members in wage negotiations which are held at national level.

National Level

Each union has a **National Executive Committee (NEC)**

What is it?

It's a committee which is elected either:
  1 at the union's national conference
or
  2 by a ballot of the members

Who runs it?

The members of the union through their representatives on the committee

What does it do?

It runs the union between conferences. (Union policy is made at the conference, but the NEC has control of the union between one conference and the next)

'The Trades Union Congress, as the central body co-ordinating the views of the trade union movement, gives advice on economic policy and a wide range of industrial and social matters. It does not itself intervene directly in collective bargaining with employers. . . . It provides a range of services to affiliated unions. . . . The TUC is financed by contributions from its affiliated organizations. Its annual income is about £2 million. . . . The day-to-day work of the TUC is carried out by a permanent staff of about a hundred and a number of General Council Committees.'

Source: NEDO Documents

Also at **national** level is the Trades Union Congress (TUC) where the trade unions come together to put their views to other interested and involved parties in industrial relations, such as the Government or the associations of employers representatives, the Confederation of British Industry (CBI).

I'll say more about the TUC in Chapter 2, but let us now move on to the second main group involved in industrial relations namely **management**. Just as there are a large number of different unions in industrial relations there are also a wide variety of 'managers' doing a wide variety of different jobs. Quite often it is hard to understand precisely what management is all about compared with the fairly easy access most

of us can have to union rule books, conferences and to union leaders' speeches and thoughts.

So, in the same way as we looked at the union branch and the NEC let us have a closer look at 'management'.

MANAGEMENT

As their name suggests, managers *'manage'* firms and businesses; but what exactly do they do when they *are* managing? In simple terms, they manage resources such as the premises and the land owned by the firm; the money and the

Assignment 1.2

Management: Some Questions

1 Check the dictionary definitions of the words:

   Manager
   Employer.

2 In what ways do you think that the relationship between the employer and the worker has changed over the last hundred years?

3 What gives the management of a firm the 'right to manage'?

4 List some of the skills you think you need to 'manage' people.

5 In what ways can you encourage people to work harder?

6 What problems do you think may arise when you try to work people harder in order to improve their productivity?

'. . . the quality of industrial relations, in my view, the state of industrial relations, will be influenced more by the management style and quality of management in that enterprise than by anything else. It's people above all other things. . . . You can point to well managed companies . . . in very difficult environments with unions known to be capable of being difficult who manage difficult situations and yet you never even hear about them! There are, of course, exceptions. There is always the possibility that even the best management will encounter a situation which blows up in its face. There are even troublemakers . . . ! There are some well documented cases of people throughout the ages who have gone from place to place and caused trouble and a place that has had no trouble has suddenly erupted. That can happen, but it's the exception.'

Source: courtesy Alan Swinden, CBI

Management

Who are they?	What is it?	What do they do?
All those who manage and run an organization. In these days these organizations are often very large, for example, ICI, British Rail, Marks & Spencer	A group of people who run organizations and who have special skills and resources to do just this. It also gives these people a 'right to manage' because they are Management'	They organize and manage. They try to improve the work performance of their workers. This is known as increasing productivity. A manager must get things done by organizing the work of others

machines that are needed to keep the firm going, and most important of all they manage the people who work for that firm. They organize the work of the workers and build up, along with the unions, good channels of communication. It is, of course, as well to remember that there are a great variety of managers. There are those running large firms and those running small- and medium-sized firms; those who run their own firms and those who are running other people's firms for them. There are firms who make products and firms who provide services and all of these need managing.

As there are wide varieties of manager, so there are wide varieties of employers and, in the same way as workers have trade unions to look after their interests, so managers and employers have special groups to look after theirs. These special groups are known as 'employers' associations' and one of their main jobs is to regulate and control relations between employers and workers. Employers from the same industry get together and agree the terms and conditions that they will then offer to workers in that industry. This happens, for example, in engineering where the employers have grouped themselves together to form the Engineering Employers' Federation (the EEF). In the same way, the various unions in the engineering industry have combined together to meet the employers. They too present a united front, in their case, through the Confederation of Shipbuilding and Engineering Unions (the CSEU).

Again, like the unions, there are a wide variety of employers' federations and they deal, not surprisingly, with a wide variety of matters.

Different People, Different View

In January 1981 the then Conservative Employment Secretary, Mr James Prior, released a discussion document (a 'Green Paper') which stressed, among other things, that good industrial relations cannot be brought about by legislation.

The following extracts (taken from *The Guardian* newspaper 16 January 1981) shows the reaction of different groups within the industrial relations field.

'*Mr David Basnett (leader of the GMBU and chairman of the TUC economic committee) said that actually to carry out the suggestions in the Green Paper ". . . would be the clearest declaration yet that the (Conservative) government do not recognize the right of trade unions to operate effectively in this country. The Department of Employment and the Government should be trying to find jobs for the three million unemployed – not just jobs for lawyers".'*
'*Mr Len Murray (general secretary of the TUC) said that there was "a latent (hidden) and often patent hostility to effective trade unionism" running through the Paper which did not come to grips with the real issue of industrial relations.'*
'*The CBI (employers' federation) welcomed the Green Paper and described it as a "useful contribution" to the debate on possible further legislation.'*
'*Mr Anthony Frodsham (director-general of the Engineering Employers' Federation) said "We are impressed by the Government's cautious, objective and responsible approach to delicate and complex industrial relations issues. Previous attempts to curb excessive union power have failed: now the achievement of a lasting solution based on wide public support is more essential than ever.'*

GMBATU	General and Municipal Boilermakers and Allied Trades' Union
TUC	Trades Union Congress
CBI	Confederation of British Industry
EEF	Engineering Employers' Federation

Unity is weakness?

'Too powerful for their own good – that may turn out to be the historians' verdict on British trade unions in the last quarter of the twentieth century.

'An American trade union leader (for example) will, very probably, have to live with the failure of his union to recruit members. AFL– CIO affiliated unions organize only 14 per cent of the workforce. But in some ways he sleeps easier in his bed at night than his British counterpart. For if he negotiates higher wages for his members, he can still legitimately claim that he is not mainly responsible for inflation in the United States, and that he is not pricing his country out of world markets.

'The buck does not stop with him.'

Source: editorial New Society 6 September, 1979

Watch events in British industrial relations over the next few years and see how this quote then applies in a changing world.

Some of these federations and associations provide back up services to firms, just like the TUC does for unions. Others discuss common problems for industry, like meeting foreign competition and the importance and impact of new laws on industrial relations.

Employers' associations really began to grow at the end of the last century at the same time as (and in reply to) the growth of the trade union movement (*see* Chapter 3). They often started on a *local* basis, and then later formed groups at national level. As time went by these, in turn, became more and more important for negotiating *nationally* with unions. Today, there is a wide variety of employers' associations, some of which are still locally based, others of which work at national level.

Over the last few years many companies (and for that matter many unions) have grown in size and so it is often easier for management and workers to negotiate at factory rather than national level. After all, individual firms do not have to join employers' associations and some large firms, such as the Ford Motor Company, for example, do not belong to any. They would rather talk to the unions at factory level. Often multinational companies prefer to bargain outside the framework provided by the employers' associations and so, in Britain at least, the power of these associations is often limited.

In addition, employers today frequently say that they are worried about the ways in which they believe the unions are getting too powerful and are out of control.

However, employers do have a major national group to look after its interests. This is the Confederation of British Industry (CBI).

The main controlling body of the CBI is its Council. Again like the TUC, the CBI holds an annual conference. This is attended by many employers and managers. The formal head of the CBI is its President who is elected for a two-year period. It is important to remember however, that the CBI has no power over individual firms. It cannot tell industrial firms what to do. Any influence the CBI has is exercised through persuasion and giving advice. The CBI is, in its relationships with the employers' groups, federations and associations, in very much the same position as the TUC is, in its relationships with the unions. Both the CBI and TUC can suggest and persuade. They *cannot* tell.

At this point a summary may be useful to help us see clearly the role of the CBI and in particular how it sees its job towards the government.

The CBI:

1 as we have seen does not engage in collective bargaining between unions and employers but does provide a wide variety of back-up services to its members who are involved in negotiations.
2 supports the **market system** in which goods and services are sold to and bought by people, major factors influencing people's decision to buy pro-

Confederation of British Industry

Who is in the CBI?

13 000+ individual companies; 200 trade associations. In all some 10 million people are employed in companies associated with the CBI, some large, some small. Indeed, one-quarter of all CBI members are companies with less than twenty employees. Member companies are involved in

1 agriculture
2 mining
3 manufacturing
4 construction
5 distribution/retail
6 finance, banking and insurance
7 the nationalized industries.

What is it?

It is the major national employers' organization set up in 1965. (The TUC was set up in 1868.) Like the TUC it is a collection of organizations which is financed by subscriptions from members (most of the money coming from individual companies).

What does it do?

It, again like the TUC, does not get involved in collective bargaining. It helps its members to help themselves by providing them with a wide variety of services (for example, in the legal and safety fields). It fights for the **market system** and the **profit motive** that underlies that system. It keeps an eye on what the government of the day does and offers help and guidance to governments so that it can, in turn, help its members.

duct 'A' rather than product 'B' being price and value for money.

3 supports and encourages the idea of the **profit motive** (If you have a successful product or service it will sell and will make large profits) and this idea of profit underlies the market system mentioned in 2.)

4 fosters the belief that the market system is in fact, the best system, in that it offers choice for individuals to buy the goods that they want at the price that they want to pay.

5 tries to ensure that the government does not take over too much of private industry (the private sector) and puts it under government control thus making it part of the public sector – for example, recently certain private firms have gone bankrupt and have been taken over by the government of the day. These firms are now run by the State for the country's benefit. (Examples that spring to mind include Rolls Royce (Aero Engine Division) and British Leyland PLC.)

Interestingly enough there is quite often a contradiction here because the CBI (like many unions and the TUC) is *not* very keen to see the government deeply involved in industrial affairs. However, if a large firm runs into financial difficulties, the firm will often generate enough popular support to keep it going as in the case of Rolls Royce (Aero Engine Division) Ltd. In general it seems that the employers want government to let industry run their own affairs but they also want it to 'bail out' bankrupt firms and keep the economy in 'good shape' so that profits will be running at a high level.

Having started to explore the relationships between employers and governments let's now go on to look in particular at the government's role in the triangle of industrial relations. Before we go any further we need to say what we mean by government. I am using the word to mean all those people in State circles who make decisions. These will include the Prime Minister and his/her Cabinet, Parliament and the political parties, etc. and also those who carry out those decisions, groups such as the civil service, the police, and the law courts.

I would, therefore, like to suggest the following roles for the government in industrial relations. The government as

 (a) '**Boss**'

 (b) the only actor in the industrial relations' theatre who can rewrite the script: that is the government as '**lawmaker**'

The Government as 'Boss'

Nearly one-third of the country's labour force work for the government. You can find them in such jobs as those of the civil service, the nationalized industries (such as the Gas Corporation, British Rail, British Steel, etc.), in local government and the health services. The jobs in which the government acts as direct 'boss' are all in what is known as the 'public sector'. We'll say more about the public (and the private) sectors in Chapter 10 ('Money to make, money to spend') but, for the moment, all we really need to know is that the public part of the economy is a very important part, indeed. It has grown a good deal since the end of the Second World War with the growth of the National Health Service, the development of widespread provision for education and with the nationalization of key industries such as coal, gas, steel and transport. It has also changed the kinds of unions that are in existence but we'll say more about that in other chapters.

One of the main points of contact for you with the public sector will be in your local community where you use State services provided by the local government authorities. For example, you go to your local GP who decides to send you on for specialist advice in a local hospital. We all go or have been to school or college. We will all make use of social services when we need them. We all have our rubbish removed! Roughly half the population live in houses provided by the local council. In all of these ways we are making use of the public sector.

Assignment 1.3

Try this assignment to see if you have understood the earlier section on different views in industrial relations

One view of industrial relations is as follows

'In particular a commitment to the removal of *restrictive practices* is required from the unions. Management can contribute to this process by the continual *improvement of communications with the work force, their greater involvement in decision-making processes* and greater efforts to raise the *level of understanding of the economic facts of industrial life*. Companies are becoming increasingly *open with employees* about policies, performances, plans and prospects. However, the support of the trade unions in *educating their members to accept the need for change to achieve greater productivity*, and therefore greater prosperity for all, would be welcome.'

Do you think that this view is that held by the workers, the employers or the government. The correct answer is given on p. 18. Incidentally, the text has been put in italics to show more clearly the main points of the piece.

There are special problems for the public sector when we look at the industrial relations' picture. For example, one of the most difficult areas to handle when it comes to pay rises in the public sector is that since it's easy for governments to keep a close check on public sector pay (particularly when government money is short), pay rises in the public sector are often kept at a lower rate than those in the private sector.

This often causes a good deal of bad feeling between workers in the two sectors particularly when private industry finds ways around the 'average' pay rise (or pay 'norm') that government suggests as the maximum. If a government suggests that pay rises should not go above 6%, a firm in the private sector if it so wishes, may well be able to negotiate various extra 'bonus' payments over and above the 6% which in reality then gives the workers around, shall we say, 10–12%. It *has* kept to the government's 6%. It *has not* broken the pay 'norm' and it *has* given the workers a better deal. However, it may not be so easy for electricity workers, or miners to do this because their purse strings are directly controlled by government.

Having very quickly looked at the government as an *employer* let's finally move on to the role of government as **lawmaker** in industrial relations. The government is the one partner in the union–management–government triangle who can actually change the *rules* of industrial relations by making new *laws*. As we shall see in later chapters on trade union history the nineteenth century highlighted the struggle between the unions and the law to allow them to be recognized by society. In the twentieth century unions are an established part of the industrial relations landscape. The law is now used (among other things) to determine what methods unions can use, for example, in key issues such as the 'closed shop' or picketing. In addition, the law is involved in health, safety and welfare at work.

So governments have not only the power to provide the legal framework, or skeleton, within which industrial relations takes place, they also have a good deal of power through the law to make a real impact on much of the detail of activity, such as negotiating, that take place at plant level. The government can not only paint in the broad legal 'picture' for those involved in industrial relations, it can paint in a lot of the local 'detail' as well. It's a very important role.

This then has been a very quick and brief introduction to some of those people involved in British industrial relations. Keep reading, you too may find you want to become more involved.

Assignment 1.4

Given the chance to interview well-known people in the industrial relations field name **three** individuals to whom you would like to talk on:

(*a*) the management, and
(*b*) the trade union side.

If you could choose **three** industries in which to interview workers which ones would you choose and why?

Assignment 1.5

Imagine a firm in the private sector going bankrupt. I want you to think about the grounds on which that firm should be 'bailed out' (that is, if you think it should be).

Make a list of the reasons you think are important enough to justify keeping bankrupt firms going: for example when Rolls Royce went 'bust' one of the reasons that people felt it should be saved was that the good names of Rolls Royce and Britain were at stake. Using that as your first reason, make a list of other reasons that you think are important.

Assignment 1.6

Neddy brings together employers, trade unions and government.

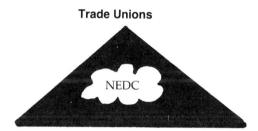

Trade Unions

NEDC

Employers   **Government**

Neddy is the only forum in the country where senior representatives of employers, trade unions and government meet together regularly to discuss ways of improving our economic and industrial performance.

Neddy has no executive powers.* It is based on the belief that discussion, mutual understanding and agreement on action are the necessary foundation for change and for helping industry to tackle its problems and seize opportunities for growth.

The name Neddy covers:

the National Economic Development Council (NEDC or 'Council')
the Economic Development Committees (EDCs) and Sector Working Parties (SWPs)
the National Economic Development Office (NEDO or 'Office)

* This means it cannot *make people* do things.

Let us have a look at the **council** (NEDC) in some more detail.

The Council tackles broad, national issues

The NEDC is at the centre of Neddy organization. Each month, the leading government economic and industrial ministers and top level representatives of the CBI and TUC, together with representatives of certain other important interests, meet to discuss topics of national importance.

The meetings are usually chaired by the Chancellor of the Exchequer or, on occasions, by the Prime Minister.

Council discussions cover a wide range of subjects, including the general economic situation, exports, imports, productivity, and the supply of skilled manpower.

Keeping the Wheels of Industry Oiled

The Advisory, Conciliation and Arbitration Service (ACAS) functions to encourage and improve good industrial relations and to develop collective bargaining by advice, conciliation, education or arbitration and by enquiry. It is directed by a council which includes members drawn from both the employers and trade unions sides of industry. ACAS does not charge for its services.

Any employer, employers' association, trade union or worker can seek information or advice about industrial relations questions. This may, for example, relate to some aspect of labour law affecting perhaps only one individual. On the other hand, it may concern an industrial relations question arising at a particular company where there is a desire to solve a pressing problem which could lead to a dispute, or possibly a longer term underlying difficulty which may be affecting efficiency and good relations. Some of these requests will be met by a short visit or discussion; others may justify a survey which may last a number of days.

Source: NEDO documents

Who is entitled to use ACAS?
Give dictionary definitions of:

  Advice
  Conciliation
  Mediation, and
  Arbitration

What reasons do you think there are for industry to need a separate group, namely ACAS, to sort out some of its problems.

Answer to Assignment 1·3

The view is that put across by a MANAGEMENT source.

Recommended reading for Chapter 1

1 *The Practice of Management* by P. F. Drucker (Pan, 1968)
2 *The Study of Organisations* by D. Dunkerley (Routledge and Kegan Paul, 1972)
3 *The Trade Union Directory* by J. Eaton and C. Gill (This is not a book to read from cover to cover but it's an excellent reference book to have around) (Pluto Press, 1981)

Books that you have read and found useful should be added below

Chapter 2
A union is a union is a union . . .

Objectives

At the end of this chapter you should be able to:

1 say what a trade union is and what it does;
2 recognize different types of trade unions, for example, general, white collar, craft and industrial unions;
3 list some of the functions of the TUC (Trades Union Congress) and outline connections between the TUC and the trade union movement.

This chapter covers the following subjects/topics:

1 what unions are for;
2 what types of unions exist in modern Britain;
3 ways in which unions are organized;
4 the TUC: why it's there, how it works and what it does.

IN CHAPTER 1 WE looked at the various groups involved in industrial relations such as the government, the employers, the CBI, the unions and the TUC. In that chapter, quite some emphasis was laid upon the first two groups, the government and the employers. In this chapter I am going to swing the spotlight round on to the unions and on to the Trades Union Congress (TUC).

As we have already seen unions are made up of groups of workers who have got together to talk to, and negotiate with, employers about wages, working conditions, holidays, and the many other matters that come up at the workplace. Rather than having individuals talk separately to their employers (which would be impossible anyway in a very large organization), unions try to get a better deal for the individual worker simply because they can represent so many of the workers in firms, hospitals, offices, mines, shops, etc.

In Britain there are roughly 500 trade unions. They range in size and variety from those with around 100 members, like the Society of Shuttlemakers, to the massive TGWU which, in 1981, had a membership of 1 886 971. They also cover a tremendously wide range of different industries, organizations, jobs and skills. On

'Not one man alone, but many, built the Union and not one man alone but many, will continue to strengthen and develop this Union in the future.'

'Unity between the leadership and the membership. That is what will count.'

Source: courtesy The Story of the TGWU, *1979*

Some Well Known Unions

APEX Administrative and clerical grades in engineering, shipbuilding and ship repair, civil air transport, finance, insurance, food and drink, tobacco, electricity supply, building and construction, etc.

ASTMS This covers workers in such varied industries as engineering, shipbuilding, the car industry, the computer industry, electronics and telecommunications, chemicals, construction, insurance, publishing, banking, universities, health service, transport, food and drink, tobacco, textiles, carpets and oil.

AUEW This union consists of four separate sections. The largest of these is the Engineering section. AUEW organizes among all the workers in the engineering industry, skilled through to unskilled, men and women alike. The Constructional and Foundry sections organize workers in the building and foundry workers' groups. The fourth section, TASS, covers staff grades in engineering and general manufacturing.

GMBATU This union organizes all levels of workers throughout industry. It includes workers in engineering, manufacturing, food, textile industries, catering, the nationalized industries, the water and construction industries, transport, local authorities, health and civil service.

NALGO NALGO recruits workers in local government, the gas, electricity and water industries, transport, health and the universities.

Assignment 2.1

During the latter years of the nineteenth century Sidney and Beatrice Webb (along with such people as George Bernard Shaw, the writer) were the main driving force of a socialist group known as the Fabians. In 1894 the Webbs wrote what has become a classic trade union text entitled *The History of Trade Unionism*.

According to the Webbs 'a trade union is a continuous association[1] of wage earners[2] for the purpose of maintaining or improving the conditions[3] of their working lives'

1 Why do unions need to be '*continuous*' associations?
2 Wage earners: today we need to include salary earners as well.
3 Describe and list some of the things that you think make up 'good' working conditions.
4 This definition is ninety years old: do you think it still describes what trade unions try to do today?

pp. 20–23 you will find a list of some of the most important and well-known unions. Check through the names, see how many you recognize. The lists should give you just some idea of the variety!

However, you do have to be very careful when you look at the very many different trade unions in existence because, as you soon discover, although there are a rather large number of them, many are very small in size. I'll just take the figures for one year to show you what I mean. For example, at the end of 1979, there were 244 unions that had fewer than 1 000 members. Of this 244 just under 200 had less than 500 members. At the other extreme, the 27 largest unions (each with 100 000 plus members) accounted for four-fifths of the total membership of *all* unions. Today, and increasingly in the future it seems, big is, and will continue to be, beautiful for the union movement.

In 1981, there were 11 601 413 members of the 108 trade unions that are affiliated to the TUC (compared with 12 172 508 in the previous year). So, however, unpopular the unions may be in the press, in the pub over a pint, or in the place of work over a problem, they enclose within their ranks roughly one-half of the **male** and one-third of the **female** working population.

Not unnaturally, the proportion of workers in a particular firm, industry, etc. who are members of a union will depend upon many factors. These will include things such as the industry concerned, the views of the workers themselves, the employers' attitudes to unions and the tradition (or otherwise) of unionism in that industry.

NUPE	NUPE organizes local government manual workers, hospital ancilliary staff, school and college caretakers, nurses, workers in universities and in the water supply industry.
TGWU	The TGWU is the largest union in Britain with over 2 million members. This union covers workers in white collar clerical and supervisory jobs, in the building and civil engineering industries, in transport, food and drink, tobacco, the power industry and engineering, chemicals, rubber, oil refining, the car industry, the docks, and transport workers.
USDAW	This union covers workers in the retail trade, but it also has members in dairies, flour mills, the cocoa and chocolate industries, confectionery, and in brewing.

However, you can make out definite differences between industries in terms of how highly unionized they are. For example, the coal industry and the docks are highly organized; the distribution trade, on the other hand, is very much less so.

Of course, it is possible for disagreements to occur between unions in the same industry. One union may try to 'poach' another union's members. When this happens, and the 'poaching' becomes serious the TUC, under what are known as the 'Bridlington Principles', can step in and, acting as 'referee', try to control and, where possible, remove these inter-union disputes.

Trade Unions: Some Common Abbreviations

A
APEX	Association of Professional, Executive, Clerical and Computer Staff
ASLEF	Associated Society of Locomotive Engineers and Firemen
ASTMS	Association of Scientific, Technical and Managerial Staffs
AUEW	Amalgamated Union of Engineering Workers
AUT	Association of University Teachers

B
BALPA	British Airline Pilots Association
BIFU	Banking, Insurance and Finance Union

C
COHSE	Confederation of Health Service Employees
CPSA	Civil and Public Services Association
CSEU	Confederation of Shipbuilding and Engineering Unions
CSU	Civil Service Union

E
EETPU	Electrical, Electronic, Telecommunications and Plumbing Union
EMA	Engineers' and Managers' Association

G
GMBATU	General Municipal, Boilermakers' and Allied Trades' Union

I
IPCS	Institution of Professional Civil Servants

M
MATSA	(part of GMBATU) Managerial, Administrative, Technical and Supervisory Association

N
NALGO	National and Local Government Officers' Association

	NATFHE	National Association of Teachers in Further and Higher Education
	NATSOPA	National Association of Operative Printers, Graphical and Media Personnel[1]
	NAS/UWT	National Association of Schoolmasters/Union of Women Teachers
	NGA	National Graphical Association[2]
	NUAAW	National Union of Agricultural and Allied Workers[3]
	NUFLAT	National Union of Footwear, Leather and Allied Trades
	NUJ	National Union of Journalists
	NUM	National Union of Miners
	NUPE	National Union of Public Employees
	NUR	National Union of Railwaymen
	NUS	National Union of Seamen
	NUS	National Union of Students
	NUT	National Union of Teachers
P	POEU	Post Office Engineering Union
S	SLADE	Society of Lithographic Artists, Designers, Engravers and Process Workers[2]
T	TASS	(part of AUEW) Technical, Administrative and Supervisory Section
	TGWU	Transport and General Workers' Union
	TSSA	Transport Salaried Staffs Association
	UCATT	Union of Construction, Allied Trades and Technicians
	UCW	Union of Communication Workers
	USDAW	Union of Shop, Distributive and Allied Trades

1 NATSOPA and SOGAT (Society of Graphical and Allied Trades) have now amalgamated.
2 NGA and SLADE have now amalgamated.
3 Now part of TGWU.

Inter-Union Relations

'Non-craft unions appear to be increasing their efforts to poach UCATT members, particularly in Local Authorities, and they are, of course, taking advantage of the fact that UCATT contributions are the highest among the unions in this field.

'We are combating this threat to the best of our ability, but have been handicapped not only by the contribution rate, but because our full-time officer strength has been depleted by sickness persistently over the last three to four years – at one period we had one Regional Organizer only to cover the whole of the region.'

Source: Viewpoint (UCATT Journal) September, 1980 in reference to an article from the South Wales region.

One of the most common questions asked about trade unions is: what different kinds of unions are there? There is no simple answer to this question. Much depends on how you go about classifying them. You could, for example, use some of the following ways to group them. Unions can be:

Large (how large?)	Small (how small is small?)
White collar	Blue collar (or both?)
Affiliated to the TUC	Not affiliated to the TUC
Affiliated to the	Not affiliated to
Labour party	the Labour party
. . . and so on.	

However, I think you may find it helpful if you divide unions into the following four main kinds: *craft: industrial: general and white collar.*

Let us have a look at each of these four types in a little more detail. First, craft unions:

Craft Unions were

The first to develop in Britain and most other countries;

Often reckoned to be the 'cream' of the workforce because their members were skilled. These skills were (and still are) usually earned by the apprenticeship method;

Not open to everyone;

Keen to encourage comradeship among their members based on their members'

shared skills and the idea that 'unity is strength';

In their early days also developing 'friendly societies'. These gave benefits such as strike pay, sickness, accident and other benefits to support their members in times of trouble;

Democratically organized, their officers elected on a regular basis.

Present day examples of craft unions include the Musicians' Union (MU), the National Graphical Association (NGA), the Society of Lithographic Artists, Design Engravers and Process Workers (SLADE) these last two having amalgamated recently.

Assignment 2.2

Check the dictionary definition of 'apprenticeship'. At the present time the apprenticeship system is disappearing. Make a *short* list of reasons why you think this is.

Closely look at the list of the various unions on pp. 22 and 23 and pick out those unions that you think are **craft unions**, i.e. unions that are based on special skills or on special tools and equipment which are used to produce some kind of article. One other example is the AUEW which, although it is a **general union** within the engineering industries, also acts as a **craft union** for skilled engineering workers.

Craft

These are based on the particular skill a person has and were the first unions to develop in Britain (*see* Chapter 3)

Examples include the MU, NGA and the Coopers Union

General

These unions, often large and powerful today, developed in the past to help the unskilled. They include workers, be they skilled or unskilled, from several different industries and occupations

Examples include the TGWU and the GMBATU

Industrial

These unions take in workers, be they skilled or unskilled from a particular industry

Examples include the NUM, UCW and the NUR

White collar

These unions have grown in the expansion of white collar jobs since 1945, and they represent people working in clerical, professional and administrative jobs

They often cover a wide range of jobs and occupations and examples include ASTMS, NALGO and NUT

Moving on to the second type, the industrial union, we can say that:

Industrial Unions are

Set up and organized on the basis of looking after workers in *one* particular industry, for example, the railway or coal industries;

Based on the fact that most of all the members are in *one* industry. This should give greater solidarity (feelings of to-getherness);

Made up of workers with different kinds and levels of skill;

(Or, in the past, were) supporters of the idea that workers in the industrial unions should, in time, take over the particular industry represented by that particular union. This movement was called **syndicalism** (*see* Chapter 4);

Often not very easy to describe accurately. For example, the NUR represents many workers in the railway industry, but there are *other* railway unions such as ASLEF and TSSA. Besides, the railway unions are just part of the transport industry and lorry drivers and coach drivers may belong to the TGWU.

Examples of industrial unions include the National Union of Mineworkers (NUM), the Union of Communications Workers (UCW), and the NUR.

The third kind of unions have some, or all, of the following features:

General Unions

They take in almost any type of worker, no matter what his/her job is, no matter what the industry is;

They originally recruited labourers and semi-skilled workers but now they re-cruit from more than one job area;

They have often been formed where other, older trade unions have joined together;

General unions are often very large. This may bring problems, although large size can also, of course, have advantages. Try to think of some of the pros and cons of having a *large* union/or a large firm or organization for that matter?

Examples of general unions include the Transport and General Workers Union (TGWU) and the General and Municipal Boilermaker and Allied Trades Union (GMBATU). Both these unions are very large and powerful as a result of amalgamating in the past with various other unions. If you look, for example, at the list of unions that make up the TGWU, you can see the tremendous collection of widely differing unions. The union covers workers in eleven trade groups.* 'As each union has merged with the TGWU, the process has brought together workers in different trades and industries into a single industrial grouping which has made the TGWU such a distinctive force' (TGWU, 1979).

Here are the *11 trade groups** in the TGWU with some *examples* to show the variety of unions involved.

*Automotive, Vehicle Building, etc.**
National Union of Vehicle Builders (pre-
   viously United Kingdom Society of
   Coach Makers)

*Power and Engineering**
File Grinders' Society
Iron Steel and Wood Barge Builders and
   Helpers Association

*Chemical, Rubber and Oil**
Union of Kodak Workers

*Docks & Waterways**
National Union of Dock, Riverside and
   General Workers
United Fishermen's Union

*Commercial**
Associated Horsemen's Union
Belfast Bread Servers' Association

*Food, Drink and Tobacco**
Scottish Farm Servants' Union
North of Ireland Operative Butchers' and
   Allied Workers' Association

*Passenger**
National Union of Vehicle Workers
Scottish Busmen's Union

*Public Services**
Government Civil Employees Association
Irish Mental Hospital Workers' Union

*General Workers (includes textiles)**
United Order of General Labourers
North Wales Quarrymen's Union
National Glass Bottlemakers' Society
Irish Union of Hairdressers and Allied
   Workers

*Building and Construction**
'Altogether' Builders Labourers and Constructional Workers Society

*Administrative, Clerical, Technical, etc.**
National Union of Co-operative Insurance
   Society Employees
Union of Bookmakers Employees
Royal Automobile Club (RAC) Staff
   Association

N.B. This is *not* a complete list of all the unions that make up
the TGWU but it does give some idea of the different groups
of workers that do go to make up a large *general* union
N.B. For further information about the TGWU, get their
excellent handbook *The Story of the TGWU* available from the
TGWU, Transport House, Smith Square, Westminster,
LONDON SW1P 3JB.

Just before we leave our brief look at the
TGWU, there are a couple of points that need to
be made about the practical reasons why unions
amalgamate. If you look at the complete list of all
those unions that have joined together to form
today's TGWU you will see that it is an enormous
one, so it's obviously important to ask 'what are

the benefits of amalgamation for unions?' Practical reasons for amalgamating into larger groupings include *better finance* (more members, generally speaking, means better financial status); *improved service to the members* because of the combination of resources from the unions that are joining together; and, thirdly, there is an *increase in the practical strength* of the union (more members, more power?), so that can be brought to bear when collective bargaining takes place with employers. A large union can also provide good back-up facilities (in research and education, for example). With the eighties being years in which amalgamations are going to become more and more common, these reasons are going to be of greater and greater importance. Keep a look out for union amalgamations and try to find out the particular reasons why they are happening.

Moving on, the final kind of union that we need to look at is the white collar union.

White Collar Unions

Cover people working in 'white collar' jobs in clerical, administration and professional areas of the job market such as central/local government, the health service and teaching. Cover many levels and types of skill.

Are generally organized on occupational lines for example the NUT which covers many (but not all) teachers.

Have grown enormously in size and power since the Second World War.

Assignment 2.3

Look over the above list of sample trade unions given and draw up your own list of *industries* that are represented with the TGWU. If a general union covers as many industries and groups of workers as does the TGWU, can you see any problems when the union leadership comes to bargain on behalf of its members? Will there be differences between what the dockers in the union want and what the road haulage people in the *same* union want for example? What advantages and disadvantages can you see to being an individual member of such a large union (over 2 million members)?

Are more likely to recruit their full time officers from *outside* the union (unlike the officers from manual workers' unions). These 'white collar' officers, are sometimes graduates rather than people who have worked their way up through the industry from the shop floor.

Examples of white collar unions include the Association of Scientific, Technical and Managerial Staffs (ASTMS), the National and Local Government Officers' Association (NALGO), and the National Union of Teachers (NUT).

One other way of classifying unions is by asking whether or not they are 'open' or 'closed'.

An 'open' union, as the name suggests, is one in which people are encouraged to join no matter what their industry. The union is open to everyone. Examples of 'open' unions include TGWU, NUPE and ASTMS, and as you can see from these examples *open* unions are usually *general* unions.

'Closed' unions usually limit their membership to those workers who are involved in a clearly identifiable trade or skill. This usually involves a formal period of training, for example, an apprenticeship. The union acts as a kind of 'gatekeeper', that is it does not encourage everyone to enter the trade but closely watches the number of entrants. Examples of closed unions include ASLEF and the Association of Boilermakers Shipwrights, Blacksmiths and Structural Workers the (ABSBSW). The printing industry also has unions which follow a 'closed' pattern.

Although it is obviously important for you to know what types of unions there are, and indeed to know how difficult it is anyway to classify some unions because they could fit into one or two categories, it is even more important to know something about the ways in which

---

Assignment 2.4

Look over the list of trade unions on pp. 20–23 and catalogue which of the unions in that list are *white collar unions*. Many of the white collar unions increased their membership during the 1960s and early 1970s. Can you explain why this was and do you think that the white collar unions will go on growing into the 1980s? What are your reasons?

---

unions are organized and to see how they go about looking after their members' interests. As we have seen most unions have a *branch* structure so the members belong to branches which may be based for example, on a particular workplace (if it is large enough to support a branch) or a geographical area (where workers from different, but smaller, firms meet).

If you join a union and you go to a branch meeting you will be involved in discussions about matters that affect you and your colleagues in the factory, office or wherever you work. At these meetings you will be asked to elect official union representatives for the branch. These worker representatives are often known as shop stewards and they are the people who bring new recruits into the union, watch out for hazardous working arrangements, arrange works meetings, etc. They are the very roots of union involvement in industry. They handle much of the day-to-day negotiations with employers. When they need to, they can bring in full-time union officials, who may be based locally or in regional headquarters. Where there are a fair number of shop stewards, as for example in a large plant, they often form a committee, the

---

Assignment 2.5

The job of the Shop Steward as seen through the eyes of the TGWU

'You carry in trust a responsibility for an organization which has taken generations of struggle and service to build up. Pledge yourself that your spell of office will keep up its high traditions. Remember that in the last resort the influence of trade unionism depends upon workers acting in unity. Trade union unity doesn't involve barrack-square discipline. We are a voluntary organization: not an army. But unity in action does mean paying intelligent regard to the policy of the Union, and doing your best to see that these policies are carried out.

'If you do your work well as a shop steward the workers will see daily evidence of the value of their trade union membership. You need nevertheless to seize every opportunity of taking action to build up the strength of the Union – by recruiting new members, by keeping existing members up to scratch, and by turning "card-holders" into trade unionists.

'As a shop steward you represent the members in the workplace. You are responsible for ensuring that wages and working conditions are a credit to the Union. If any of your members has an individual grievance or a problem, you have the responsibility to see that you do your best to help him. In dealing with many of your problems, the Union will expect you to be able to manage on your own. If you cannot, you know you have the help and resources of the TGWU behind you.'

Source: TGWU Shop Stewards Handbook, 1979

From this description give a list of the various jobs the shop steward in the TGWU is expected to do. If possible, list some of the difficulties you think the shop steward may have to face in his/her day-to-day duties.

---

chairperson of which is known as the senior steward or 'convenor'.

Shop stewards (and full-time officers) often have a very difficult time trying to reconcile what their members want and what the employers are prepared to give. In addition, they often are working very much on their own. In 1975 the TUC carried out a survey which reckoned that there were just over 400 000 voluntary union officers, just over 290 000 of them being shop stewards, nearly 3 000 being full-time officials, the majority of the remainder being lay (that is worker) branch officers (for example, branch secretaries, etc.).

Branch meetings will also (usually) elect representatives (delegates) to represent them at the union's national conference that the union's plans and policies will be made for the forthcoming year. Between the times that the conferences meet the union is under the control and guidance of the union's National Executive Council (NEC). The NEC is made up of officials who have been elected to the Council by the members, or in some cases, by the conference itself. The conference will in turn be made up of delegates who have been elected by the members at the workplace. In this way unions hope that they can achieve an organization that is democratic in that it allows the voices of the members to be heard right through to the people who make the key policy decisions of the unions. (For more on union democracy see Chapter 6 'What strange ideas you have about industrial relations!').

One of the major criticisms of the trade unions

is that individual workers' needs and wishes somehow 'get lost' in the journey from the shop steward in the workplace to the union's national leadership. Critics of the unions also argue that the people who go to union branch meetings are the most militant and so the view that gets sent to the union bosses is also one of militancy. If you do decide to join a union you should, wherever possible, try to go to branch meetings in order to ensure that the majority view, whatever that may be, is the view that goes across to the shop stewards and to the full-time union officials. However, many union members are not keen to become involved in the workings of their union. An article on the trade unions in *New Society* made the following point:

> *'Yet while more than 12 million workers belong to unions, very few of them play an active part in union affairs. Research suggests that most workers treat membership of a union as a kind of meal ticket which will bring with it obvious economic rewards with higher pay, better working conditions, longer holidays and so on. They do not see the union as a collective expression of democratic self-government, which is the way unions like to see themselves.'*
>
> *Source:* courtesy 'Trade Unions' (Society Today) in *New Society 15 November 1979*

Union democracy will only work if people can be bothered to participate in it to make it work, and most people evidently see the union as a way of getting better pay, etc., rather than a movement trying to get better conditions for the workers in general.

Although trade unions rely on a good deal of voluntary workers, like shop stewards, they also have full-time officers who are involved with negotiation, co-ordination between firms and between local activities and national activities, etc. One of the difficulties in looking at what a full-time local officer does is that (just as is the case with shop stewards and national officers) there are so many different *unions*, in so many different *industries*, in so many different *places* (factories, offices, steelworks, shops, hospitals, etc.) and so because of this it is almost impossible to generalize about what full-time officers do. All you can really do is try to show some of the activities officers have to be involved with, such as negotiating, planning, etc. On p. 32 there is a timetable showing a week in the life of a full-time official in the footwear and leather industry.

Remember this timetable can only show some of the activities with which full-time trade union officials are involved. It does not mean that all full-time trade union officials do *exactly* the same things, although, in many ways, the *general* activities are *roughly* the same.

This week is based on a real person's workload – let's call him Les! The events outlined here may not actually have

> *'Every pit has its lodge or branch and each lodge is governed by the rules of its constituent association. Those who run the lodge are part-timers, who work in the pit. The lodge committee consists of officers plus six to fifteen other workers. All of them are elected every year or biennially. Each lodge elects a delegate to the area council. Unlike most union branches the NUM lodges are vital and active parts of the union, and they practise a degree of democratic involvement unknown in many larger unions. Miners live in tightly knit communities close to the pithead. It is true that modern transport and rehousing has dispersed many farther away from their workplace, but the solidarity and comradeship of the pit village is still strong on most of the coalfields.'*
>
> *Source:* Courtesy The Fifth Estate, Robert Taylor, 1980

happened all in one week, but the timetable does give you a sample of the kinds of activities full-time trade union officials may have to do.

In order to balance the picture, on p. 35 you will also find a week in the life of a full-time union official at *national* level. The official concerned works for the union, USDAW.

In many communities, most of the trade union branches in different firms and industries join together to form local *trade councils*. In the same way, at *national* level unions have collected together to form the TRADES UNION CONGRESS or TUC. Unions 'affiliate' to the TUC by paying a fee for each member and the money goes towards the running of the TUC. The TUC is a broad alliance of more than one hundred

	MORNING	AFTERNOON	EVENING
M O N	**1** Go into office, clear up some letters and some admin. Deal with telephone enquiries	**2** Urgent 'phone call from local shoe factory — dispute over short time working. Visit department concerned for talks	
T U E S	Local dispute continues. More talks with members and management. I have to leave at lunchtime when one of my colleagues takes over	Magistrate court meets this afternoon I'm on the Bench !	
W E D S	After further talks, workers go back. In the afternoon I am visits to another factory some problems and a bonus — one	able to make one of my regular 30 miles away. No real or two new members	**5** Chairman local Labour party meeting
T H U R	**3** Into office, write some notes on some rate re-negotiations I am involved with — read some new reports	on Health & Safety at work visit to most distant factory **4** under my care Some problems here	Overnight stay ←----→
F R I	→ Return from factory X Fairly quiet visit this time — some routine problems	More letters waiting back at the office. End of the afternoon — phone call — could I go Monday first thing to Factory Z	

unions representing nearly 12 million members. In fact, well over 90% of all the British trade unions' memberships are affiliated to the TUC. Its current general secretary is Len Murray.

It is through the TUC that discussions, negotiations and consultations take place with government, the CBI and various other agencies such as 'Neddy'. The TUC brings together the views of the British trade union movement. It gives unions advice on a wide variety of indust-rial and social matters. It provides a range of services to those unions affiliated to it. It gives help with education and training. It provides legal advice. It settles inter-union disputes where it can and maintains contacts with unions in other countries. It does *not* enter into collective bargaining with employers but it does suggest guidelines to those actually involved in negoti-ating.

Number on Diary
(*see* p. 32)

1

ACTIVITIES
Many full-time officers working at local (and other levels) have to do a good deal of routine office work, like writing letters, looking over agreements, etc., etc. You can never get away from the paperwork it seems!

COMMENTS
General increase in paperwork in society. Importance of keeping good records!

2

It's very important that full-time union officials at district, regional and national level keep very closely in touch with their members. In this way any troublesome areas at work can be spotted and things can be done to avoid the problems. Negotiations with management are an extremely important part of

Watch the communications! Your members pay your salary (and may have to re-elect you). Important to keep the lines open!

the job and good communications and personal relations are crucial.

3 Les has to keep up-to-date with all kinds of new laws and technology. He needs to be prepared when his members and his colleagues ask him awkward and difficult questions. In his busy week it is often hard for him to sit back and read about new laws etc., simply because of the pressure of work.

Note the importance of good research and preparation especially in the legal field.

4 Again, Les is keeping in touch with the 'shop floor'. It gives his members and his shop stewards a chance to air their views and to ask him those awkward questions we were talking about in 3.

As 2
Say no more!

5 Les is also involved with the local community. In this case, you can see that he is both Chairman of the local Labour Party as well as being a member of the local Bench (Justice of the Peace).

The Labour Party and the unions are rarely far apart but see the chapters on history and issue Chapter 9.

MAKE A NOTE OF ANY OTHER POINTS THAT YOU FIND INTERESTING

TUC policy is decided at and by its annual Congress which meets in the first week of September usually either in Blackpool or Brighton. Here, around 1 000 delegates* (elected union representatives) meet for a five day conference. They consider the report that the TUC's General Council has prepared on the previous year's work. The Congress discusses, and votes upon, notions submitted by affiliated unions. The Congress also elects the members of the General Council for the following year.

The day-to-day work of the TUC is carried on by a full-time staff of about a hundred people. There are also a number of TUC committees which carry out work in various areas such as education, economic matters, welfare problems, etc. The TUC is now very much part of the 'establishment'. Before leaving the subject of the TUC however, we need again to stress that it does not have much direct power. It is true that it has a good deal of *influence* with governments, employers and unions but that does not mean that it can force those groups to do anything. It can only persuade, cajole and hope that its view is taken up by the other parties concerned.

* N.B. Each delegate union can send one delegate for every 5 000 union members, while it can have a vote for every 1 000 members. Each delegate votes, not as an individual for whatever policy is put forward, but the votes are cast *in blocks* by each union according to the number of members for whom the unions have paid the affiliation fee.

	MORNING	AFTERNOON	EVENING
MONDAY	Go into office. Deal with correspondence. Check weekly programme with Research Assistant. Bring diary up to date. Study draft of NEW TECHNOLOGY Agreement	Discuss various company proposals for self-certification with Legal Officer. Deal with various telephone messages. Collate files/papers for week's meetings.	—
TUESDAY	Meeting of JNC at Mail Order company. Areas of discussion:- 1. Warehouse representation. 2. Warehouse Strategy.	Meeting of WAREHOUSE STRATEGY GROUP on future warehouse developments (mechanisation etc.).	—
WEDNESDAY	Go into office. Telephone calls. Correspondence. Meeting with Ind. Rel. Director of retail company (PROCEDURAL MATTERS)	Meeting at RETAIL DISTRIBUTION DEPOT. Dispute on transfer of work between depots. Dispute resolved by 3 months trial with pay safeguards.	—
THURSDAY	MEETING WITH TGWU/USDAW — Senior reps. Matters not settled in joint grievance procedure. 2 resolved / 1 Company to respond within 4 weeks.		Meeting of local Labour Party.
FRIDAY	MEETING National Committee - To discuss office strategy - 1982/83. Consultation on planned changes to office systems on jobs.	Go discuss 1982/83. planned changes and effect Grading etc.	—

Assignment 2.6

List six functions of trade unions.

Without referring to this chapter *name* four important points about each of the following unions:

1 Craft
2 Industrial
3 General.

Take a particular union (or industry, for example printing, construction), and *list* some of the industrial relations problems facing that particular union or industry.

Assignment 2.7

Without referring to this chapter, write in your own words, a *list* of *five* aspects of the TUC's work.

Once you have your list, and not before, go back to the diagram on p. 36 and see where you were right and where you were wrong.

Assignment 2.8

Below is a list of trade unions. Do you think they are concerned with the same aims to the same extent? For example, do you think some are *more* concerned with *working conditions* than others in the list? Are some known more for their *pay claims* than anything else?

Here is your list

National Union of Miners (NUM)
Amalgamated Union of Engineering Workers (AUEW)
National Union of Agricultural and Allied Workers (NUAAW) (now part of the TGWU)
National and Local Government Officials Association (NALGO)
National Union of Teachers (NUT)
Association of Scientific, Technical and Managerial Staffs (ASTMS)

Assignment 2.9

Here is an assignment that will help you to find out for yourself whether or not you have 'got the message' about the four types of unions. Below is a list of unions. You have to try and classify them into CRAFT, INDUSTRIAL, GENERAL and WHITE COLLAR.

Before you start, you must obviously know what the initials mean. Make sure you do. Check the list on pp. 22 and 23.

One of the questions you need to think about is this:

Does the union you are looking at 'fit' neatly into just one of the four groups? It might well do, or you might find you can squeeze it into other categories!

NUR NUM NUJ TGWU AUEW MU

Craft
Industrial
General
White collar

Assignment 2.10

In 1965, the TUC gave the following list of points that it believed its affiliated unions were trying to achieve.

1 Better terms of employment
2 Better working conditions, for example, warmer and safer buildings
3 Everyone in a job and greater prosperity for the country
4 A secure job and a secure wage
5 Better social security benefits, for example, better old age pensions, etc.
6 A fair share for the workers in the wealth of the country

7 Industrial democracy (workers more involved in the running of industry)

8 Some influence in the way the government runs the country

9 Better public and social services such as education and health services

10 Greater public control and planning of industry

Read through the list, make sure you understand each and *all* of the points. Take half a dozen of the points mentioned above, explain carefully what each one means and then say whether you think it is a *good* or *bad* thing that the unions should be trying to do this and say why.

This list was put forward in 1965. Do you think trade unions are still trying to do the same kinds of things or have they moved on?

Group Activity

As a group discuss which of the *ten points* you think are the most important and why? Make a group list showing your conclusions and the reasons for those conclusions.

Secondly, as a group, discuss which of the ten points you think the *trade unions think* are the *most* important? Again make a group list. *Are the lists roughly the same?*

Recommended reading for Chapter 2

1 *Unions and Change since 1945* by C. Baker and P. Caldwell (Pan, 1981)

2 *Getting Organised* by A. Campbell and J. McIlroy (Pan, 1981)

3 *The Trade Unions* by H. Williamson (Heinemann, 1981)

Books that you have read and found useful should be added below

Chapter 3
To find out where you are going, you must know where you've been (1800–1900)

Objectives

At the end of this chapter you should be able to:

1 list some of the key events in industrial relations history over the last 180 years:
2 describe ways in which past events in trade union history still affect present day trade union practice:
3 carry out some research into trade union history.

THIS CHAPTER COVERS the following subjects/topics

1 early origins of trade unions 1800–30;
2 first National Unions (Robert Owen, Chartism and Marxism) 1830–40;
3 growth of 'New Model Unions' 1850–80;
4 growth of General Unions 1880;
5 the role of women in the early unions.

IN THESE DAYS of very large unions (and amidst cries that the unions have far too much power for their own good) it may be quite difficult for us to remember that there was a time when unions were small, illegal organizations, feared and kept down by the governments of those far off time. Trade unions had very small beginnings and they can often be traced back to the craft guilds of the Middle Ages. We shall take up the story however around the late 1700s when trade unions, as we know them now, started out on their difficult route to become the well-known institutions that they are today.

late 1700s

The early trade unions were known as 'combinations' because of course, that is precisely what they were; groups of workers *combining* with other workers to get an increase in wages, or an improvement in working conditions. Combinations were, generally speaking, of two kinds. In the first kind, workers got together for a short time in order to air a particular grievance or problem. They may just have had a *particular* difficulty with their employer and it was for this that they collected together. Once they had succeeded (or

'*History does nothing, it "possesses no immense wealth". It "wages no battles". It is man, real living man, that does all that, that possesses and fights; "history" is not a person apart, using man as means for its own particular aims; history is nothing but the activity of man pursuing his aims,*

Source: courtesy The Holy Family, *K. Marx, 1956*

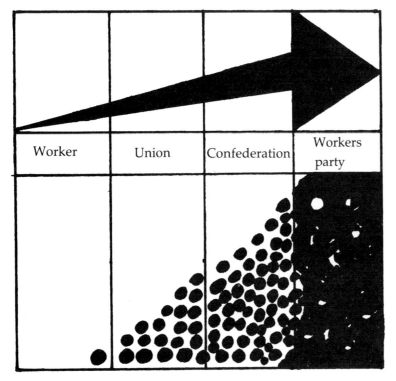

Worker	Union	Confederation	Workers party

One man on his own is weak, many united are strong

more likely, failed!) in their demand, they may well have split up again. It was the brief time that the groups were together that is important to notice here. In the second type of combination, the time the groups were together was again important but in their case the combination was a *more permanent affair*. It was usually confined to the members of a single workshop or trade and it will have been made up of men who were all involved with a single craft, or who were all working in the same local area. (Remember communications were nothing like as good in those days as they are now!) These men got together to look after their interests in the *long* term and quite often they were very concerned about who they 'let into' their particular trade or skill. This point about *ADMISSION* to a particular occupation is a very important one in trade union development as we shall see later in the chapter when we are discussing the 'New Model Unions'. (The New Model Unions were the skilled, elitist craft unions such as the ASE which were exclusive and charged high subscriptions.) It remains an important general point even today, as for example, in the professions where only certain well-qualified individuals are allowed to join a 'professional group' such as that covering doctors and lawyers.

The combinations however developed other aspects to their activities that related *to work* but were not concerned directly with what actually went on at work. For instance, what were known as 'Friendly Societies' and 'Sick Clubs' grew up and these were the only guard that the working man had against the difficulties of the age in which he found himself. They provided small amounts of money when he found himself without work. They also provided help with such things as funeral grants! Again, if we bring the situation up-to-date it is all too easy for us to forget that today we have the benefits of the welfare state in terms of medical care.

Indeed, one of the most important things that we need to remember when we study the trade union movement from an *historical* viewpoint is that the way the trade unions have grown still very much influences and reflects the ways of the trade unions today. What happened to the trade unions during their development comes through today in their attitudes, views, etc. For example, there has always been a difficult relationship between the trade unions and the law. It is still true as we shall see in the chapter on law and industrial relations that the role of law in industrial relations is even now being questioned and, in many cases, viewed with suspicion. Many trade unionists distrust the use of the law in industrial relations. This distrust has a long tradition going right back to those early days we have been talking about.

1799
1800
It became illegal under the **Combination Acts** of 1799 and 1800 for workers to join with other workers to get wage increases, less working hours or any improvement in working conditions. The Combination Acts were readily taken up by Members of Parliament of the time. This was because of the real fear felt by many people in all levels of society that the influence of the French Revolution, which had taken place in 1789, might spread into Britain through the dangerous formation of these workers' combinations. Those in power at the time,

Banner of Amalgamated Stevedores Protection League

Banner of Amalgamated Society of Carpenters and Joiners

the landed gentry and the merchants, were very worried about conflict and revolution, although in many ways they had little to worry about because the new combinations had very little industrial muscle. The workers were *'kept down' politically* in that very, very few workers could vote while, because of the large difference in power and wealth between employer and employee, it was so often the case that the worker was also economically exploited at work. The employer had all the 'ace' cards and had an almost total right to 'hire and fire' his workers. It was therefore not unnatural that workmen should get together to form combinations because times were so hard. In addition, they got together with people who were in the same situation as themselves. People who were suffering the same kinds of hardships. It is in this way that unions have grown. *Men and women facing common problems have formed groups together in order to fight a 'common foe'.* We have here the beginnings of the idea of *solidarity*: an agreement as to what the problems are and some kind of collective approach to finding and solving that problem.

In the adjacent article* about Arthur Scargill, the miners' leader, Noreen Taylor gives us some insight into Scargill's home and work background and the importance of the community and collective approach in that background.

It cannot be denied that the workers at the end of the eighteenth and beginning of the nineteenth centuries had a good many problems to face. In addition to the problems already mentioned that they had at work there were more general problems. As now, people were worried about the 'state of the nation' and high prices in particular. The war against Napoleon had put prices up. There was unemployment, job insecurity and low wages and so it was not at all surprising that people were concerned, particularly the working people. There was a general discontent amongst workers. If, as an individual, you had no security, then it was hardly surprising that there was no group security. In addition,

---

'He represents thousands of disabled miners and has fought hard for their injury compensation.

'He is proud of the skill and productivity of the miners and never stops battling to improve their quality of life.

'Such pride and closeness is understandable because, until 1972, Arthur Scargill was crawling along two feet high tunnels, choking on coal dust, and using sign language to communicate above the machinery noise.

'He was born . . . in a one-up, one-down cottage with no electricity, hot water, or inside lavatory. 'At 17 he went below.

. . . 'The strength of his commitment to his family and to his men can be explained by the close, almost tribal, society of Yorkshire mining villages.

'A shared background of poverty and danger has produced communities whose support for each other is equalled only by their disdain for Coal Board bosses, Tories and a public which complains about "greedy miners".

"There is only one place I want to live and that's Yorkshire", he said. "My roots are here, my friends are here".

Source: courtesy   Daily Mirror, 25 November 1980

---

one other cause of general discontent was the way in which society in those days was so much more unfair than it is today with vast differences between the very rich and the very poor.

In addition to all the problems we have already discussed changes were taking place in society due to the consequences of the *Industrial Revolution*. People were leaving their well-established way of life, working on the land, and moving in to the towns that were then developing. Here they worked in large factories so different from the small cottage industries and farms to which they had been accustomed. Assignment 3.1 may help you to see just how different life in town and country is today from then.

In the early days of the Industrial Revolution conditions in new factories were often extremely bad. People had to work long hours for low wages.

You can get a good idea of just how severe these fines were when you compare them with the expenditure for selected items for a family living during the first quarter of the nineteenth century. For example, a fairly typical skilled artisan's house rent would be about 1s 6d (7½p). This would give the family a room and a kitchen. Milk for the week would cost 1s 0d (5p), as would potatoes and other vegetables. It would seem that it has always been difficult for some sections of our society to make ends meet!

1808 It is interesting to note, however, that in spite of all the political, legal and social
1810 constraints, strikes by combinations did occur. For example, in 1808, the weavers about whom we have been talking came out on strike. Two years later, there occurred the first general strike of miners in Northumberland and Durham. The miners' tradition of militancy in order to gain better pay and working conditions obviously began early in trade union history. One more interesting link that we could make between the early 1800s and the present time concerns the introduction of new technology. Some workers, the so-called *Luddites*, were blaming the troubles in the industrial field on the machinery

N.B. If you want further information about this period read, *Milestones in Working Class History*, N. Longmate, BBC Publications, 1975

Assignment 3.1

TOWN   COUNTRY
1980   1980

Make a list of a typical day's activities for a farmer in the country and a worker in an office in the 1980s. Discover differences and similarities between the two life styles. (You will need to do some research for this.) Try to talk to *people* wherever possible.

Assignment 3.2

If you want a real challenge, think about the differences and similarities of a country worker and a town worker living in 1800. For this you will definitely need to research life on the land and life in the city by reading books about life at that time.

TOWN   COUNTRY
1800   1800

then being introduced. Their answer was to go around and smash machines. Workers today have a similar fear of redundancy, of course. They feel that, with the developments in the micro-electronics industry, the silicon chip, the microprocessor, for example, their very livelihood is being threatened. This often leads to strikes about the introduction of new technology such as those that have occurred in the British newspaper industry.

However, in the early 1800s, in spite of all the restrictions, labourers still met in secret. Indeed, it would seem that all the Combination Acts had, in fact, done was driven

For example, early in the nineteenth century a Lancashire cotton worker was employed for fourteen hours a day in very hot, damp conditions. He would be sweating all day long but not allowed to stop for a drink of water. If he lost concentration for a moment and left an oil can out of place he would be fined. He could also be fined for many other "offences" such as whistling. The owners felt that harsh discipline was essential. Some workers were children aged five or more, who would be beaten if they lost their concentration or failed to work hard enough.

Source: courtesy Investigating Society, D. Lawton, 1980

'The fines for such offences were of the following order:

	s	d
"Any spinner found with his window open	1	0
Any spinner putting his gas out too soon	1	0
Any spinner leaving his oil can out of place	1	0
Any spinner spinning with gaslight too long in the morning	2	0
Any spinner heard whistling	1	0
Any spinner being five minutes after last bell rings	1	0
Any spinner being sick and cannot find another spinner to give satisfaction must pay for steam per day	6	0
Any spinner having a little waste on his spindles	1	0"*

Source: courtesy Milestones in Working Class History, N. Longmate, 1974

---

the working men 'underground'. They still met, except now their members were sworn to secrecy. In 1824 the Combination Acts were repealed. One interesting side-effect of these was that the Friendly Societies (which had never been made illegal incidentally) grew in membership from roughly 700 000 in 1803 to 925 000 in 1915, although, like the combinations themselves, were still *small and locally based*. Once the early unions became legal again after 1824, many new ones were formed. Some of the former unions, such as the Northumberland and Durham Colliers' Union, were reformed. However, many unions, being only local in character, had financial problems and, in the depression of 1829, many of them were forced to throw in the towel and accept the employers' terms, however bad they may have been.

One of the unions that collapsed at this time was that of the Lancashire Cotton Spinners. Their leader, John Doherty, shrewdly reckoned that the only way for unions to be really effective was to build up 'national' unions so that they would be financially sound because of the large membership. A national union would also stop smaller regional unions competing for members. Again, it's interesting to note that one of the criticisms often thrown at unions today is that they are often in conflict with one another in the local factory rather than being a truly coherent, cohesive overall group of unions. In order to put his

ideas into practice, in 1829 Doherty formed the Grand General Union of all the Operative Spinners of the United Kingdom which he saw as the first step towards the setting up of a national union of *all* workmen. Towards this end, in 1830 he succeeded in establishing the National Association for the Protection of Labour. It prospered and by 1831, it had 100 000 members. However, the employers fought back and by 1832 it had collapsed, although many of the member unions survived separately to go on to fight another day.

In 1833, new developments inspired by the disappointment felt by working men that the 1832 Reform Bill had given the vote to the middle classes and not to them, helped in the setting up of the Grand National Consolidated Trade Unions. This was promoted by Robert Owen, a socialist philanthropist*. A mill owner who had practised his own beliefs, he felt that it was no good having a system whereby profit was made on a totally competitive basis. For him, co-operation between individuals was much more important. One of the stated aims of the movement was to bring about:

'an entire change in society – a change amounting to a complete subversion of the existing order of the world.

* *Philanthropist:* one who practises philanthropy. One filled with a love of mankind, who spends time, energy and money in helping others, a person who makes large and frequent gifts to charity.

Here you can see the beginnings of another of the roles that the trade unions later took on, that of bringing about wider changes in society.

As now they were concerned with getting more money and better working conditions for their members but later in the nineteenth century they became increasingly interested wth power in society. These kinds of views were taken up by the writer, economist, historian and philosopher Karl Marx during the middle of the nineteenth century (*see* p. 50 for more information). For him, and for some of the individuals in the early unions (and in unions today as well), the important thing was the role that the unions could play in bringing about a change in the power structure of the country.

1834   However, few people held these kinds of views in the 1830s and by 1834, the National Union of Robert Owen had started to fall apart and its membership of over half a million workers from all trades and all parts of the country became disillusioned. The workers turned their attentions to political action again with involvement in movements such as the Chartists (*see* p. 50 for further details).

The Chartists were the most important element in the working class political scene during the 1830s and 1840s, but from the 1840   end of the 1840s a new type of union began to emerge. These unions drew their strength from hierarchy created by the

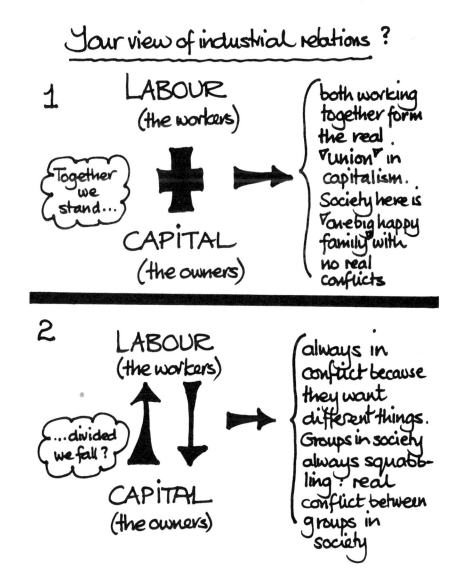

Assignment 3.3

New Model Unions:

		Is this true of unions today?		
1	Wanted to be accepted by society	**Yes**	**No**	DK*
2	Often rejected the idea of going on strike	**Yes**	**No**	DK*
3	Wanted to control who came into the trade they were representing	**Yes**	**No**	DK*
4	Were generally well organized	**Yes**	**No**	DK*
5	Were not concerned with revolution	**Yes**	**No**	DK*

* If you 'don't know' the answer at this point read the book right through and then come back to the question again.

Assignment 3.4

Was striking an act of courage on the part of an individual worker in the nineteenth century? Is it now?

Having read some of the history of trade unions, in what ways do you think that striking in 1830 differed from striking in the 1980s?

What effects at work and at home did and does striking have upon adults and children then and now?

The Tolpuddle Martyrs: The Most Famous Unionists of Them All?

'*Memories bind the farmworkers together in their scattered isolation in the English countryside. Every July union stalwarts gather in the tiny village of Tolpuddle in Dorset for the annual rally in commemoration of the events of 1834 when six farm workers were deported to serve seven years hard labour in Australia for daring to organize themselves as a union. A leading Labour politician heads the procession of gaily coloured banners through the main street of the village to the churchyard where a*

'division of labour'. They were not general unions open to all but were based on individual skills or trades, and so, not unnaturally, these developments were led by the 'aristocrats of labour', the skilled craftsmen. These workers were fairly safe in their employment. Their jobs were stable. They received fairly high wages, were usually quite literate and had apprenticeship systems that allowed them to control who came into the trade. They were not concerned with revolution but thought it much more important that they obeyed society's rules and won the support of the Victorian middle classes. They wanted better conditions at work and at home and felt that the best ways to achieve this was through political reform. Many of them thought that striking was dangerous and was not to be encouraged and so they

looked after the economic interests of their members through *constitutional* methods.

One of the first successful unions organized on this basis was the forerunner of today's AUEW (Amalgamated Union of Engineering Workers) which, in those early days was called the ASE, the Amalgamated Society of Engineers. This was formed in January 1851 and members paid a shilling (5p) a week subscription (out of their wages of between 24 and 25 shillings a week: 120–125p). By the end of the year 11 000 members were paying their subscriptions to develop a union that set the pattern for what was later to be called the *New Model Unions*.

Assignment 3.3 lists some important points about the 'New Model Unions'. Look down the list and see how many of the aims still apply today.

Steady growth of the trade union

1860s   movement continued on through the 1860s and 1870s with such developments as the local Trades Councils. These were made up of representatives of all the different trade unions in a particular town. The first of these, the London Trades Council, was set up in 1861. The TUC followed in 1868 and in 1871 the TUC 'Parliamentary Committee' was established. All of these were trying to build a recognized place for the trade unions in nineteenth century British society.

In 1867 the Royal Commission on the Organization of Trade Unions and other Associations started work and eventually their conclusions led to the passing of the

1871   Trade Union Act in 1871. This Act recognized the *legal* status of trade unions and

1875   this, along with another Act in 1875, which recognized the unions' right to bargain collectively with their employers and to strike and peacefully picket, allowed further trade union growth to take place in the latter part of the nineteenth century.

However, it must not be forgotten that progress was still difficult. For example, the unions wanted to have, through members of Parliament sympathetic to their cause, some voice for their views in Parliament, and the Reform Bills of 1867 and 1884 had certainly allowed more people to vote. (Even so after the 1867 Bill only 16% of all adults were entitled to vote, while even after the 1884 Bill the number had only increased to 28%.) There was still a good

deal of opposition to there being a workers' party set up with the aim of trying to change the power balance in society.

It is very easy when one talks about 'the unions' to think that they are all very much the same. This is of course completely untrue in that there were and still are very marked differences between unions. So it was with *the workers* in the latter quarter of the nineteenth century. The skilled 'aristocracy of labour', who were after all but a small section of the total work force, were slowly but surely improving their own position. But what about the other workers, the army of unskilled individuals who were not organized and who were the first to suffer the ups and downs of the capitalist economy? Why were they so difficult to organize? There were several reasons. First, if there were a strike it was very easy to replace an *unskilled* man. In many cases, the unskilled worker still had not seen the benefits that being organized into a union could bring, and even if he had, with his low wages and the then relatively high union subscriptions, it would have been unlikely that he could have afforded to join anyway!

Where could you find these workers? They were in the factories, steelworks, coalmines, docks and railways created during the Industrial Revolution. They were local and regional workers in developing industries such as coal and cotton. They were workers in those unions de-

wreath is laid on the grave of James Hammett, the only Tolpuddle 'martyr' actually buried in the village. When Hammett was laid to rest at that spot in 1878 the local squire stood by the graveside to make sure nobody spoke for or on behalf of trade unionism. The brass bands play and the assembled faithfully munch cucumber sandwiches and reminisce, beside the row of martyr memorial cottages built in the 1930s. Tolpuddle – like the Durham miners' gala – has a hallowed place in Labour's commemorative history.

Source: courtesy The Fifth Estate, *Robert Taylor, 1980*

'The dockers' marches through the City, stage-managed by Burns and made spectacular by the banners and emblems and totem poles crowned with stinking fish-heads and rotting onions – current samples of the docker's diet – went from strength to strength; but the strikers' relief funds sank lower and lower. . . . Then suddenly, out of the blue from Australia, money began to pour in for the sustenance of the London strikers. Money from the wharf labourers of Brisbane; from almost every Australian trade union; from Australian football clubs. About £30 000 in all: a sum to make the dock companies jittery, and reluctantly disposed to meet with a mediation committee that was set up . . . by the Lord Mayor.

'The dockers obtained the major part of what they wanted. A famous victory, which lifted the hearts not only of the London dockers, but of other workers – gas workers, railwaymen, textile workers, building workers, ship building and metal workers, miners and boot and shoe operatives. . . .'

Source: *courtesy* The History of the TUC 1868–1968

veloping in large cities, such as the gas-workers, the dockers and the railwaymen. Their strength would lie in their numbers. Here were the beginnings of the large, general unions of the present day. These unions were very different from their 'Model Union' counterparts. They catered for the unskilled and the poorly paid. They had low subscription fees, and open membership. Anyone could join. Their rule books were simple and often showed socialist tendencies. Even today the National Union of Railwaymens' rule book states that one of its aims is 'to work for the suppression of the capitalist system by a socialist order of society. The *New Unions*, as they came to be called, provided strike benefits. This was important since the 'New Unions' were quite prepared to strike for what they wanted and this was precisely what these newly emergent unions did (even though the majority of the TUC were opposed to these kinds of tactics!).

1880s Towards the end of the 1880s there was a series of successful strikes on the part of **1888** unskilled workers. In 1888, 700 match girls from the firm of Bryant and May went on strike. Much to everyone's surprise and with good organization on the girls' part, the strike was a success and their claims were met. In 1889, the gas workers led by Tom Mann, John Burns and Will Thorne, agitated for an eight hour day. Again, success went to the workers. A few days **1889** later, on 13 August, 1889, a strike of a few

labourers at the West India Dock, in the East End of London, led to the famous London Dock Strike. The strike, led by Tom Mann, John Burns and Ben Tillet, paralysed the port. The quote on this page describes some of the incidents that occurred during the great docker's strike which led to their claim of 2½p an hour (the 'dockers' tanner') being fully met.

Before we leave this chapter I want to highlight the *role of women* in the early unions. In fact, perhaps, I should say '*non role*' for, quite often, when we read accounts of trade union activities that have taken place in the past we might be forgiven for thinking that the only important things that took place were those carried out by men! Since we've just been looking at the match girls' strike of 1888 it might be a good idea to have a quick look at the struggle women had (and, for that matter, are *still* having) in making their way in the union movement.

One important point that has to be remembered is that the early trade unions were often reluctant to accept women members at all. Women were put in special 'womens' sections' where they paid lower subscriptions and had fewer rights than the male members. In 1886 the *Women's Trade Union League* had been formed. The League had, as one of its aims, the wish to get women included as *full* members in the general unions which, as we have just seen, were then growing in strength. The League also encouraged women to set up their own trade unions so that womens' interests could be better looked after for, it was felt, then (as now), that the women's viewpoint was not being considered or communicated by the male-dominated unions. This point about male domination will crop up again in the next chapter and, of course, in Chapter 11 where the role of women in the trade union movement is examined in more detail.

Assignment 3.5

If you were living in 1850, what technological developments (cars, hot and cold running water, television, etc.) would you *miss* most and why?

Assignment 3.6

In what ways did improvements in communications (railways, better roads, postal services etc.) help the growth of the trade unions?

Assignment 3.7

In what specific ways are workers and their families better protected from the economic 'ups and downs' of capitalism today than the early trade unionists and their families were in the early 1800s. Make a list. Once you have read this chapter and Chapter 4, see if you can add to your list.

Dockers at work

Miners at work

If possible, do the above exercise again but this time in a *group*. Compare your own list with that of the group and see how the two lists compare and contrast.

Assignment 3.8

For each of the photographs on p. 49:

(*a*) describe what work is taking place;
(*b*) describe what you think are the dangers associated with each of the jobs;
(*c*) describe how the work in each industry has changed and try to give some of the reasons for those changes.

Assignment 3.9

As an assignment, find out what happened to the Chartists and see whether or not their movement was *successful*.

Think also why the Chartists campaigned for 'universal *male* suffrage'. Why didn't they campaign for suffrage for both men *and* women?

Chartism: Some Notes

The charter (from which Chartism gets its name) was originally drawn up by the London Working Mens' Association (LWMA) with the help of Francis Place and a number of radical MPs. The aim of the exercise was to draw working men together to support political reform. The Charter put forward the following *six points*:

1 universal male suffrage;
2 secret ballot;
3 annual elections;
4 equal electoral districts;
5 payment for MPs;
6 Abolition of property qualifications for candidates.

Marxism: Some Notes

Karl Marx lived from 1818 to 1883. His writings have had a profound effect on many peoples' thoughts. His ideas, some of which are very briefly outlined below, are key factors in the systems of belief known as *socialism* and *communism*.

MARX believed:

1 in the importance of *economic* forces and factors in society. He said they underlay all that went on in capitalist society.
2 in the importance of the *class struggle* between the *bourgeoisie* (the middle classes) and the *proletariat* (the workers);
3 that the capitalist system exploited the workers and that, in the capitalist system, the 'rich get richer and the poor get poorer';
4 that because of 3 the workers would get so fed up with capitalism that they would overthrow it and build a fairer society that was *socialist* in outlook;

5 that the workers would take control through a *revolution* (as happened in Russia in 1917);
6 that this fairer society would be run by the workers (the proletariat).

These are only a few of Marx's complicated and varied ideas. Because Marx is difficult to read try the following two *sources* as an introduction to his thoughts.

1 'Society Today' in *New Society*, 14 February, 1980
2 *Marx for beginners* by RIUS published by Writers and Readers Publishing Co-operative (1976).

Chapter 4
To find out where you are going, you must know where you've been (1900 to the present day)

A New Century – A New Party

'*In Queen Victoria's reign Britain became the 'workshop of the world' – but at a price; the ordinary man was over-worked and under-paid, his family condemned to the poorest housing, education and social welfare. In protest, workers formed trade unions . . . , revolutionaries founded Marxist organizations . . . , intellectuals publicized socialist ideals and a true party of the people was begun (Independent Labour Party 1893). In 1900 these groups formed the Labour Representation committee. In*

Objectives

At the end of this chapter you will:

1 have a basic overall picture of some of the key events in industrial relations' history over the last 180 years;
2 see ways in which past events in trade unions' history still affect present-day trade union practice;
3 have carried out some research into trade union history.

THIS CHAPTER COVERS the following subjects:

1 the development of the Labour Party (1890s/ early 1900s);
2 industrial relations during World War I (1914–18)/the role of women during the war and after;
3 trade union growth and decline between the wars (1920–39);
4 World War II and after (1939 until present time).

1890s

1906

Earlier in our story we saw how important it was for the unions to have working with them Members of Parliament who were sympathetic to their cause. Until the 1890s, this connection was particularly strong with the Liberal Party. However, during the 1890s things got harder for the unions. The employers became better organized. Economic conditions got tougher and various legal decisions went against the unions in the late 1890s and early years of the twentieth century. Under the influence of Keir Hardie, the key socialist figure of the nineties, the beginnings of a new party came about. The extract below shows how the Labour Party describes its own growth. Note how it highlights the close connection, then as now, between itself and the trade union movement.*

In the election of 1906 twenty-nine LRC candidates were elected to the House of Commons and the Labour Party was here to stay in British politics. During the 1900–14 period, events particularly in the law

*N.B. For more information on this *see* Chapter 9.

courts, swung for and against trade unions, although in the main at this time the law, the various governments and employers 1910 were still hostile to them. In the 1910–14 period wages fell behind prices and some large scale strikes took place in various heavy industries such as shipping, shipbuilding and mining. In spite of all these problems, however, the unions continued to grow in the years before the First World War.

With the outbreak of the First World War 1914 in 1914, the government became increasingly involved in industrial affairs, as, for example in the production of munitions and for the first time, the trade unions and labour leaders actually became part of the governmental decision making process. During the war the *Triple Alliance* made up of the railwaymen, the miners and the Transport Workers Federation, did a good deal to contribute to the war effort. The 'Triple Alliance', incidentally, had been formed in the spring of 1914, and was a result of those pre-war problems that we have just been discussing.

The First World War obviously had important effects upon the trade union movement just as it led to marked changes in peoples' everyday lives. Some important trends that are, perhaps, worth remembering are these. After the war, the unions had greater confidence. The workers *were* important and the work that they had done towards the war effort had

shown that to be the case. A second trend, one that, interestingly enough, has implications for what goes on in present-day industrial relations, was the rise of the Shop Stewards' Movement. These rank and file workers, generally militant in outlook, were very much concerned with what was happening on the shopfloor. Indeed, if we follow this development we can see evidence of a split between the more militant shop stewards and the national trade union officials, who were, at that time, working with the government to set up national negotiating groups such as those suggested by the Whitley Reports.* What makes the difference of opinion so interesting is this; one of the real problems in studying industrial relations is that it is very complicated to understand. Here we have an example of this complexity, because if we look deeper into the war situation we can see that although we talk of the 'unions and the war' reality was not as simple as that statement makes it appear. We need to be able to look at different sides of the same situation. For example, when the war broke out we have seen how the established trade unions

* The Whitley Reports of 1917 were put into action by the Ministry of Labour immediately after the war. On a voluntary basis, they did a good deal to encourage the setting up of *national* collective bargaining groups (*Joint Industrial Councils* or JICs, such as those we have today, for example, in the Health Service). These groups or councils were made up of people from the trade union and employers' side and they developed in the period between the First and Second World Wars.

1906, *twenty-nine of their candidates were elected to Parliament, and the Labour Representative Committee became the* Labour Party. *At this time MPs were not paid and so financial support was necessary. For the first Labour MPs this came from the* Unions *and so a close and enduring link was forged.*

Source: courtesy Labour Party Documents

Syndicalism

('Workers' control of industry leading to ultimate workers' control of the state')

TUC, 1968

This movement (which had grown up in Italy and France) wanted to overthrow the existing way of things by means of a 'general strike'. Syndicalists aimed to have workers' control of a country's economic resources. The movement had some influence on British trade unionism in the difficult 1910–14 period. For example, in 1912, a group of miners' leaders issued a pamphlet called The Miners' Next Step.

'This pamphlet . . .' proposed that the miners' unions should re-organize themselves on industrial lines with a strong central direction of policy, the object of which would be to bring the industry to a standstill, with strike after strike, until the system of private ownership collapsed. Then the miners would take over the paralysed industry and re-organize it on the basis of workers' control. The ultimate aim of the authors was to see their lead followed by the trade unions on other industries'.

'The revolutionary implications of this syndicalist policy were in due course, overwhelmingly rejected by the Trades Union Congress of 1912.'

Source: courtesy The History of the TUC

tended to take the view that the best thing to do was to call an 'industrial truce' to help keep the factories going. These people were then given power within the government to help keep the 'wheels of industry' turning. On the other hand, people such as the shop stewards saw this as a 'sell out' to the government. They saw the 1915 *Munitions of War Act* (which among other things made strikes illegal) and *dilution of labour* as a surrendering of power to the employers and the government.

Incidentally, when we talk of the 'dilution of labour' we simply mean that semi-skilled and female labour were introduced into jobs that had, up until that time, been reserved for skilled craftsmen. During the First World War women took over many jobs that had previously been carried on by men. They worked in factories. They worked as nurses and were also to be seen working on buses and trains. During the war the *National Federation of Women Workers* became an important group in the labour movement, and, in the 1920s, it brought pressure to bear on the unions and the TUC until the latter eventually established two seats on the General Council especially for women. It's worth noting, I think, that no further increase in 'womens' seats' took place again until 1981!

After the war there was a dramatic reduction in the number of women employed. This, in turn, led to a dramatic reduction in female trade union membership. Very quickly the unions took control of areas of skilled work. Both women (and young men who had not 'served their time') were left 'out in the cold'. However, for a short time after the war there was an industrial boom and, for men at least, jobs were plentiful.

When this happens, workers are in demand and the power of the unions is strong. When times get harder, and there are fewer jobs about, it becomes much more difficult for the unions to bargain from a position of strength. They may simply have fewer members and less cash because of that. It is important to remember this when we look at the history of the unions during the 1920s and 1930s when depression and high unemployment were the norm rather than the exception. (It might also be worthwhile to think what will happen to the membership and power of the unions in the 1980s if unemployment remains high.)

1920s   However, back in the early 1920s the unions were responding to changing circumstances by joining together to form fewer but larger federations (or groupings). We have the further development of large general unions led by men who were prepared to strike for what they want. From 1920 onwards strikes and threats of strikes brought the unions into conflict with the government of the day. Things went from bad to worse. There was in-

Match girls on strike outside Bryant & May, Bow, July 1888

The General Strike 1926: a cartoon of the time

creasing economic gloom. Unemployment rose. Wages fell. Bitter conflicts developed between employer and employee and, in spite of a minority Labour government in 1923, conditions worsened, culminating in 1926 in the *General Strike*.

The strike was part of the old battle between the miners and the coal owners (the coal industry was not nationalized

As the History of the TUC says, however,

'in fact the "general strike" was not, in any real sense, general. (The trade unions themselves preferred the name of "national strike".) The only principal unions initially called out in support of the miners were those of the railwaymen, the transport workers* the builders, and iron and steel workers – and the printers, engineers and the ship-yard workers were called out after the first week, when it was almost all over bar the recriminations.'

* Note the members of the old Triple Alliance

until 1947). Very simply what happened was that in 1925 there were further falls in general trade. The mine owners announced that they would be cutting wages. They also insisted that the men worked a longer day. The miners' leaders had had enough and were determined not to give way again, as they had on previous occasions. Their slogan was *Not a penny off the pay, not a second on the day*. The miners successfully appealed to the General Council of the TUC for help, and it agreed to call a general strike which began on 4 May.

1926

Insufficient cash in union coffers and uncertain leadership from the General Council led to the strike's collapse. The miners, however, went on fighting but even they were forced to go back, seven months later.

The defeat heralded a steep decline in union membership. The strike had shown that the unions could not 'deliver the goods' on pay. The figures speak for themselves (*see* graph on p. 57). In 1920 6½ million people were members of the movement. By 1929 membership had fallen to 5½ million; by 1932 4½ million.

The government followed on the unions' defeat by passing the Trade Disputes and Trade Unions Act 1927. This made strikes where workers come out in sympathy with other workers illegal. It also made strikes illegal where the strike was called to *force* the government into doing something that

1927

THE GREAT PENNY STRIKE;
OR, THE BLOATED CAPITALIST AND THE AUTOMATIC DOCK LABOURER.

The Great Dock Strike 1889: a car oon of the time

the *workers* wanted. It also banned civil servants and workers in local government from going on strike. In addition, the law on picketing was altered. Finally, and from the Labour Party's viewpoint, most importantly, it made it necessary for union members *expressly* to say that they wanted to pay into the unions' 'political fund' ('contracting in'). This meant that instead of the money being paid into the fund automatically (as had been the case under a

1913 Act), members had to say quite specifically that they wanted to contribute. In effect, this meant that the apathetic members of the union simply did not pay into the fund. The Act ensured that the Labour Party was weakened because it received less cash through unions' funds, while on the union side, due to declining membership, they too declined in strength.

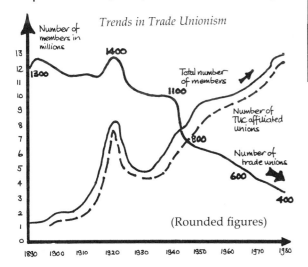

Trends in Trade Unionism

(Rounded figures)

Together, the general world recession and the unions' failure in the general strike made the unions 'back off' from the forceful positions they had taken up after the First World War. There was little contact with the Labour government of 1929–31. The thirties were terrible years of world recession and not until late on in the thirties did the trade unions begin to recover. By

Assignment 4.1

Carry out your own research into the 'General Strike'

Find out as much as you can about the General Strike, the people involved, and the issues at stake. Use the following sources:

1 people who were living at the time;
2 local libraries;
3 local newspapers of the time;
4 books such as:

(a) *The History of the TUC 1868–1968* (TUC)
(b) *Milestones in Working Class History* (Longmate) BBC
(c) *Learning from Industrial Relations* (Stuttard) Longman

the time the Second World War broke out, they had again grown in size and status. By this time many workers were covered by

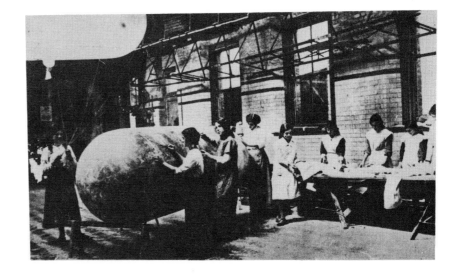

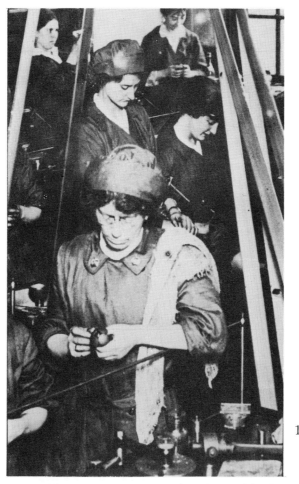

*World War One: women working in munitions'
factories*

nationally agreed pay rates, etc. The TUC
has now become accepted in society at large

and the 'Establishment' had come to
recognize that the TUC had itself become
part of the 'Establishment'.

The strong rank and file militancy of the
1914–18 war was not repeated during the
Second World War. The view taken by the
established trade unions in the First World
War was strengthened in the Second. The
unions worked with the government and
the employers and, in return, were given
decision-making responsibility. More and
more agreements came to be made at a
National Level and more and more bodies
were set up to allow this to happen. After
the war, collective bargaining and collective agreements through these national
groups went on growing.

Once the war had ended, the Labour
Party swept to a landslide victory in the
1945 general election. In 1946 they passed
the Trade Disputes and Trade Union Act;
this abolished the hated 1927 Act which
had been so bitterly resented by the unions.
With this the unions and the Labour Party
moved back again to a closer working
relationship.

1950s   The welfare state (free health, education,
social services, etc.) and the consumer
society developed through the fifties and
sixties and the TUC was increasingly
consulted, by governments and employers, about broader matters than just the
straightforward   industrial   relations'
business. They became increasingly involved in a wide range of social and welfare

issues. Post war, the trend towards *national* bargaining for whole industries continued to increase until, by the mid-sixties, out of a total of 23 million working people in Britain, 18 million were covered by more than 500 national agreements covering entire industries.

However, like so many things in industrial relations changes have taken place once again. Since the 1960s there has been a new trend (a trend which really began after the Second World War) in which the national agreements we have been talking about became increasingly 'backed up' by *local* agreements made between shop stewards and managements at local, plant level. This is an attempt to get the best of both worlds and has led to the growth of more and more local agreements. It has also meant that the importance of the shop steward has grown tremendously over the last few years although the recession of the 1980s has, without a doubt, checked the power of the shop stewards at local level.

On top of all these changes there have been very important changes in the laws applying to industrial relations. We have already seen throughout Chapters 3 and 4 that the relationship between the law and the unions has been both complex and controversial. The 1970s were notable for the vast amounts of industrial relations' legislation that appeared on the statute books. (The full list can be seen in Chapter 7.) The 1980s seem to be going the same

Assignment 4.2

Themes Past and Present

Use the following guidelines and questions to put into some clear order the effects of history on today's trade union thinking.

Shall I join a trade union or not?

Yes
Joining with others gives me increased power

No
Staying on my own is a basic individual right

Historical Point : Think back to the *Closed Shop* argument of the early unions

If I join a union should it be:

Militant
Willing to resort quickly to strike action

Non-militant
Unlikely to resort quickly to strike action

Historical Point : Think back on the *New Model Unions* of the 1850s and the *General Unions* of the 1880s

Collective bargaining should be at:

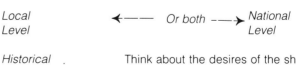

Local Level

Or both

National Level

Historical Point : Think about the desires of the shop stewards' movement to get power to the factory floor

Keep the *law*
out of industrial   ◄─────────►   The *law* has
relations   a place in
                                    industrial relations

Histroical
Point   :   Think about the relationship between
                     the unions and the law as outlined
                     in the last two chapters

                     Economic demand for labour

High demand   ◄─────────►   Low demand
for workers   for workers

Historical
Point   :   When was demand for labour high/low?

Having looked at some of the factors that have been (and still are) important in the ways that unions grow and change, ask yourself a question like '*as a group of workers* should we strike?*' and see how each of the different themes have to be taken into account when you are thinking of your answer.

* For example, nurses, shop workers, miners, civil servants, farm labourers.

way and, even as I write, the Conservative government is adding to that legislation with their very important, and controversial, 1982 Employment Act. That legislation, like so much industrial relations' legislation in the past, is concerned with curbing the power of the unions. With this last point in mind we arrive back rather well to the comments we made in the beginning of Chapter 3 where we were talking about early unions and how little power they had!

Today, the wheel seems to have turned full circle and, nowadays, some people say that unions are too powerful because they can 'hold the country to ransom'. At the same time, unions are often powerless to stop local unofficial strikes by their own members. How much power do they then have? With questions like these, we need only look at the current industrial relations scene to find plenty to keep us thinking about trade unions and their development. Whatever conclusions you come up with however, remember that if you want to understand what is going on today, you have to go *back* into time to find the roots of today's behaviour in yesterday's events, issues, and individuals.

Summary

The last two chapters have tried to make clear some of the *themes* underlying the history of British industrial relations. They have taken *some* of the ideas present in contemporary trade union thinking and, hopefully, have shown how these ideas have developed, and also how thoughts and ideas coming from the past still influence trade union thinking.

Assignment 4.3

What are some of the advantages and disadvantages of joining a union. Look back over the history of the last 180 years and ask the question again as it applied to times gone by.

Assignment 4.4

Which of the following do you think are important factors for unions to develop and grow:

(a) a group feeling of 'solidarity' against employer, governments, other workers;
(b) a political party to 'back them up' in Parliament;
(c) the support of the legal system.

Assignment 4.5

In the Industrial Revolution the factory system replaced the small workshops etc that people had formerly worked in. How do you think this change would affect:

(a) methods of production?
(b) job style?
(c) daily routine?
(d) ways of family life?

Assignment 4.6

In the past the employer had a good deal of power over his workers. Give examples to show whether you think employers have more or less power over employees *today*.

Assignment 4.7

Examine some of the ideas of

(a) Robert Owen;
(b) Karl Marx;
(c) Keir Hardie;

and show how these ideas have influenced trade unionism in Britain.

Assignment 4.8

List some of the effects that:

(a) the Great Dock Strike 1889;
(b) the First World War 1914–18;
(c) the General Strike 1926;
(d) the Second World War 1939–45;

have had upon industrial relations.
This assignment would need supporting material in the form of extracts from newspapers of the time, people living at the time (where possible), etc.

Assignment 4.9

Having looked at some trade union history, we have seen some of the *forces* that 'knock' the worker, for example:

(*a*) trade recessions ('slumps' in trade);
(*b*) political pressures (governments not accepting the legality of trade unions);
(*c*) monetary pressures (being sacked if you go on strike);
(*d*) social pressure (people believing that unions are dangerous and revolutionary).

From trade union history, give examples of each of these.

Books that you have read and found useful should be added below

Recommended Reading for Chapters 3 and 4

1 *To Build Jerusalem* by J. Gorman (Scorpion, 1980)
2 *Milestones in Working Class History* by N. Longmate (BBC, 1975)
3 *Women at War 1914–1918* (A Marwick Fontana, 1977)
4 *The History of the TUC* (An excellent book regrettably out of print but your local library should have a copy) (Published by the TUC, 1968)
5 For histories of individual unions I suggest you refer to *The Trade Union Directory* by J. Eaton and C. Gill (Pluto Press, 1983)

N.B. If you have enjoyed reading about trade union history, why not visit these museums or send to them for further information:

The National Museum
of Labour History
Limehouse Town Hall
Commercial Road
LONDON E14

The Rochdale
Pioneers Museum
31 Toad Lane
ROCHDALE
Lancashire

Section Two

Chapter 5
You've got to work at it . . .

Objectives

At the end of this chapter you should be able to:

1 show, by giving examples, the importance of work in our Western society and show how work affects our life outside work;
2 outline the work of particular individuals and list some of the advantages and disadvantages of the particular job under discussion;
3 list some of the reasons why people work;
4 show, again by giving examples, some of the important aspects of working with people;
5 explain some of the important industrial relations' events that happen at the place of work;
6 think about and discuss the future of work;
7 think about more critically the relationships between work/women

THIS CHAPTER COVERS the following subjects/topics:

1 work: what is it? How does it affect us?
2 work: who does it, when and where?
3 work: for what?
4 work: with whom?
5 work and industrial relations;
6 people without work;
7 work and women.

THIS CHAPTER is all about work, the work group, the workplace and industrial relations at the place of work. The workplace is crucial in our discussions of industrial relations. Unions started and became firmly embedded in the workplace. It was at the workplace back in the 1800s that men and women got together in groups to discuss the relationship they had (or more likely were unable to have) with their employers. That is one thing that is still true today. Whether or not the workers belong to a union work is still an important topic for group discussion at work. Indeed, for many people their work follows them home and affects their lives at home. For many women, of course, the home is not only their place of work it is their work. If we are lucky we enjoy our work. At the same time there will be readers among you who do not enjoy their work particularly, but who enjoy and make the fullest use of the money that

'Work is the curse of the drinking classes.'
Popular saying

'The less I say, the more my work gets done.'
'Philadelphia Freedom' Elton John, 1975

When you work with people it may pay to remember that:

'There is no other way of guarding one's self against flattery than by letting men understand that they will not offend you by speaking the truth; but when everyone can tell you the truth, you lose their respect.'

Source: Machiavelli: The Prince

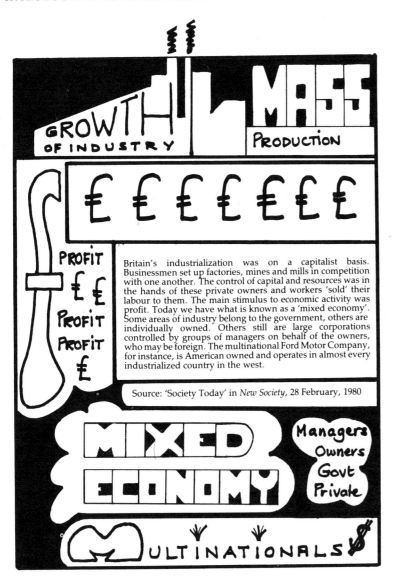

GROWTH OF INDUSTRY

MASS PRODUCTION

£ £ £ £ £ £ £

PROFIT £ £ PROFIT PROFIT £

Britain's industrialization was on a capitalist basis. Businessmen set up factories, mines and mills in competition with one another. The control of capital and resources was in the hands of these private owners and workers 'sold' their labour to them. The main stimulus to economic activity was profit. Today we have what is known as a 'mixed economy'. Some areas of industry belong to the government, others are individually owned. Others still are large corporations controlled by groups of managers on behalf of the owners, who may be foreign. The multinational Ford Motor Company, for instance, is American owned and operates in almost every industrialized country in the west.

Source: 'Society Today' in *New Society*, 28 February, 1980

MIXED ECONOMY

Managers Owners Govt Private

MULTINATIONALS

work provides. So whatever else, for workers, managers, unionists and the unemployed, work is important because we do it since we need money.

Let us make that our starting place. For many, indeed, for most of us, work is something we have to do to live. Essentially, *we work to live*. On the other hand, it's also true to say that some people enjoy and need their work so much that *they live to work*. These people have been nick-named 'workaholics' and for them work is their main interest, goal and aim in life.

For many work gives life some kind of meaning. It fills our days with things to do. It gives us money, friends and status. It is so important in our society that the key question we often ask someone when we meet them for the first time is 'what kind of work do you do?'. So many of us are committed to the idea of work that when someone answers the above question by saying that they are unemployed we often offer sympathy and hope that they get a job in the near future. Work gives us an identity and to be unemployed implies rightly or wrongly no clear identity or direction in life for the person concerned. For example, the job a person does is a pretty good guide to the amount of job satisfaction that the person will get from their job. Where the job demands a fairly high level of skill research shows that people feel a higher level of job satisfaction than where levels of skill are low. Often jobs where you are helping others to develop and solve their own problems, such as teaching and nursing, give high job involvement and therefore high job satisfaction. In these cases work is often part of their social lives as well as their professional ones.

So like it or not, the influence of work is very powerful. We may think we can leave an unpleasant job at work but what happens at the workplace will so often affect the way you feel, your general attitude to life, your choice of friends, your future prospects, in fact, all kinds of things. On the positive side, if you really enjoy your work and it becomes part of you, you will, where possible, be only too pleased to take it home with you. For example teachers prepare lessons at home. Architects may have their own drawing office at home while research workers may do a good deal of their reading and writing at home. For these people work and leisure merge gently together.

In addition, the kind of *work* we do gives us a place on the social class ladder and in Britain particularly we seem especially concerned with our position on the social scale. Since work (and the income we get from work) are important factors in determining where we are ranked on the social class scale it might do us good to think about the relationship between our job and the social standing it gives us in other peoples' eyes. However, work affects our *own* lives much more deeply than this. We have seen how a job and the money you get from that job will determine your standard of living. It will determine how expensive a house you can afford (to buy or rent) and how costly the furniture will be that goes into that house. It will determine whether you spend your holiday in the Bahamas or in Blackpool. Indeed, it will almost determine whether

or not you can afford a holiday at all! The money you get from your job is obviously crucial in so many ways. However your job also deeply influences many of your own *personal characteristics*. Just as your personality influences the kind of job you apply for so your job will affect you and your personality. For example, your job will affect your health. Have a look at the table on p. 69. Certain jobs have a high level of stress and, where this is the case, it is often true that workers in those jobs get certain diseases associated with this stress. For example, bus drivers, who are subjected both to stress and to sitting for long periods (therefore not getting any exercise), often suffer from duodenal (stomach) ulcers, unlike farm workers whose lives are relatively stress-free.

Moving on from here into other individual activities, such as leisure, it is clear to see another

Assignment 5.1

Rate the following jobs (from 1 [most important] to 10 [least important]) in terms of:

(a) how important *you* think the jobs are;
(b) how important you think society in general thinks those jobs are.

How closely do the two lists match?
The jobs are as follows:

nurses, electrical power workers, dockers, teachers, civil servants, agricultural workers, railwaymen, lorry drivers, firemen and miners.

'The best way to spot a workaholic is to look at how he spends his leisure time. Dr Oates says: 'A true workaholic doesn't know what to do when he's not working. For him, Sunday is dreadful.'

'Workaholics are notorious for making a shambles of their personal lives. . . . For example, the wife of a Los Angeles accountant talks about how distressed she was when, soon after their marriage, her husband began staying out until midnight several nights a week and leaving the house on Saturdays and Sundays. She was convinced he was having a clandestine love affair. Now, five years later, realizing that her husband is a workaholic, she laughs at her earlier suspicions. 'He would never take the time to have an affair', she says.

My favourite quotation highlights the care we need to take in deciding how seriously we ought to take our work:

'Workaholics have been known to die of heart attacks within a few days of going on vacation.'

Source: all above quotes: Thank God, It's Monday *by N. Howard and S. Antilla in Dun's Review, No 6, 1980*

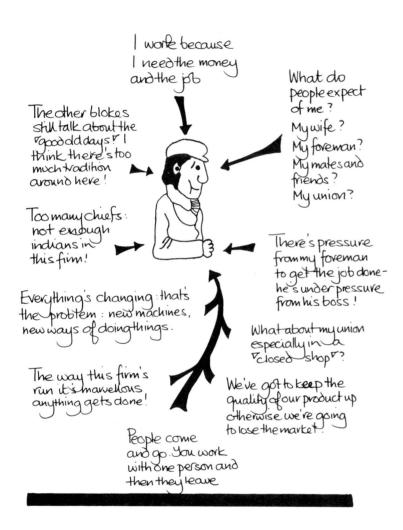

I work because I need the money and the job

What do people expect of me? My wife? My foreman? My mates and friends? My union?

The other blokes still talk about the 'good old days'! I think there's too much tradition around here!

Too many chiefs: not enough indians in this firm!

There's pressure from my foreman to get the job done — he's under pressure from his boss!

Everything's changing: that's the problem: new machines, new ways of doing things.

What about my union especially in a 'closed shop'?

The way this firm's run it's marvellous anything gets done!

We've got to keep the quality of our product up otherwise we're going to lose the market.

People come and go. You work with one person and then they leave

Some of the 'forces' that can put pressure on the worker at WORK

important link with work. The amount of leisure time the job gives, the amount of cash you have to spend on sports, hobbies, etc. and the reasons why people follow certain hobbies and activities are all-importantly related to the work a person does. Certain sports may be so expensive to follow that only a certain number of people in the population can afford to play. People, for example, may take up golf because they truly like the look of the game and they want to get some exercise and do something that relaxes them. They may also see joining the golf club as an important step up the social ladder.

In these cases work is spilling over into the person's leisure time. On the other hand you can, of course, cut work completely off from leisure. You are literally a different person at work from the person you are at home. It would seem that more involvement at work leads to a greater involvement in an active leisure life. Boring occupations on the other hand seem to have two alternative reactions: boring work leads into boring leisure or boring work is made up for by a really active leisure life.

But what is 'boring' work? Many factory workers whose work is often very repetitive, simply do not expect too much from their work. In this way they are not disappointed when the work is boring. It may simply mean that they get their main pleasures from life in their non-work activities, for example, during their leisure time. In this way they may not actually get satisfaction from their time at work but are able to spend their (relatively) high pay on things that they want and enjoy, for example, on a caravan, or a boat or

HOW THE OTHER HALF DIES

The table below shows the death rate per 1 000 of men aged 15–64 in different occupations

High Death Rate		Low Death Rate	
Electrical engineers	19.04	Medical practitioners	4.94
Bricklayers' labourers	16.44	Postmen	4.84
Policemen	12.70	Civil service executive officers	4.67
Labourers and unskilled workers, all industries	12.47	Architects, town planners	4.43
		Sales managers	4.21
Fishermen	10.28	Primary and secondary school teachers	3.96
Steel erectors, riggers	9.92	Ministers of the Crown, MPs, senior government officials	3.71
Coal miners (above ground)	9.72		
Watch repairers	9.46	Local authority senior officers	3.42
Machine tool operators	9.34	Managers in building and contracting	3.19
Shoemakers, and shoe repairers	8.98	Paper products makers	3.02
Leather products makers	8.95	Physiotherapists	2.97
Coal miners (underground)	8.22	University teachers	2.87

Source: courtesy The Sunday Times, 31 August, 1980

Work is good for you

'Nathanson argues that work is a source of accomplishment, self-esteem and social contact, and that these are important factors in maintaining mental and physical well-being. Housebound women are socially isolated – and competence at housework is not widely acclaimed, although successful child-rearing is a valued activity. Women with the largest number of obligations as housewives, mothers and employees, are therefore healthier. They have no time to be ill.'

Source: courtesy Social Science and Medicine, Vol. 14A No. 6

an expensive holiday in the sun somewhere.

A good deal of research has been carried out into what makes work interesting for an individual and the following assignment leads you into thinking of the particular aspects of a job that really makes that job interesting. Michael Argyle, a psychologist with a particular interest in groups and the ways in which they work, writes about this as seen in Assignment 5.2.

Assignment 5.2

Your job and you –
a two way fit?

You
Job

'There are, of course, some jobs which need a special kind of personality, such as light-house keepers, wrestlers, spies and monks'.

'Persons and Work', M. Argyle in New Society 16 November 1972

Before we leave the relationship between work and time outside work it is important to remember that a large number of people (journalists, engine drivers, nurses, power workers) work hours that are unsocial. Many of these do night work which has all kinds of implications for a person's social life.

Night work is, perhaps a good way of looking at work somewhat differently. Just before we move on to pay at work, etc. I want to cast a passing, but nevertheless very important, glance at *women and their relationships with work* both at home and at the workplace.

Before reading on, do Assignment 5.5.

Although Chapter 11 will tell us a good deal more about women's role in the unions, there are a couple of points about *women and work* that need to be made here.

Women make up over 40% of the total work-force. In general terms, they earn considerably less than men even once you've taken into account the fact that they work shorter hours and do less overtime than men. Women are still, in very many cases, cheap labour. In addition, they work in a much narrower range of jobs than do men.

Women are spread very unevenly throughout the workforce. They are usually in *low paid jobs*. In the late 1970s nearly 60% of all women worked in just three service industries. These were (*a*) the *professional and scientific services* area (typists, secretaries, technicians, teachers and nurses), (*b*) the *distributive trades* (shops, supermarkets, mail order warehouses, etc.) and (*c*) a mixture of *other*

Work should be varied and interesting in itself[1] and that workers should have freedom to choose both the speed at which they work and the ways in which they work[2]. In addition, work should give workers sufficient security and pay[3]. Work teams should be small[4]. Supervisors should be democratic in the ways in which they supervize those workers working for them[5]. Units within the business should be small and there shouldn't be too many levels within the firm[6]. Finally, wherever possible, workers should be involved in taking decisions[7]. It's a lot to ask for and Argyle does suggest that these points require someone who has a certain work personality. They need to be interested in co-operating in groups and in actually becoming involved in decision making and, of course, not everyone wants (or, for that matter, feels able) to do all of these things.

Assignment 5.3

Have a look at the following comments and questions. They help to explain and get you to ask further questions about the above quote.

Point 1 What makes work 'interesting' for you?

Point 2 Doing things in your own way and in your own time!

Point 3 How much is 'sufficient'; for example in terms of pay – £50 per week; £100 per week; £500 per week?

Point 4 How 'small' is 'small' – 4, 14 or 40 in a group?

Point 5 Does your supervisor treat everyone in the groups fairly and equally?

Point 6 Quite a mouthful this one . . . but basically it's concerned with how *large* the organization is in which people work and how many levels there are from the top of the organization to the bottom.

Point 7 Are you given a say in the decisions that affect you and your job?

services such as catering, hairdressing, and cleaning. In clothing and footwear manufacture, professional and scientific services, the distributive trades and banking, finance and insurance women markedly outnumber their male colleagues. On top of this, of course, in spite of attitude changes, women still take the main responsibility for the home and for children. From this it's very easy to see how a man's view of what work means can be, and often is, very different from that of a woman.

Don't get your rag up !

'TUC backs dirt cheap Mrs Mops

The TUC yesterday told five unions it will back a recruitment campaign for Mrs Mops in Britain's contract cleaning industry, whose average earnings of 105p an hour are described as "appallingly low". A recent ACAS report showed that cleaners are among Britain's lowest paid industrial workers.
Len Murray, the TUC General Secretary, said:

'There is extremely limited or non-existent provision for pensions, holiday or sick pay schemes. Collective bargaining covers less than 10% of the employees, and union membership is around the same level.'

The five unions are the transport workers' (TGWU), General and Municipal Boilermaker and Allied Trades' (GMBATU), the Civil Service Union, the public employees' union (NUPE) and the shopworkers' union (USDAW).

Source: courtesy The Sunday Times, *19 April, 1981*

Assignment 5.4

Below, a list of jobs is given. Go through the list and see whether or not you think each job meets up to each of the points mentioned in the quote. Check each job in the following way:

Job		Yes	No	Difficult to say – It all depends
Window cleaner	Point 1			
	Point 2			
	etc.			

Here is the full list of jobs I want you to look at:

1	Window cleaner	**7**	Car worker on assembly line
2	Housewife	**8**	Nurse in community
3	Hairdresser	**9**	Car mechanic
4	MP	**10**	Vet
5	Miner	**11**	Shop assistant
6	Secretary	**12**	Architect

Once at work, hopefully in a job that you like, you will encounter many problems and questions that you will have to think about. These will include topics such as *pay*, (how much do I earn before and after tax and do I get paid weekly or monthly?); *working conditions* (how many hours do I have to work in a week; am I expected to do overtime; how long am I given for my holidays, when can I take them?) and your relationships with *your fellow workers* (do I get on with them well; do I want to; do they like my company; do they need to if I'm doing my job

Night Work: The Loss of Social Life

'Night work is anti-social.
'In fact, the inability to take part in normal social activities is one of the most important causes of the harmfulness of night work.
'Night workers usually feel a greater sense of freedom at work because there is less supervision than there is by day.
'But there is also a strong feeling of isolation, of not belonging to society.
'Night workers cannot undertake further education courses. They cannot take part in community projects designed for the day worker. They cannot join clubs that meet in the evenings.
'Night workers attach more importance than other workers to trade unionism, because they are aware they are being exploited, but are often prevented from taking a full role in their branch activities.'

Source: courtesy Our Health is Not for Sale, *by R. Lacey, NUJ*

A dirty business?

'The nature of the cleaning industry makes its workforce vulnerable to low pay and poor conditions. Many cleaners work in small, isolated units, and because of the hours they work are unlikely to be in contact with other members of staff and are not considered an integral part of the workforce by other workers. This, together with the fact that the choice of employment that allows them to fulfill commitments is restricted, increases their vulnerability to exploit-ation. In 1977 the Unit* published its own investigation into the problems of those working in the cleaning industry.

In this we reported the evidence collected by Bruce George MP in Walsall in 1976 on the pay and conditions of a group of eighty-nine cleaners: poor pay (hourly rates ranged from 40p to 68p, most earning less than 60p an hour); lack of organization and communication; differing rates of pay paid by the same employer to separate groups of cleaners and the lack of local alternative employment opportunities. The absence of holiday pay, sickness pay and overtime provision for most contract cleaners was also highlighted in the report.'

* *Source: courtesy* The Brush Off, *Jill Sullivan, Low Pay Unit Pamphlet, No. 5*

well?). In addition, you may decide to join a union (what do I do to join the union, partic-ularly if I'm not approached by a union repre-sentative; if there is more than one union, which one should I join?) and so with these practical topics in mind, the rest of the chapter will look at

the following aspects of work at the workplace:

1 *Pay and hours*

2 *Relationships with people in and at work*

3 *Industrial relations at work*
   and some of the ways in which they could affect you as an individual.

Having said then that money is obviously important we need to say something about the ways in which people are actually paid at their place of work. Most white collar (or 'non

Assignment 5.5

By now it's fairly obvious, I think, that this chapter is most certainly written by a *man*! Go back over the pages of the chapter and see if you can discover 'proof' of this fact in the text.
   Once you have done this, think about the following question:

*In what ways does work
differ for men and women:*

(a) in terms of the kinds of work that women do?
(b) how much women get paid for that work; and the
(c) kinds of work women themselves value.

As the TUC itself admits:

'*The biggest job a union does is to talk to the management every year and ask for improvements in pay, the hours you have to work, holidays, and so on.*

It can sound very complicated because there are often hundreds of details – different pay for different kinds of work, overtime, pay when you're off sick. And then there are schemes for making work safer, schemes for training people to do new jobs, and schemes for changing the way you work so you can get more done in the same time.

Usually the union has to see the management over and over again before both sides agree on the details. All these meetings are called negotiations. *And when it's finally sorted out, they've got an* agreement *– or* settlement *– which lasts for the next year.*'

manual') workers get an annual salary which is generally paid to them on a monthly basis. Manual workers on the other hand usually get *paid by time or by results*. For example, if a man in a factory is paid for 'day work' he will get paid a certain amount of cash for working from say eight in the morning to five at night. The same will be true for many clerical workers who work from nine to five. They are not paid by how much they produce because quite often workers are very busy in an office or a factory one day and slack the next.

With payment by results (for example, 'piece-work') people get paid for what they produce. Management and unions will have agreed rates at which people can reasonably work and workers will then get paid a certain rate per item,

this rate having been worked out by experts in the field of time and motion study.

Most piecework rates are negotiated at plant level but there are many different practices. For example, in the shoe industry *minimum* rates are negotiated at national level but individual firms and factories argue out their own rates *above* the *minimum* because there are bound to be local differences. Different firms, for example will be able to afford different rates of pay depending on how good their sales and their profits have been and how generous they feel they can afford to be!

In addition, firms and unions often agree on incentive and 'bonus schemes' which are related to the work done by individuals and groups, so that in order for an individual to earn a *group bonus* (s)he will have to get on well with colleagues and workmates to make sure that the group gets through the work. Another way of paying workers occurs when you get a mixture of 'piece' and 'day' work. For example, in an industry where the work comes in dribs and drabs when things are quiet, the workers will 'sign off' piecework and go on to day work until the time that the flow of work builds up again.

In some industries, for example, catering, hairdressing, clothing and in the retail trade (shops, stores, supermarkets, etc.) minimum wages and conditions are determined by *Wages Councils**. Nearly 3 million employees, many of

* The minimum wages of the agricultural workers is also fixed by an Agricultural Wages Board, one in England and Wales, and another in Scotland.

Assignment 5.6

1 'One (wo)man on his/her own is strong, many united are strong: does this apply to the cleaning industry?
2 Make a list of the problems faced by cleaners as outlined above and, if possible, talk to a cleaner and find out what the job is really like.

them women working part-time, have their pay and the conditions under which they are employed established by Wages Councils. These are made up of representatives from the employers and the trade unions sides. They also have independent members, one of whom acts as the Council's chairperson. However, Wages Councils are not necessarily a permanent part of the wages and working conditions scene because once satisfactory arrangements are established for voluntary collective bargaining, trade unions and employers can approach the Secretary of State for Employment to set in motion the process by which the particular Wage Council can be abolished.

We've talked about cash; what about the number of hours people have to work for that cash? In general terms the law does not set any limits on the pattern or number of hours worked by men. There are some exceptions to this rule, however, two examples being coal miners and long distance lorry drivers. On the other hand, the hours of women and young people under eighteen are in fact limited. In reality, the standard working week laid down in many (male) manual workers' collective agreements totals forty hours, while this figure is slightly less for women. Non-manual employees usually have a shorter working week with thirty-seven and a half hours being a common figure.

Having talked about work and having given some examples of work, we moved on to talk about the cash we work for and the number of hours we work. Let us now move on and look at people at work, our relationships with them and

Assignment 5.7

Make a list of some of the advantages and disadvantages, problems and possibilities that a shorter working week brings?

with those people involved in industrial relations events at the workplace.

Throughout history, people have lived and worked in groups. They've grown up together, hunted together and worked in groups together. Often to do a job at all in our modern society we rely on and co-operate with other people individually and in groups. In this section of the book I want to start looking at groups of people at work and see in what ways working in groups can bring both pleasure and pain.* Quite often we take the people we work with very much for granted since we see them everyday. They are simply there and it is only when a particular person is ill or on holiday, perhaps, that we

* If we had the space it would be useful to explore some of the ways in which people react to and with *machines*. It is important to remember that human beings develop relationships not only with one another but also with the machinery that they use. This pattern of relationships is known as the *socio-technical* relationship and is an important aspect of the workplace. For example, if a typist has trouble with her typewriter then there is a good chance that it will upset her rhythm for quite some time, perhaps, even for the rest of the day. In industry when a machine breaks down it will upset the operator's rhythm to a certain extent, although a good deal will depend on the operator's skill in how quickly he or she will get back into a good working routine.

appreciate his or her contribution to the workplace. We do not question or think too much about the ways in which other workers' behaviour can affect ours; and yet, of course, it does. Before we look more closely at how this happens we need to make it quite clear who is actually involved at the place of work.

In Chapter 1 we saw how the three major groups involved in industrial relations were first the workers and their representatives the unions, secondly the management and thirdly, the government who had a particularly important role to play in the 'public sector' part of the economy. At the workplace I want to concentrate on the *workers*, the *unions* and the *management*. However, I want us to remember that not all workers belong to unions and that quite often groups of workers, even though they may belong to unions, do not necessarily agree with their full-time union officials or with their shop stewards for that matter. For us, the workplace highlights the relationships that take place between workers, unions, and management.

Each of these groups is represented at the workplace. You the reader could well be the worker. You could also belong to the union and have a foot in that camp. In addition, the management has its own representative and source of authority in that every shop floor or office has its own foreman or supervisor to keep the work flowing through. Supervisor, shop steward and you, the worker, these are three basic starting points when we look at work relationships.

The Workplace

The Union

1 The union *fights* for better conditions
2 The union *protects* the individual
3 The union acts as a *voice* for its members
4 The union is a *fraternity* bringing members together.

The Union and the Workers

One shop steward told me that he saw his job as follows. He reckoned that you have to:

1 organize the workers;
2 represent the members and their interests;
3 negotiate on behalf of your members;
4 inform;
5 communicate.

Assignment 5.8

Think about and then list some of the ways in which your friends and co-workers affect you at work (and at home).

The Management and the Workers

'He (Sir Terence Beckett, CBI Director General) . . . feels the real answer to good industrial relations is to get the relationships right . . . he thinks the answers to most of our problems lie in an experienced, energetic management that is well motivated and determined to get results. . . . Employees in turn must accept the reality of having to earn their living in the world. And both parties have to be able to accept the need for change and then work effectively together.'

Source: courtesy 'Sir Terence Beckett' by S. Lawrence in Personnel Management, *November, 1980*

'The work group does not derive its power from the union. The printing chapel with its chapel father, the best organized of all work groups, existed before the printing unions and was subsequently incorporated into their branch structure. Work groups can exert considerable control over their members even where there are no trade unions, or where unions refuse them recognition.'

'These instances show the basis of the shop steward's power. He could not of his own volition impose a limit on output or a ban on non-unionists. This can only be done by decision of the group of workers he represents. "Custom and practice" which settles so much in British industrial relations, consists of the customs and practices observed by work groups. If workers did not keep to them, the customs would cease to exist.**'*

Source: *The Donovan Report, June, 1968*

* In simple terms this passage could be expressed as 'It's been done like this for ages now and it's always worked so why go and change things now? It's all right as it is, I think. . . .'.

'Unions have long been scapegoats for the UK's economic troubles; but are the unions to blame for Britain's feeble productivity performance? It is often the work groups, *not the unions themselves, that control disruptive strikes and restrictive practices, and are unwilling to depart from tradition to accept manpower reforms.'*

Source: *courtesy 'Why workers weaken output', R. Taylor in* Management Today, *November, 1980*

Common Interest

All groups need a *common interest* to survive and grow. On the face of it the common interest of a work group is work. However, that does not necessarily follow. Many women, for example, particularly those who work part time, get a tremendous amount of pleasure working with other women who have similar interests as themselves. They do the work because many of them need the cash but they also chat and have their needs for company and friendship met. Groups can give individuals all kinds of satisfaction and this is obviously true of work groups where you get satisfaction from getting on well with the group and feeling at home in their company or where you have done a good job and one of your mates, or the supervisor, or, for that matter, the firm's boss congratulates you on a job well done. The group setting can give real satisfaction. It can encourage co-operation and the members of the group get pleasure (and sometimes a good deal of argument as well!) from working with other people. Colleagues help us to put up with things when they get difficult at work. They are around for a moan when the organization is difficult to work for or is inefficient.

Pattern of interaction

Once the group is formed a clear *pattern of interaction* develops. This means that the people within the particular group relate to one another in particular ways. It may be, for example, that two men on the production line work very well together, so much so that outside work they go fishing at the weekends and often the two men and their wives go out for a drink at the local pub on a Saturday night. Within any work group there will be one or two of the members who are not keen on one another's company and so the supervisor may have to separate them by having them work at different ends of the factory floor. Of course, it is often the case that because of noise or distance between the members in a work group it is difficult for relationships to form and develop. On a busy machine shop floor the levels of noise can inhibit the development and growth of healthy social relationships.

Involvement at the WORKPLACE

The
MANAGEMENT
keeps its eye on workplace practices through its **SUPERVISORS** and **FOREMEN**

The
UNION
keeps its eye on workplace practices through its
WORKPLACE REPRESENTATIVES
SHOP STEWARDS
FATHER of CHAPEL
(in printing industry)

The **WORKERS** belong informally to a **WORK GROUP** which in turn has :—

1 on the face of it at least a COMMON INTEREST

2 a PATTERN of INTERACTION

3 its own STRUCTURE

4 its own RÔLES (for example TASK and SOCIAL leaders)

5 its own NORMS

6 its own IDENTITY

Roles

Once a group of people have been together for some time certain people within that group will take on certain roles. They will play 'parts' just like actors and actresses on the stage. For example, most (work) groups will have someone who is the group's comedian. (S)he is always telling jokes, too much so perhaps at times because none of the others in the group gets anything done!

There is usually someone in the group who has a lot of useful contacts and friends. If you want a cheap, but reliable car, (s)he knows a good garage. If the plumbing at home needs servicing (s)he knows a good plumber. If you want information about people in the factory or office (s)he is the person to whom to go.

Leadership

One of the most crucial roles that a group member can play is that of group leader. There are many types of leader but one kind at which I would like to look is the leader who is either very closely concerned with the *TASK* with which the group is involved or who pays special attention to the *PEOPLE* in the group. Taking each in turn. *Task* leaders want to get the job done. They encourage the group to get the task completed. The other type of leader, let's call them *people centred*, are more concerned to see that people are happy and enjoying their work. They do things that will encourage a 'group spirit' in order to get the group to 'stick together'. This feeling of 'togetherness' in groups is often very important because it leads to all kinds of benefits for the management, for the union and for the work group itself.

'Here is a foundry worker:
'Oh, there's all sorts, millions of them (jokes).' 'Want to hear what he said about you', and he never said a thing, you know. 'Course you know the language at the work, like. "What you been saying about me?" "I said nothing." "Oh, you're a bloody liar", and all this.'
They play jokes on you. . . . They asked, the gaffers asked, Charlie to make the tea. Well it's fifteen years he's been there and they say 'go and make the tea'. He goes up the toilet, he wets in the tea pot, then makes the tea. I mean, you know, this is the truth, this is, you know. He says, you know, 'I'll piss in it if I mek it, if they've asked me to mek it' . . . so he goes up, wees in the pot, then he puts the tea bag, then he puts the hot water in. . . He was bad the next morning, one of the gaffers, 'My stomach isn't half upset this morning'. He told them after and they called him for everything, 'You ain't makin' our tea no more'. He says 'I know I ain't, not now.'
Source: both extracts 'Shop Floor Culture, Masculinity and the Wage Form' by Paul Willis in Working Class Culture, Clarke, Critcher and Johnson (Eds). Hutchinson, 1979

'The noise on our line is what drives you almost mad. You can never really get used to it, and I have been there ten years (and in another factory ten years before that). It would drive you mad if you let it. Imagine nine men beating hammers and mallets on steel. If there were some sort of rhythm to it, it wouldn't be so bad.

Source: courtesy Work by R. Fraser (ed.), Penguin, 1969

'A foreman is like, you know what I mean, they're trying to get on, they're trying to get up. They'd cut everybody's throat to get there. You get people like this in the factory. 'Course these people cop it in the neck off the workers, they do all the tricks under the sun. You know what I mean, they don't like to see anyone crawlin'. . . . 'Course instead of taking one pair of glasses from the stores Jim had two, you see, and a couple of masks and about six pairs o' gloves. 'Course this Martin was watching and, actually two days after, we found out that he'd told the foreman see. Had 'im, Jim, in the office about it, the foreman did, and . . . well I

Group cohesion

Group cohesion (or how much the group holds together) is a very important factor. Being in a close knit group gives individual members of that group, satisfaction. At the same time it also produces low rates of absenteeism. In addition, group members will want to stay with that group (this is obviously an important point to remember when new methods of working have to be brought in) because they are content. The firm will have a low labour turnover. People like the place and want to stay.

Quite often whenever work groups face common dangers there is a very strong feeling of group cohesion, 'belongingness' and solidarity. One of the things I remember most clearly when I visted Lea Hall Colliery in the Midlands was the friendliness and co-operation of the men at the pit. After all once underground you might need the assistance of your mates if anything goes wrong and so, above all else, you have to feel that you can trust and rely on the people with whom you are working. The same applies to the fishing industry where people are literally 'all in the same boat' and if anything goes wrong the work group needs to be able to work well together to get out of that trouble, be it bad weather, bad health, bad accident or problems with the boat itself.

Norms

All groups have *norms*. These 'norms' are the informal, unwritten rules by which the group abides. One of the most important 'norms' within a work group is the one about how much work the group feels is acceptable to do. Student groups often 'pick on' individual students who are seen to be working too hard. They are often called 'swots' and 'creeps'. In work groups pressure is often brought to bear upon those members of the group who work too hard or, if there is group bonus involved, not hard enough. Those members who slack within the group will soon be told to 'pull their fingers out' because they are letting the group down.

We've said that groups can be rewarding for individuals but they can also be very hard upon people when an individual does not do what the group wants him or her to do. The group has all kinds of sanctions to put upon the person who 'deviates' from the group 'norm'; for example, a worker can be 'sent to Coventry', ignored and despised by the rest of the group. Groups often ridicule members, are sarcastic to them, rob them of the benefits which a cohesive and friendly group can give. There are other 'norms'

Work groups seem to stick together strongly when the members

Working close	work physically close to one another and where talking and working with one another is easy
Backgrounds close	do the same kind of work and where members' backgrounds (e.g. age, status, etc) are similar
Socially close	are socially skilled (or have a leader who is socially skilled) and where none of the members are very 'bloody-minded'! are doing work that encourages them to be sociable
Close and closed (the 'in group' (*us*) and the 'out group' (*them*)	belong to a *small* group (under threat perhaps by a larger group), which is on a *group* bonus scheme (you get your bonus on what the entire *group* does!)

about the quality of the work the group does, the ways in which you can save time on jobs and yet still produce a reasonable product and there are, of course, 'skives' that groups know about that help to make the working day move along more easily.

One of my printing apprentices once told me that he used to enjoy the night shift for a publishing firm for whom he was working because he and his mates had a system whereby he could get one or two hours 'kip' every so often because his mates would cover their own machine and his as well. It was a way that the men had come up with to make the time pass more pleasantly. At the same time, the apprentice said that he knew that the management knew that this was happening but they had done nothing about it because it kept the industrial peace that way.

From what we have said above, group norms are very important in terms of how *productive* the work group will be. However, one other very important factor in productivity matters is that of *group participation*. The more people feel involved the more productive they seem to become. Brian Walden on LWT's current affairs programme *Weekend World* (Sunday 12 April, 1981) had this to say about one example of getting individual workers involved in a group to check just how well the firm's product are being made. They were also encouraged to put forward any good ideas that they had so that the management could go on to improve their product even more.

However, we need to remember that just because the scheme has worked at ITT's Harlow

mean, his life hasn't been worth living, has it? Eh, nobody speaks to him, they won't give him a light, nobody'll give him a light for his fag or nothing'. . . .

'Well, he won't do it again, he won't do it again. I mean he puts his kettle on, on the stove of a morning, so they knock it off, don't they, you know, tek all his water out, put sand in, all this kind of thing . . . if he cum to the gaffer, "Somebody's knocked me water over' or, er. "They put sand in me cut", and all this business, "Who is it then?" "I don't know who it is." He'll never find out who it is.

Source: Working Class Culture, *Clarke, Critcher and Johnson (eds), Hutchinson, 1979*

Brian Walden on 'Weekend World'
Sunday 12 April, 1981

''At the ITT Components factory at Harlow in Essex, 2 500 workers make a wide range of electronic parts for industries like telecommunications and computers. Over the past few years the firm has faced a growing challenge from the Japanese, who've been turning out high quality components at very competitive prices. About twelve months ago ITT executives resolved that if their firm was to survive they'd have to match the quality of these foreign rivals, but to get the quality they needed they decided they'd have to change the attitudes of their work force. Work force attitudes would only change, the management believed, if there was more worker participation in decision making, so ITT chose to adopt a Japanese form of industrial participation, called the quality circle. Under this scheme, small groups of workers meet regularly in the firm's time to discuss ways of improving the quality of their product.*

'These meetings turn up a number of simple suggestions . . . and these are passed on to management. And already worker participation achieved through the Harlow quality circle scheme seems to be bearing fruit. Managers . . . have not only found that the circle's recommendations have contributed directly to a boost in quality, they've also had an indirect effect, for through the circles the work force has come to feel more deeply involved in the company's fortunes, so they've become more enthusiastic about every aspect of their work.',

Reproduced by kind permission of London Weekend Television

CIRCLES

factory that it will not necessarily work (or be wanted at other firms in the country). Brian Walden continues:

''Trade unions are highly suspicious of schemes which involve management talking to workers behind the backs of their union representatives. They fear that their position is undermined by direct worker–management communication. And though the unions haven't interfered with the quality circles at ITT, they might well obstruct similar initiatives elsewhere.

But it isn't only trade unionists who might stand in the way of moves to break down the barriers in industry. . . .

Some managers dislike worker participation at least as much as some shop stewards. Many middle managers guard the right to manage jealously. And they see this prerogative ('right') as threatened by demands that they should constantly consult the workers before they take decisions.'

Reproduced by kind permission of London Weekend Television

Assignment 5.9

Give your own examples and descriptions of industries and jobs that:

(a) give the individual freedom to work in the way (s)he wants, for example, a small shop keeper;

(b) give the individual very little freedom to work in the way (s)he wants (for example a car worker on a production line);

(c) forces different groups of people working in a factory, office, etc. to work very closely together (for example, in an industry where various parts are made by various individuals and firms, for example, the car industry);

(d) forces different groups working in a factory, office, etc. to compete against one another to get a product finished (for example, groups working on a piece work basis: you get paid on what you produce!).

With these introductory ideas about quality circles we come to the end of our quick survey of work and the workplace. Let's look back over what we have been saying. We've looked at what work means in a Western, industrialized society such as that existing here in Britain. We've seen how it can mean many different things to many different people and, in particular, we've started to think about some of the ways in which the reality and meaning of work can be very different for women and men.

We've also investigated and explored some of the connections between our work and the rest of our lives such as our choice of friends, our health and where we live, for example. We've discussed pay, hours and the relationships we have at work. All of these things assume (rightly or wrongly) that you and I regard work as important and also, and perhaps more importantly even, that we *expect* to work when we leave school or college. We expect (or increasing unfortunately, do not expect?) that there will be a

Assignment 5.10

'In industry, a form of social apartheid exists in many plants, where workers eat in different canteens with different menus; use different lavatories; and drive into different car parks.'
Source: "Why workers weaken output", by R. Taylor in Management Today *November, 1980*

Mrs Thatcher may talk of a new mood on the shop floor but the comments had a sense of *deja vu.* 'Look at the V8 Rovers and Princesses in the staff car park,' said one man, complaining about the delay in carrying out redundancies among white collar employees.

Source: courtesy The Sunday Times *9 November, 1980*

Does it really matter that workers and managers park their cars, eat their meals and wash their hands in places specially reserved for the two separate groups? If you think that it does, list your reasons.

job waiting when we leave the educational system. For many young people there will not be jobs waiting when they leave school, and today unemployment has become a very real and deep seated problem both for the country and for individuals who are faced with it in their own personal lives.

Recommended reading for Chapter 5

1 *Women on the Line* by R. Cavendish (Routledge and Kegan Paul, 1982)
2 *Work: 20 Personal Accounts* by R. Fraser (Penguin, 1969)
3 *Work* (3rd Edition) (A New Society Social Studies Reader, 1981)
The *New Society* reader is available from 2613 King's Reach Tower, Stamford Street, London SE1.

Books that you have read and found useful should be added below

Chapter 6
What strange ideas you have about industrial relations!

Objectives

At the end of this chapter you should be able to:

1 recognize the importance of ideas in industrial relations' work;
2 give examples of the differing roles union members often see their unions having to play;
3 discuss in some detail the idea of 'democracy' and to explore the ways in which the idea applies to both society in general and the unions in particular;
4 investigate the idea of democracy as it applies to one particular union, that of the National Union of Mineworkers (NUM);
5 tie in the idea of democracy in the unions with that of 'industrial democracy' as it's discussed in Chapter 12 (It's the way they tell it . . .).

THIS CHAPTER COVERS the following topics:

1 some ideas in industrial relations;
2 some ideas union members have about the roles of their unions in Britain today;
3 some ideas about 'democracy' in society and in the unions.

THIS CHAPTER is all about certain key ideas that people in industrial relations' activities often think about. It may seem strange to include a chapter on 'ideas' in a book on industrial relations. After all, it could be argued that industrial relations is all about practical, down-to-earth things like money, machinery, men and women and the relationships between these. From what we've already said, it's obvious that industrial relations is based in experience, is set in workplaces, offices, shops, etc. It is all about *practical* issues, like grievances, and it's these that are at the heart of things. You can quite clearly see workers negotiating with managements: why then have an entire chapter devoted to woolly 'ideas'?

The answer to that question is very simple. *Ideas are important to people.* You and I actually behave in certain ways because of the ideas we have and believe in. When we get paid at work the cash is clear for us to see. However, whether we think that what we have received is *'fair'* is another matter. It will all depend on what we regard as 'fair'. We may look at other people doing the same job as ourselves and compare

'*A democracy, that is a government of all the people, by all the people, for all the people . . . for shortness' sake, I will call it the idea of freedom. . . .*'

Source: courtesy Theodore Parker in a speech made in 1850

Democracy

'*. . . the ability of the rank and file to affect decisions, replace leaders and to change policies. . . .*'

Source: The worker views his union *by J. Seidman University of Chicago Press, 1958*

'We do use phrases in the trade union movement like ''social justice'' and ''equality''. I think what we're talking about is ''fairness''. . . . One of the biggest problems in industry at the present time, which reflects un-fairness, is the fact that there are workers who are employed on entirely different conditions from other workers . . . (after all they are all workers at the end of the day). . . . It's truly ludicrous that we have certain groups who are working longer hours . . . who don't enjoy a company pension, who face total hardship when they are off ill whereas other employees in the same company, working side by side with them, have some protection when they're off ill, through sick pay schemes and so on. Therefore we immediately create a cleavage, a gulf between the one group and the other group; and yet industry in this country cannot survive unless these two groups work to-gether. . . .

Source: courtesy Alex Ferry, (CSEU)

their earnings with ours. Do they get similar wages for similar work? If not, why not? For example, are men and women who are doing the same jobs treated by management and unions in the same way? Is 'fairness' taken into account? Of course, as soon as you start talking about 'fairness' you are in the realm of ideas.

I think it's also essential to stress at this point just some of the other ideas that are import-ant when considering industrial relations. On the management side we have the idea of the 'right to manage'. In other words, the very important idea in-volving authority that by simply being part of management managers have a right, a duty and an obligation to 'manage'. For unionists one key idea is that of 'members' wishes', that is, that the union is there to serve the member and to satisfy his or her 'wishes' whatever they may be. It's very important in the members' mind that the union does this. After all, if it doesn't, what's the point of belonging to the union in the first place?

On the union side, the full-time officials and the shop stewards (like all human beings) have certain 'roles' to play. The idea of 'role' is very important in

that it dictates and influences the kind and scope of job the person in that job feels he or she should do. For example, as part of the role of shop steward, the person doing the job has to recognize that part of the (shop steward's) role is a recognition that if they don't do as their members wish, they will quickly come unstuck. All of these ideas may seem rather 'wishy-washy' but, since they all have an effect on people's behaviour within industrial rela-tions, they do, in fact, have very real importance.

One problem that comes up in a chapter like this is that quite often the idea you want to talk about is difficult to define. It is often hard to 'pin down' exactly what the idea is all about. In addition, it is also difficult to get to grips with the large numbers of ideas that people have. These ideas are often very different and, even more interesting is the way in which the *same* idea (take *'fairness'* as an example) will be seen very differently by two people. It may be, for instance, the case that my idea of *'fairness'* may be very different from yours. Likewise your picture of what is 'wrong' and what is 'right' in industrial relations could very well be different from mine. This is not unreasonable when you see just how many different groups and individuals there are involved in industrial relations. We saw in Chapter 1 how workers, unions, employers and governments were all involved. These groups are often trying to achieve very different things and so is not surprising that there will be many different views and ideas in and about industrial relations.

Having talked generally about the importance of ideas in industrial relations, we are now going to concentrate on just *three* sets of ideas in order to give you a brief, but close, glimpse of the ways in which ideas can affect the thinking of people involved and interested in the study and practice of industrial relations. These three sets of ideas are concerned with:

1 the ways in which the student of industrial relations 'sees' the various approaches that can be taken to the study of industrial relations;

2 the ways in which members 'see' the role of their union; and

3 the ways in which the idea of democracy is 'seen' both in society at large and in the unions in particular.

In this first section on ideas I want us, as students of industrial relations, to look at the overall ideas that have been put forward about the ways in which you can 'look at' the field of study known as industrial relations. Just as different individuals 'see' unions and managements in different ways, so writers on industrial relations have had different approaches to the study of industrial relations.

Various writers have suggested that if you look at the entire field of industrial relations (and this, in itself, is a very difficult thing to do) you can pick out *four main approaches* to the ways in which you can see the relationship between the kind of society you have and the activities of those involved in industrial relations. These various approaches reflect the differing ideas, views and perspectives that people have about the society in which they live and, since they have different ideas about that society, they will also have different ideas about the ways in which the industrial relations' set up works within our society.

Let's look at each of these four approaches and see if we can make the matter any clearer. The four that I want to look at are as follows:

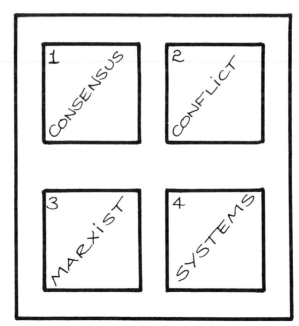

CONSENSUS

IR

WORKING TOGETHER FOR THE SAME THINGS

CONFLICT

IR

WORKING FOR DIFFERENT AIMS

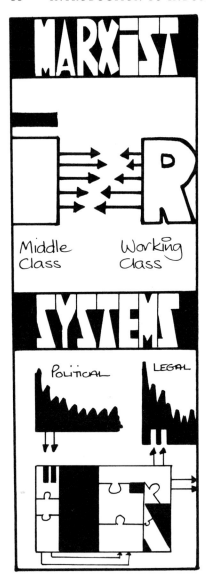

Consensus view

The consensus view emphasizes the idea of working together in industry; that the aims of both employees and employers are basically the same. The idea of there being 'common ground' on which both sides can build is also important; rather than the bosses and workers fighting one another, they ought to be fighting the Japanese and West Germans in the international trade market.

Conflict view

The conflict approach to industrial relations highlights the idea that employees and employers have different aims and objectives and that the two groups are often working against one another. Conflict exists because of the variety of different groups in modern society, many of whom have very different needs and goals. In a plural society (that is one where there are many different groups) conflict is an almost inevitable part of a person's everyday life and because of this the people involved with industrial relations are, to a certain extent 'managers of conflict'. Finally, it's perhaps as well to remember that often conflict is a good thing in that it leads to changes for the better.

Marxist view

In the Marxist view of industrial relations the emphasis is still on conflict but in this case it is on the particular conflict between the 'bosses' and the 'workers' (in Marx' words, the bourgeoisie and the proletariat). For the Marxist, the important struggle of life is the class struggle between the workers and the owners. The workers, Marxists believe, are exploited and in order to overcome this exploitation they must change the capitalist way of running things. For Marx this change would be brought about by a revolution of the workers.

Systems view

In this view of industrial relations, society could be seen as a jigsaw in that it is made up of various 'sub-systems' (or sub-groups) that 'fit together' to make up, what we call, 'society'. The various sub-systems include the work sub-system, the family and the educational sub-systems, the political and belief sub-systems and so on. The industrial relations system is itself part of the work sub-system and can be broken down again into groups (workers, unions, management, etc.).

Assignment 6.1

Check the dictionary definition of each of the following terms: *Consensus/Conflict/Marxist/ Systems.*

The second set of ideas connects to the last chapter and its emphasis on the place of work. In that chapter we looked at those groups involved at the workplace and now, having emphasized the importance of ideas to the ways in which people behave, I want to weave these two themes together and have a look at the ideas that union members have of unions and, in particular, the *various roles union members think unions play in our modern society.*

In an excellent, and interesting, piece of research carried out by the Tavistock Institute for the National Union of Seamen the following different 'types' of unions emerged as being important in NUS members' minds. It was discovered various members had very different ideas as to what 'their' union was actually like. Different members 'saw' the union in different ways and had different ideas as to what the union was doing for them.

The seven roles produced by the research were:

1 The *agent union*   5 The *active union*
2 The *meal ticket union*   6 The *usurped union*
3 The *co-operative union*   7 The *alien union*
4 The *umbrella union*

Looking at 'each' union in turn, we find that they can be described as follows:

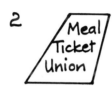

1

2

3

4

5

6

Agent union

The full-time officers are paid to do a job and we expect better pay and conditions from them!

Meal ticket union

The union helps us to get a job and then keeps us in that job.*

* Particularly relevant to employers and unions that have closed shop agreements and to the National Union of Seamen from whose research this list is adapted.

Co-operative union

We, the members, work together on committees and we vote in the union's elections, but that's about it.

Umbrella union

We, the members, are the *real* union, not the officials at head office!

Active union

We belong to a union and we fight for that union. We have the full-time officers to help us but quite often we do the work ourselves.

Usurped ('seized') union

What's the point? This union is not run in the way that the majority of members want it run.

7

Alien union

We don't think that you even need unions at all!

Whatever views you may have about society or the unions, you can be sure that these views and ideas will affect and influence your opinion about the next set of ideas at which we are going to look. For, in the next section, we are going to examine an idea that is important not only to the study of industrial relations but to the study of society in general as well. We're going to look at *the idea of 'democracy'* and see how this, extremely important, idea applies to our industrial relations' studies. As an idea it's obviously a very important one because it is connected with other very significant human values such as 'justice' and 'freedom', ideas which are crucial to all of us as human beings.

Before we go any further in our discussions we need to say exactly what we mean by the term 'democracy'. The word itself comes from the Greek *'demos'* (meaning people) and 'kratos' (meaning power) and, like the word itself, democracy has its roots in the ancient civilization of Greece, in the famous city state of Athens to be exact. Here the citizens, with the notable

---

Assignment 6.2

Bosses and workers together can lead the way to recovery

We must reject utterly the idea that a division between management and workers is an inescapable fact of life. (There were Mrs Thatcher said four vital lessons to learn.) I call them the four lessons for industrial recovery. The first is that management and workforce have a common interest in keeping companies profitable. . . .

. . . the second lesson is that this common interest in the company will be brought about by action and leadership – not exhortation. . . .

. . . the third is to recognize the common interest in the business of creating new markets and keeping existing markets. . . .

. . . the fourth lesson is the common interest of employees in using resources to the full to maximize output. . . .

. . . those who achieve a partnership between management and workforce, whose productivity is rising, who create a market and then satisfy it, will be leading the way to industrial recovery. . . .

Extracts are taken from a speech given by Mrs Thatcher the Conservative Prime Minister in Hereford in 1980

Which view of society do you think the above quote represents? Is it (a) Consensus (b) Conflict (c) Marxist (d) Systems?

Answer is on Assignment 6.3.

Assignment 6.3

The Tavistock/NUS research has shown us that different people 'see' the role of their union in very many different ways.

Look back over the seven roles that the research identified within the NUS and say which of those seven roles *you* think:

(a) unions *should* play
(b) unions *actually* play

Repeat the assignment by asking for the opinions of friends, family, co-workers, unionists, foremen, supervisors, etc., etc.

Answer to assignment 6.2: (a) Consensus.

exceptions of women and slaves (!) used to gather together in the market square to discuss those issues of the day that were important to them. Decisions on these issues would be made, the final outcome being decided on a majority basis. As a system it seemed to work fairly well in the small Greek city.

However, it immediately raises problems when the city becomes a country of nearly sixty million people such as that of modern, industrialized Britain. The total population cannot all meet in Trafalgar Square in London to discuss key issues! Today, we have *'indirect'* democracy where the people elect *representatives* to put forward and represent their views in the governing body and in Britain this is, of course, made up of the House of Commons. These elected representatives (*or Members of Parliament*) represent the people and make decisions on their behalf. Basically, the same kind of thing happens in the unions where members elect representatives (shop stewards, etc.) and pay full-time officials to make crucial decisions on their behalf between the union's national conference (for a recap on this turn back to Chapter 2).

If we look more closely at democracy as a form of *government* we can say that it seems to work quite well when certain social, economic and political conditions are to be found. In the next few paragraphs I want to look at what these conditions are. I want you to bear each of them in mind and think about whether you think they exist (or not), first in *Britain* and, secondly, in *British trade unions*. Actually, it might be a good idea to see if you think they exist in *British firms*

and offices as well. Are these, indeed, run on democratic lines?

First, people in a society that is supposed to be democratic must actually *want* democracy. They must see it as a 'good thing' and something valuable to have. Secondly, in any democratic society everyone should have the *right to vote*. Remember, even in Athens, two major groups (slaves and women) were not allowed to do this.

Tied in with the right to vote there should be a *democratic law-making body (or legislature)*. This should be made up of a group of freely elected representatives who have been voted into office at free elections. The latter should, of course, be held at regular intervals. In Britain elections are held at roughly five year intervals. If the system works well these elected representatives make laws that represent the 'best' interests of the people who elected them into power. In addition, democracy is helped along if the Prime Minister (that is the leader of the political party with an overall majority in the House of Commons) is freely elected into power, either by his or her colleagues, or, by the mass of the party (s)he represents.

It's also very important that *institutions, such as the courts* for example, that carry out the plans and policies of the law-making body *should be both independent and impartial* so that legal decisions are both fair and are seen to be fair. In fact, many trade unionists believe that, generally speaking, the law is (and always has been) anti-union and so they are dubious about bringing it into industrial relations. (*See* the following chapter for more on this.)

Democracy in Britain

Assignment 6.4

For this assignment I want you to:

1 list those reasons that help democracy survive and grow;
2 discover whether or not you think Britain is democratic using the reasons found in 1;
3 make a list of the kinds of information you would *really* need to have to answer 2.

If you have a society where the (social, economic, political and legal) groupings *are* democratic one further important ingredient in the democratic 'mix' is the willingness of people in that society to make use of (and involve themselves in) those groupings. In an industrial relations' setting, for example, it's obviously important to have unions that are democratically organized. However, if, once they *are* set up on a democratic basis no-one bothers to attend the meetings then it's hardly surprising if the views of the activists (that is, those who regularly attend the meetings) are the only ones heard. *For a truly democratic way of working many members have to become involved.* Once involved, *people also have to be well informed.* If you want to take part in industrial relations' work you obviously need to know what's going on in firms, unions, government circles, etc. Democracy needs active, critical, interested and informed individuals to survive.

The democratic cause is often helped if there is general agreement (or *consensus*) about the direction in which the country is (or should be) going. Increasingly, in societies such as our own, there is a very real mixture of groupings, ideologies (these are sets of beliefs about the world) and outlooks. Our own society has a richness of these groupings such as black and white, young and old, middle and working class. It also has groupings that split our society such as workers and unemployed and rich and poor. These groups often have different ideas about the ways in which society should be going. They believe in different policies to get a 'better'

society. It helps if people can all pull in the same direction, in that way we may get peace, or an improvement in the lot of the poor and black groups in our society. *A sense of democracy is helped if people pull with one another rather than against one another.*

Since we've mentioned money and the rich and the poor, democracy can be said to exist where a country has a *wide distribution of wealth* throughout its population: where the gap between rich and poor is not a very large one. On this basis we could say that some of the 'best' instances of democracy are found in Europe where, for example, Scandinavian countries, such as Norway and Sweden, do not have the very great extremes of poverty and wealth unlike some of the other 'democratic' countries such as Britain and the USA.

If, in a democratic country, all the conditions we have talked about until now have been met (and when all's said and done, that's a very big 'if') then there's a good chance that the last condition will already exist. That key condition is the one of *tolerance*; of letting other people 'do their own thing' (providing, of course, no-one else gets hurt in the process!). People accept one another and, more importantly, will still accept one another even if they disagree with one another. There can be said to be a *'spirit of democracy'* in the country concerned and that's very important.

This may be a good place, incidentally, especially since we've talked a good deal about democracy (government by the many), to talk briefly about some of the other common forms of government. There can be *government by one person* (dictatorship, for example) or *government by the few*. This latter form of government is known as *'oligarchy'* and it has a very important place in our study of ideas in industrial relations. In a study of European trade unions and socialist parties a man named *Robert Michels (1876–1936)* suggested that even in these groups, which had, after all, been set up to encourage change and democracy a point was reached when, instead of the organization (trade union, political party or whatever) being run for the benefit of the members, it was in actual fact being run mainly for the benefit of the officials and leaders of that organization instead. As a modern-day example, it's sometimes said within education that schools and colleges are often run, not for the good of the students, but for the benefit of the *staff*. The organization's real aims and goals somehow get changed!

In politics some people suggest that, although the Labour Party was set up to help the working classes, it has now, itself, become part of the middle class 'Establishment', that it was set up to overcome and, in some people's minds, overthrow. It's now part of the State, which by definition in Britain, is *middle class*, so how can it really help and fight for its *working class members*? Incidentally, Michels' original idea that, in time, the interests of the members become less important than those of the officials, he called the *'iron law of oligarchy'* and, I think, it's fairly easy to see how this 'law' could apply to our discussions of democracy both at, say, a general (society) level and at a particular (union) level.

We've talked at quite some length about some of these 'democratic' ideas and I think that we now need to apply them at 'grass-roots' level. First, we will have a look at democracy at the workplace and then we will go on to examine union democracy nationally by taking an example of a union that most would regard as a 'democratic' union, namely the National Union of Mineworkers (NUM).

Since the early 1970s there have been increasing demands from many quarters, including the so-called 'man in the street' (who, of course, is often a trade unionist himself) to make the unions more 'democratic'. They have become the scapegoat for most of the country's economic ills. They are often accused by people of differing political persuasions of being 'out of touch' with their members, so let's try and find out more about this.

To start our look at union democracy let's go back and see what happens at the workplace and, in particular, at the branch meetings themselves. As we have already seen most unions believe strongly in the importance of the branch in their structure. To show this let's take as an example the quote opposite from the TGWU's shop stewards' handbook.

However, the reality is often very different. Unfortunately, in many unions many members are simply not interested in industrial relations. Branch meetings are poorly attended and are restricted to the union's activists. Unfortunately, it's also true that many (although obviously not all) union meetings can be boring and routine. One industrial relations' writer wrote this:

The branch is the place where the rank and file member has a chance to make his (!) contribution to the Union's policy. It is the springboard of union democracy. On the floor of the branch, local decisions are made which may then be transmitted through the . . . machinery of the Union. . . . In its turn, the branch is the point of transmission of the Union's policy to the membership. Here, members are informed of the decisions of the governing bodies. It is, therefore, a vital part of the Union's machinery. Its liveliness is a measure of the vitality of the whole Union. . . .

Source: TGWU

The union branch of today is often so dull an affair that the member not holding any office in the branch, who has been persuaded by a keen member to attend, comes home with the impression that he has wasted his time. To some extent this is unavoidable. There is a great deal of routine business to be transacted and important decisions are taken at a higher level of authority.

Source: *Trade Unions*, A. Flanders, Hutchinson, 1965

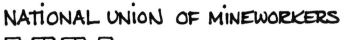

NATIONAL UNION OF MINEWORKERS
NUM

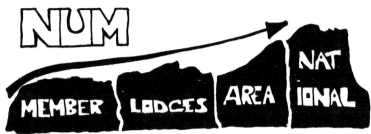

MEMBER | LODGES | AREA | NATIONAL

Members form lodges : lodges elect area   : The annual
officers and area   conference:
councils   delegates
elected by
areas.
President
General
Secretary
Vice President
elected by
whole
membership

'*Every pit has its
lodge or branch and each
lodge is governed by the rules of
its constituent association. Those who
run the lodge are part-timers, who work in
the pit. The lodge committee consists of officers
plus six to fifteen other workers. All of them are
elected every year or biennially. Each lodge elects a
delegate to the area council. Unlike most union branches
the NUM lodges are vital and active parts of the union,
and they practise a degree of democratic involvement
unknown in many larger unions. Miners live in tightly
knit communities close to the pithead. It is true that modern
transport
and rehousing has dispersed many farther away from their
workplace,
but the solidarity and comradeship of the pit village is still
strong on most of the coalfields.*'

Source: **The Fifth Estate**, Robert Taylor, 1980

General apathy on the part of the mass of the members means that, in most unions, levels of participation are generally poor. We are talking about 10% of the total branch membership who are regular attenders. We've said that participation is one of the really crucial aspects of democracy. People must be involved and so, however democratic the union's structure may be, unless the broad range of membership use it, then almost automatically a minority view will go across at branch meetings.

In the case of the NUM branches, unlike so many other unions, they are well attended. They are still seen to be important and people *are* actively involved. The union has real 'grass-roots' participation, and being part of a mining community means, among other things, that miners rely on one another when they are underground. There still is a feeling of solidarity and standing together (collectivism) that many other unions can only envy. However, having said that it cannot be denied that there are other unions, particularly white collar unions, where turnout can be quite good (40–50%, for example). Unions that can be included in this category are NATFHE, NUT and NALGO.

Within the NUM two other important points about democracy can, I think, be usefully brought together at this point: first, that full-time

Take a second look at p. 42 and the description of Arthur Scargill since it's worth another look.

officials are *elected* by the membership into their posts and secondly the way in which the union allows different views to be taken into account by use of the secret ballot. Within the NUM the president (Arthur Scargill), vice-president and the general secretary are *all elected on secret ballots*. These ballots often have high turnouts at the pits themselves. They also mean that everyone can vote the way they please and, at the same time, different views can go across. Incidentally, the different views expressed get reflected on the National Executive Committee (NEC) where members' views range from broadly left to broadly right on the political spectrum.

In addition, the secret ballot is used within the NUM to decide whether the miners should resort to strike action. An official, national miners' strike can only be called where 55% of those voting in the ballot are in favour. The secret ballot is also used to get the agreement (or otherwise!) of the members to the annual pay rise. The union has involvement, secret ballots and a concern for what the members actually want. This is surely what democracy is all about?

Election for the delegates who go to the annual NUM conference are at area level and each area of the union (these areas include Yorkshire, Scotland and South Wales) is entitled to elect two delegates for the first 5 000 members within the area. After that figure a further delegate can be elected for every further 2 500 members. From this we can see the importance that the union attaches to both branches and areas. The latter have a good deal of power although they cannot finance strikes, for example. Permission for

industrial action of that kind has to come from the NUM's headquarters. In this way you get a reasonably good balance between the national level (the NEC) and the area and branch levels. There is, incidentally, one point that I think has to be made and that is that the NEC isn't strictly representative of the coalfields themselves. Due to historical factors, the NEC of the NUM does actually give some of the smaller areas of the British coalfields more power than they are really worth in membership terms today.

So, it's important to remember that there is real concern in many unions that democracy should be worked towards and that it's an important idea to get across to the members. However, this is not a perfect world by any manner of means and the unions do have real hindrances to the democratic ideal being achieved; and so, before we finish our brief look at democracy we need to have a look at some of the things that make the achievement of democratic working within the unions such a difficult thing to accomplish.

Rule books and change

As we have already seen, unions are organizations that vary from the very large to the very small. Most importantly they are *organized* and have rule books about the ways in which they should be run. If change of a democratic kind is to come about then unions will have to change their rules. With some unions' rule books this may be easy; with others it may be very difficult indeed.

A democratic approach to trade unionism often comes through in a union's rulebook. These extracts from the NUM's rulebook show what I mean:

'1 *RULE 14 There shall be three National officials, the President, Vice-President and Secretary. The President and Secretary shall be full-time permanent officials, and shall continue in office during the pleasure of the Union. . . . A ballot by vote of the Members of the Union shall be taken to appoint the President. . . . Upon any vacancy occurring in the office of a National Official, the position shall be filled by a ballot vote of the Members of the Union. . . .'*

'2 *RULE 24 Each area shall be entitled to elect two Delegates for the first 5 000 members (or fractional part thereof) and one further delegate for each additional 2 500 members (or fractional part thereof). . . .'*

'3 *RULE 25 When under the Rules a ballot vote of the Members is to be taken the ballot shall be conducted in accordance with the regulations and directions laid down by the NEC, but when it is on the question of the Election of a National or Area Official it shall be taken on the principle of 'the transferable vote' as defined in Section 41 of the Representation of the People Act, 1918.*

At the same time, some unions may not want to change (although with the rough years of the 1980s ahead of them, many of them will have no choice). Change, in the form of falling memberships, difficult financial times ahead and a government that is opposed to their existence, will be forced upon them.

Turnover of members

A very real, and practical, difficulty that many unions bump up against is that of a fairly rapid turnover of members. Members come and go. They join a union and then, for various reasons, they let their union subscription lapse. This often happens in jobs where there are large numbers of part-time and women workers. Unions such as those in the distributive trade (shops, supermarkets, etc.) are notoriously difficult to get, and keep, organized. In the meanwhile, of course, if a member's subscription goes unpaid the union quickly gets into financial trouble and, these days when money is tight, they need all the cash they can get!

Elections

Without going into too many complicated details about the various forms elections take within unions it's fairly obvious that there will be problems no matter what form you use. One of the problems that we ought to mention is that in craft and general unions that hold elections for full-time officials' jobs, *big turnouts of voters are*

unusual. They do happen, a good example being that of the election of Jack Jones to the general secretaryship of the TGWU in 1968.

In addition, because of the nature of the job, very few of the candidates for full-time officers' posts actually face any competition. It seems that not too many people want those kinds of jobs, anyway! There is a lack of participation and interest once more. Incidentally, in *most white collar unions* it is common for full-time officials to be *appointed* rather than elected into the job. This appointment work is carried out by an *elected* (lay) executive committee. There are all kinds of interesting questions here for the student of democracy to start thinking about.

One other problem before we leave the subject of elections is the human ones for the actual individuals involved. They can become 'marginal': pulled between workers and unions. In their important work *Industrial Democracy* the Webbs summed it up rather well when they said:

Directly the working man representative becomes properly equipped for one-half of his duties, he ceases to be specially qualified for the other. If he remains essentially a manual worker, he fails to cope with the brain-working officials; if he takes on the character of the brain-worker, he is apt to get out of touch with the constituents whose desires he has to interpret.

From the quote we can, perhaps, see the 'iron law of oligarchy' coming through once again?

Different views

Another very important aspect of democracy is that, within a large group of people, such as a union or a society at large, *there should be some opportunity for many different voices to be heard.* In the unions (and in our larger society), some of the voices that aren't heard as frequently as they should be include those of women and black workers. Although women are increasing their say and influence within the trade union movement, they are still badly under-represented as are black and coloured workers. We'll say more about this in Chapter 11, but it's obviously an important subject and, over the last few years, the TUC has realized this and has highlighted the importance of increasing black and female representation within the union movement. At least it's a step in the right direction. After all, unions cannot be held responsible for all their members' attitudes!

Democratic leadership

For our final point in connection with barriers to democracy I want to look at the question of *leadership within unions.* If democracy is reckoned to be important by the leadership then there is a good chance that it will be seen to be important generally within the union. A good example of democratic (or 'open' style of) leadership occurs on p. 153 of the public sector chapter where a NALGO official tells of the way he runs his own branch. It's good to see that there are examples of

general secretaries who are showing a lead and are genuinely concerned to make democracy more than just an idea but who want to try and make it a state of affairs within their unions. Good examples of democratic leadership come, I feel, from such people as David Basnett (GMBATU) and Tom Jackson, formerly General

---

Assignment 6.6

Democracy within unions

Which of the following do you think are important to make and keep a union 'democratic'?

A union:

1 that has a set of rules and principles which make it quite clear that this particular union thinks that what its MEMBERS want is most important;
2 that encourages its members to go to local branch meetings;
3 in which different views can be heard and taken account of without minorities being 'picked on' for holding those views;
4 in which most of the full-time jobs are given to those people who have been *elected* by union members;
5 in which the members give that union support for its ideas and its policies;
6 in which people *think* democracy is important;
7 which tries to overcome problems of:
   (a) size;
   (b) meeting the various needs of all its members;
   (c) a membership which is scattered (all over the country) for example the farm workers, or (all over the world) for example, seamen.

Make a list of the numbers of those points that you think help a union to be democratic.

You will find the answer, as I see it, on p. 96.

Secretary of the UCW. Just as 'good' leadership from the top can encourage democratic workings below so authoritarian leadership can often have the reverse effect and that can be a real barrier to the 'democratic spirit' of which we were talking earlier.

One very important point must be made before we leave this chapter and that is that before we think that the unions are particularly undemocratic (and I would not want to suggest that at all) I would ask you to think about how democratic firms and businesses are (or are not, as the case may be!). Very few shareholders, for example, turn up to a company's Annual General Meeting (AGM). The leadership of the firm throughout the year is left to its directors and management. Isn't that undemocratic? At the same time many managements do not want to give up what they see as their 'right to manage'. So, it's very important to remember that democracy does *not* just apply to unions, it applies to governments, multinational and national firms, schools, hospitals, even work groups!

I hope this chapter on ideas, and particularly the idea of democracy, has really interested you. It is an important idea and one that really matters. It's a very large area to cover and so, even if I have done no more than started you thinking about (union) democracy, then I am content. If you particularly want to broaden your knowledge of the idea of 'industrial democracy', then pay special attention to Chapter 12, '*It's the way they tell it. . . '*.

Recommended reading for Chapter 6

1 *Democracy at Work* by P. Burns and M. Doyle (Pan, 1981)
2 *The Fifth Estate* by R. Taylor (Pan, 1980) (This is an excellent *reference* book on industrial relations and it contains a good chapter on union democracy)
3 *The Trade Unions* by H. Williamson (Heinemann, 1981)

Books that you have read and found useful should be added below

Answer to Assignment 6.6

In my own view the answer to Assignment 6.6 is that for a union to be *very democratic* all of the points outlined in the assignment should be met.

Chapter 7
Rules are there to be broken

Objectives

At the end of this chapter you should be able to:

1 differentiate between statute law and common law, civil and criminal law;
2 list and discuss the differences between 'norms', rules and laws;
3 list major Acts of Parliament relating to British Industrial relations;
4 to discuss and keep up to date with (legal) developments connected with the 'closed shop' and picketing.

THIS CHAPTER COVERS the following topics:

1 social order and social control in industrial relations;
2 the role of 'norms', rules and laws in industrial relations;
3 Acts of Parliament connected with industrial relations;
4 the 'closed shop' and picketing.

In Britain we have collected a body of labour law. This has grown up over the years, particularly over recent years. In the future we will be affected more and more by another source of law, namely the EEC. The subjects, however, that British labour law cover include:

(a) the definition of the status and rights of trade unions and employers' associations;
(b) the establishment of minimum standards of pay in industries where voluntary collective bargaining is not effective. This is done by setting up *Wages councils* (*see* Chapter 5);
(c) the minimum standards governing contracts of employment;
(d) laws relating to:
   Dismissal
   Redundancy
   Sex discrimination
   and equal pay and
   Racial discrimination.

1 *'The good of the people is the chief law'*

Source: Cicero 106–43 BC
2 *'Custom, that unwritten law, By which the people keep even kings in awe'*

Source: Charles Davenant 1656–1714

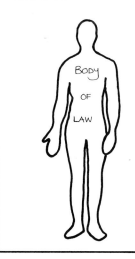

BODY

OF

LAW

In any group of people there has to be some kind of order. As a member of a family at home; as a student at school or college or as a member of a group at work or in the union, people have to be able to control both themselves and others in order for everyday life to go on. Not only is this true of small groups, it's also valid for much larger collections of people such as the 'British' or the 'Americans'. There has to be some order and control rather than disorder and chaos for people to live in safety and security. This chapter looks at the rules, both informal and formal, that exists in the industrial relations field and examines very generally the role that the law has to play in making and keeping those laws and rules.

In Chapter 5 ('You've got to work at it . . .') we had a look at some of the ways groups work *at work*. We saw how groups set up their own informal laws or *norms* which were the taken-for-granted standards of acceptable and unacceptable behaviour within that particular work group or place. We saw how work groups have much to say in deciding how fast (or how slow!) people will work in groups. One of the group's norms may be that individuals joining that particular work group will be expected to do a good day's work and not let the rest of the group down. If one of the group's members is having problems at home the others may agree (unofficially) to work a little harder and 'carry' him or her through the day.

This all works fine until one member of the group decides not to do what the other members of the group want him/her to do. In the language of the sociologist they become 'deviant' in that

HOW TO KEEP PEOPLE IN ORDER
[FOR BEGINNERS]

1 (FORCE)

▽Let me persuade you a little...▽

2 (COMMON INTERESTS)

▽We've got common interests you and I : if you scratch my back I'll scratch yours▽

3 (COMMON VALUES) ▽Well, you and I are agreed: the only trouble is now we've got to convince those on the other side that what we believe is right...▽

4 (STATUS QUO)

▽Why don't we leave things like that: it's worked alright for years▽

they deviate from the accepted rules of the group. However, it is equally important to remember that not all social rules are equally important. In Western societies distinctions are made between manners, customs, morals, and laws. Manners and customs are ways of behaving that are not particularly important. If people break them they may get other people annoyed but society will not shake or crumble away! On the other hand we keep words like 'immoral' and 'illegal' for far more serious breaches of society's rules.

In families and groups of friends (indeed, in industrial relations, as well) it is obvious that, although laws are very important, it is the informal understandings that are the crucial ways of keeping the group together and in good order. For example, in a family's private squabble it's thought wrong to bring in the law in the shape of the local police. Indeed, the police themselves, rightly or wrongly, often feel that problems between husbands, wives and children are better left to the individuals concerned rather than get involved officially. Indeed, in many cases the families themselves reject the idea that police can help in this kind of situation; just like the family has its own ways of doing things, so do many employers and unions. Both sides often feel that if they are left to their own devices they can get their problems sorted out on their own without the interference of the law in the form of Acts of Parliament. (Hence the expression *'free'* collective bargaining.)

In any workplace, if we start with the individual worker, you, at your place of work, will have certain constraints and controls placed upon you. Imagine a stone has been thrown into a lake. You, the worker, are that stone and once you hit the water (the workplace) you will have an impact on that water and the water will have an impact upon you. The first ripple will be the group of people with whom you regularly work. The group will have its own norms and sanctions

for making sure that those norms are kept. Workmates will encourage you to keep to the rules of the group (even if they are unwritten and often, unspoken as well, although most members in the group will know unconsciously almost, what the group's norms are). However, wherever you go there are individuals who cannot, or will not, follow the codes of behaviour that are accepted by *other* members of the group.

If these deviants do not conform, pressures, in the form of 'social sanctions' are brought to bear on them. In our society there is the idea that 'the punishment ought to fit the crime'. Being rude to someone at work and tampering with their equipment at work require different punishments. The pressure to apologize will almost

---

Assignment 7·1

Control, constraint, and conscience

We have seen how important keeping social control is in any society. Think about your:

(a) family
(b) school or college
(c) work
(d) friendship

group(s) and list some of the sanctions which the members have for controlling other members of that group. These sanctions might include force, persuasion, gossip, ridicule, sarcasm, informal understandings of various kinds, agreed (work) rules, custom and practice, formal and informal agreements, the law, etc.

Union Rules OK?

Rules

'Members should examine these rules carefully. The rules will be strictly enforced; and ignorance of them will not be accepted in mitigation of any breach of them.

Rule 1

1 The name of this Trade Union is 'Musicians' Union'.
2 The objects of the Union are to secure the complete organization of all persons eligible for membership for their mutual protection and advancement, to regulate their relations with their employers and with each other, to improve the status and remuneration of its members, to afford pecuniary or other help in time of need to its members and their dependants, to maintain a fund for the furtherance of political objects as hereinafter provided and to further the interests of its members in all ways.'

Source: courtesy Rules of the Musicians' Union

Sticking to the Rules

'Let me say this . . . the trade union movement cannot duck out of its responsibilities of intelligent labour relations. My union says that once we have made an agreement we will honour it, and if there is any member of ours that starts to kick over the traces we exercise great discipline on them. That's firmly in our rule book and anybody that goes back on decisions that we take (and I'm talking not about me taking action but our national executive committee and our annual conference) he's accountable to us, and we make him measure up to our rules.'

Source: courtesy Sidney Weighell, formerly General Secretary, National Union of Railwaymen

certainly be brought about *informally* by the group whereas making equipment unsafe in some way will mean that the person concerned is indulging not only in a very unpleasant act he may also be doing something *illegal*.

The second 'ripple' in the pond happens at the level of the firm itself where management has made rules about timekeeping, about those actions that can lead to dismissal, about job responsibilities and so on. Firms need to know what to do when you are absent from work and so there will be agreed procedures about when and who to contact if for any reason you are unable to turn up for work. Again at this level the

employer in this case makes it clear to us what we can and cannot do through clearly laid out written rules (in our contract of employment, for example).

At the workplace we have already seen how there is a third group of interested parties and that is the trade union itself. Not surprisingly, just as the workgroup has its unofficial rules, the employer has his (official) rules so the union has a set of (official) rules as laid down in the union rulebook, a fairly typical example from the rule book of the Musicians' Union can be seen opposite. Having talked about norms and rules, let us now move on to explore the concept of the 'law'.

Until now we have talked about the 'law' in a rather vague way. We must be very careful to say exactly what we mean by the terms which we use when we talk about law in industrial relations. First, we need to understand the difference between what is known as *statute* and *common* law.

Basically *statute law* is a law (or Act) that has been made by the British Parliament. These are relatively clear, written statements about what is 'right' and 'wrong' in certain areas of our everyday life such as education and schooling, the family and divorce, our rights as consumers, and industrial relations. Statute law is meant to provide a clear guide about the area in question but because our world is rapidly changing Acts need to be applied to different facts and changing situations. These applications and interpretations are made by the courts and other legal tribunals. These interpret what they think the

Act of Parliament means in relation to the particular facts of the situation under discussion. A law on industrial relations, for example, may not be very clear when it is applied to a particular situation in a particular firm and so an industrial tribunal, for example, will have to look carefully at the law *and* the new situation to which it relates. It will then pass a decision on how the law applies to what is happening here and now at that place of work.

However, there is another kind of law that has developed over hundreds of years and that is *common law*. It is very much the informal kind of law that 'like Topsy has just growed!'. Common law is the *unwritten* law of the land. It has developed from events that have happened to ordinary people in the past. Disputes have arisen and have been taken to court to be dealt with. Here a judge has made a ruling, that is, has come to a decision about that case. His decision has then set an example, or 'precedent' which has become accepted as law until changes in society have made the judge's decision no longer valid. It was then changed by the ruling of other judges of a higher court, or by Parliament passing an Act to bring about a change. As you can see, this kind of law is also 'judge made' whether that judge be in a Crown Court, a Court of Appeal or the House of Lords which is the highest court in the land. With common law, judges decide cases as they arise and give the reasons as to how they have come to their decisions. As time has gone by these decisions have grown and have formed a body of law. This body of law is based on certain principles that judges have tried to make

clear when explaining their decisions to the Court. Obviously some parts of the common law are out of date and are no longer important. Other parts have changed as society itself has changed.

One important point to note is that when a common law decision clashes with a statute law, *statute law always takes priority over common law.*

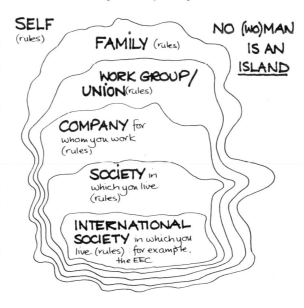

'I don't see why there should be any need beyond that (that is the 1906 and the 1913 Acts) to have judges making decisions about industrial relations; in many cases they don't understand the problems and, secondly, they seem to inflame the situation. In fact, that is why we had the 1906 and the 1913 Acts put on the Statute books because of judgements made in the House of Lords, which seems to teach us something, that they got it wrong then and there was such a bloody uproar that these two Acts have been put on the statute books. So, it seems to teach us something. . . .'

Source: courtesy Sidney Weighell, formerly General Secretary, National Union of Railwaymen

Indeed, many Acts are passed to change and replace common law decisions. So we can see that judges are a key group of people working within the legal system in that:

1 they *interpret* statute law;
2 while they also make law by their decisions under common law

and it is for these reasons that the *decisions* that *judges* make are so crucial in the ways in which the law grows and develops. It is also because of the importance attached to what judges say that trade unions watch legal decisions made by judges who are dealing with industrial relations' matters. They can see very quickly whether or not the judge concerned is interpreting the law in a way that is sympathetic or hostile to the trade union movement.

As we have just seen judges are employed to make decisions about disputes and arguments that people and groups have with one another. Basically these disputes are seen to be of two kinds: namely:

(*a*) disputes between private individuals; and
(*b*) disputes between individuals and the State (that is, society in general).

In (*a*) two neighbours may have had a disagreement. They are unable to sort it out on their own and so they take the case to court so that a judge may decide who is right and who is wrong. This kind of law is called *civil law*. The argument may not be just between two individuals: it may be between groups of people, for example, a union and an employer.

Take as an example the following case. A firm builds a motorway and after the road has been in use for ten years large cracks start appearing in some of the bridges on which the motorway is carried. The group for whom the motorway has been built (in this case the Department of the Environment) may feel that they have not had good value for money and may decide to take the contractor to court. The judge will then decide who is in the right and who is in the wrong. Having come to a decision he may feel that the injured (or 'wronged' party) should receive some compensation in the form of damages. Cases of this kind are dealt with in the *civil* courts as you would expect.

In (b) the dispute is with the State, that is society in general. These laws, the *criminal laws*, deal with problems and incidents that society at large feels are very important in the keeping of law and order. Indeed, very often these 'crimes' are felt to be wrong not only by the State, but by religious groups and by the ordinary person in the community. They include murder, manslaughter, theft, assault and rape. Crimes are more serious breaks in society's rules and are tried, naturally enough, in the *criminal* courts.

Although agreements made between workers and employers have always been entered into *voluntarily*, such relationships have always been guided by Common Law and Acts of Parliament (Statute Law). These Acts include many familiar ones such as the Factory Acts, the Contract of Employment Act and the Equal Pay Act. They have provided workers with a minimum/fair/good/overgenerous (depending on your viewpoint!) level of protection. Indeed, the last Labour Government (1974–9) introduced a number of new laws designed to strengthen the legal rights of the trade union movement. At the present time, the current Conservative Government is starting to weaken and take away many of those rights.

Throughout trade union history notable Acts of Parliament have played an important part in guiding the fortunes of the trade unions and the climate in which those unions dealt with employers and governments. We have seen how when the Industrial Revolution started to change the ways in which people lived at the end of the eighteenth century, particularly with the change from working at home to working in factories, trade unions came in contact almost immediately with statute law. In 1799 the *Combinations Act* was passed. This Act, along with another passed a year later, made trade unions virtually illegal. These Acts were repealed in 1825 only to be replaced a short time later by a new Act which, although it gave trade unions their legality, meant they had to be very careful in how they made use of their greatest weapon, the strike.

1870s It was not until the 1870s that the strike problem was really tackled again. In 1871 the then (Liberal) government passed two Acts. The Trade Union Act gave encouragement to the unions in various ways. However, at the same time as this Act was passed the Liberals under their leader, Gladstone, passed the Criminal Law Amendment Act which wiped out almost all the advantages given under the first Act. In 1875, with a change of government, the Conservatives scrapped the Criminal Law Amendment Act and replaced it with the *Conspiracy and Protection of Property Act*. This Act accepted the right of workers to bargain collectively and to make their case to their employers by striking and by peaceful picketing.

1901 Major legal problems again faced the unions in the very early years of the present century. The first of these was in 1901 when a strike occurred on the Taff Vale Railway in

'. . . We are covered by two Acts of Parliament at the moment, the 1906 Act and the 1913 Act.* The 1906 Act governs our responsibilities for industrial conduct which emerges as a consequence of a dispute with my union way back at the turn of the century, this gives us freedom to take action in furtherance of an industrial dispute without any fear of government or employer charging us with the damage we cause to the undertaking. Now if that was reversed there would be an explosion in Britain and I don't think the trade union movement would accept that at any price. So that's fundamental to our existence. . . .'

Source: courtesy Sidney Weighell, formerly General Secretary of the NUR

'As far as I'm concerned . . . industrial relations should be "free", it is a matter between management and the unions. You've got to have laws and the right to do certain things but a law can't establish good industrial relations. . . .'

Source: courtesy Ray Buckton, General Secretary, ASLEF

South Wales. The company tried to break the strike by using volunteers to do the work of their regular men. The railwaymen's union (The Amalgamated Society of Railway Servants, the forerunner of today's NUR) gave cash backing to its striking members. The company took the case to the (civil) courts. Here it was granted an injunction and a ruling that a union could be sued in its registered name. The union appealed and was successful. However, the company took the case to the House of Lords (the highest appeal court in the land) and there the original decision was upheld. The union was obliged to pay damages of £23 000 to the company and another £19 000 in court costs. This ruling meant that a trade union could not help its members in a strike without fear of being sued. Even worse, if the union did win a strike, the damages and costs of the strike could well ruin the union involved.

1906   In 1906, with the help of the then new-born Parliamentary Labour Party, a Bill, introduced by Keir Hardie, passed into law to become the *Trades Disputes Act*.

This:

(a) legalized PEACEFUL PICKETING;
(b) gave full protection of UNION FUNDS;
(c) and said that no *civil* action could be taken against unions for 'TORTS', or wrongdoings like calling members out on strike. They were given immunity. If men came out on strike because of conflict and dispute with their employer and broke their contracts of employment with their bosses, their union would not be liable for damages in the courts.

More developments occurred in the courts and in parliament towards the beginning of the First World War. These had a serious effect upon the development of the Labour Party. More will be said about these in Chapter 9 but at this stage all that is really important to know is that in *1913* 1913 another *Trade Union Act* was passed which allowed trade unions to spend funds on political matters and this led to an increase in the unions' strength and power *politically*.

In Chapter 4 we have already seen how the government of the day and the employers won a total victory in the 1926 General Strike. This strike led to an Act (*the Trade Disputes and Trade Union Act of 1927*) which until the end of the Second World War put severe controls on the freedom of the unions. The TUC official history puts it well when it says 'The strikers go back to work and the Tories reach for the law'. This belief by many Conservatives that the law should have greater powers over what happens in industrial relations is still an important one held by many members of the Tory Party today. On the other hand, the unions want the law out of industrial relations as much as possible.

Over the last twenty years there has been a

growth in the role that the law has played in British industrial relations, particularly when it comes to providing statutory rights for individual workers. Having said that, however, we must remember that even today collective bargaining and everyday industrial relations between the workers, unions, and management are still very much in the hands of custom and practice. The voluntary tradition is still strong, and it is important to remember as well that's the way both management and unions usually want it (generally speaking).

The 1970s have seen an absolute mass of legislation on industrial and trade union matters. If I simply list the major Acts I think it will give you some idea of the amount of work that these laws have brought about for employers, trade unionists and individual workers who ought and need to know their individual rights and responsibilities. You can understand the comments of those on the shop floor or on the management side when they say they have trouble simply keeping up with the changes in the law. In addition, having joined the Common

---

In Britain we have collected a body of labour law and most people involved in industrial relations accept the need for a basic 'skeleton' of labour law to provide a framework within which to work. The question then arises: how much law do you need to provide this basic framework? Indeed, many observers would say that you need much more law than just this basic framework.

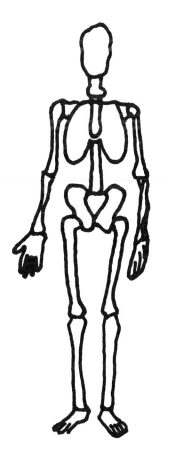

Market means that on top of the workplace 'norms', on top of the workplace rules (both union and management), on top of both civil and criminal laws that apply only to Britain, will be added a variety of Common Market laws.

Acts concerning industrial relations that have recently been passed are as follows: the **Equal Pay Act** (1970), the **Industrial Relations Act** (1971), the **Trade Union and Labour Relations Act** (TULRA, 1974), the **Health and Safety at work Act** (1974); the **Employment Protection Act** (1975); the **Sex Discrimination Act** (1975); the **Trade Union and Labour Relations Act** (**Amendment**, 1976); the **Employment Protection (Consolidation) Act** (1978), the **1980 Employment Act** and, last but by no means least, the **1982 Employment Act**.

The 1971 Industrial Relations Act, made law by the then Conservative Government of Edward Heath, was one of the most controversial industrial relations Acts of recent years. It received a good deal of opposition both in Parliament and in the community at large. The Act, among other things, set up a National Industrial Relations Court. This had wide-ranging powers to consider complaints arising under the Act. It could impose penalties and punish those who disregarded the Court's orders.

The Act caused much conflict during 1972 and

'I have never subscribed to the view that the law has no real part to play in industrial relations. The law has a vital role in providing the basic framework within which industrial relations are conducted. The law has to protect the right of employees to combine in trade unions and to take collective action to defend their interests. Equally, I believe that the law must define the limits of industrial action and protect the individual and the community as a whole against the abuse of industrial power.'

Source: James Prior, former Secretary of State for Employment in a speech to the CBI, 1981

A union view on the law:

'However, one word of warning! Don't expect these Acts to provide magical solutions to the thousand and one problems that trade unionists face every day at work. They will undoubtedly be of assistance in the struggle to achieve decent conditions of service for all workers. But in the

1973 because the unions saw the Act as using the law, the courts and the judges to achieve objectives which were *'political'* rather than *'legal'*. Various disputes during the three year period that the Act was in force persuaded many union members and their leaders that the judges were not to be trusted. We have seen how in the past unions had been wary of the role of the law in industrial relations. For many, the 1971 Act confirmed their worst suspicions, that the judges were biased against them, as were the Conservative politicians of the time. The Industrial Relations Act was repealed in 1974 when the Labour Party returned to power.

Bargaining or battleground? The choice in Industrial Relations

'I had thought that by 1974 the Conservative Party – and the CBI – had learned something about how not to improve industrial relations. The bitter experience of the operation of the 1971 Industrial Relations Act is still fresh in my memory, if not in theirs. It demonstrated that in this field attempts at detailed legal regulation are both irrelevant and counter-productive. Now the Conservative Government, abetted by the CBI, is in danger of committing the same errors all over again.'

Source: Len Murray, 2 October, 1979, TUC Documents

One of the more controversial issues covered by recent legislation is that of picketing. Imagine that you work for a small firm and that for various reasons the generally good communications between the union and the employer have broken down: so much so in fact that the union has called an official strike which the majority of workers have agreed to support. However, a small group of workers at the firm have decided that they wish to work and because of this group your union branch decides to set up a picket line to persuade these workers not to go in to work. You have been asked to form part of that picket line. You and the law come face to face. You decide to do some research into your rights as a member of the picket line and these are some of the questions and answers that you find.

You discover that one of the latest Acts in a long line of Acts of Parliament that has something to say about picketing, is the Employment Act of 1980. With this Act the Conservative Government released *codes of conduct* (that is suggested ways of behaving) on two important matters in industrial relations namely, *picketing and the closed shop*. We will follow up our discussions of the closed shop (later in the chapter) but for the moment let's work at the Act and the codes of practice and see what they have to say about picketing.

The word 'picket' comes from the French word 'piquet' which means a stake and, in fact, its original meaning was that of a sharp pointed stake or peg used in the making of a palisade or fence. It did, however, have a military use in that the word also meant a group of men who were selected as an outpost or for special duty. In the industrial relations sense the word ties in with this last military meaning in that today we use the word 'picket' to mean someone who keeps watch at a factory or an office, etc. to make sure that 'blacklegs' or 'scabs' do not work and so break the strike. A picket can try and peacefully persuade someone not to work but (s)he cannot threaten or cajole that person.

Picketing is nothing new. It has happened throughout the course of trade union history. One reason, however, that it is an important subject for discussion at the moment is that there have been, of late, several changes in the ways in which unionists have picketed. The first major change is that the so-called *Secondary Picketing* has become more common. This form of picketing was used by the miners with great success in their 1972 dispute. Rather than picket their own collieries, where no-one was working anyway, they decided to picket the premises of the people who actually used and stockpiled the coal such as the CEGB's power stations. In secondary picketing the strikers not only picket the works of their own employer but they also send out 'flying' or travelling pickets to firms that supply the raw materials or to customers to make sure that their action really has an impact. For example, if a furniture-making factory goes on strike 'flying pickets' could well be sent to the timber merchants that supply the firm. They might also go to the DIY supermarkets that sell the firm's products. The other main change in picketing, that the mass media in particular have

been very quick to highlight, is that of the mass picket where large numbers of strikers have gathered. The strike at Grunwick, the photo-processing laboratory in North London, and Hadfields, the private steel making firm in Sheffield, have shown how ugly things can get when large numbers of striking workers and police get together. The possibility of conflict is

final analysis, the Union can rely only on the strength of the organization it has built up. These Acts should be seen as part of the tools of our trade which, used effectively, can bring considerable benefits.

Source: NUPE Documents

Earlier in this chapter we talked about the role of the judge as an arbiter ('go-between') in a dispute. It is very interesting to see what Sir John Donaldson (President of the National Industrial Relations Court under the 1971 Act) had to say about the part the NIRC could play in industrial relations. Stressing the importance of guidelines (a need for a basic structure, like our legal 'skeleton') he said:

'With such guidelines, the courts could be given their traditional role of investigating the merits of disputes and helping the party who is right. . . . The public suffers from every industrial dispute. Ought they not to know who is right? Adopting this new approach they would know, for the court which investigated the dispute would tell them. Those who suffered injustice would then be supported by the courts.

However, one of the problems with this approach is that most industrial disputes are not clear cut 'black' and 'white', 'right' and 'wrong' situations. They are very much in the middle grey area where there may be right and wrong on both sides. The solution would come through discussion and compromise rather than through the law courts?

The Abuse of Bargaining Power

'One reason is the framework of law which is uniquely favourable to trade unions. They can organize and cause industrial disruption with wide immunity from legal action. Many rights under employment protection legislation apply only to unions and their members. Yet in return for their privileged position, unions have not been obliged to assume parallel responsibilities toward the community at large. Indeed, while the short-term costs of industrial disputes for employers may be extremely high, the cost for employees can be cushioned in a variety of ways, for example through the payment of supplementary benefits and PAYE tax rebates. Our competitors do not give as much support to those on strike.'

Source: Pay: the Choice Ahead, CBI, February 1979

'It has recently been suggested that changes be made in the laws* affecting trade unions. Do you agree or disagree with the following?'

	All Voters		Union Members	
Percentages	Agree	Disagree	Agree	Disagree
No strikes being called until there is a postal ballot of union members concerned	86	6	84	11
A limit on the number of pickets allowed at any location	77	15	72	23
A ban on secondary picketing: that is, a ban on picketing a company not directly involved in a strike	76	16	67	28
The introduction of postal ballots in the election of union officials; to be paid for by the government	60	25	62	31
Social security benefits to strikers' families being made subject to income tax	54	35	44	51
The removal of the right of those in key industries to strike, in return for guaranteed wage increases	46	37	39	51

Source: courtesy MORI/The Sunday Times, 31 August, 1980*

built into the situation and when violence flares the TV cameras and the newspapers are always ready to show some of the unpleasant scenes that have occurred at both of these places.

Much of today's law on picketing is deeply rooted in laws passed in the last thirty years of the last century and the first thirty of this and so much was written before the age of the lorry and the car. This fact of history is still important for pickets today because a picket can only try peacefully to persuade someone not to work or to give someone information about the strike and the picket. (S)he cannot make a lorry driver stop: all that a picket can do is signal them to stop.

> '. . . A really decisive case on the right of pickets to stop lorries in order to communicate information and peacefully persuade is the decision of the House of Lords in (the case of) Broome v. Director of Public Prosecutions (1974). They decided that Mr Broome was guilty of wilful obstruction of the highway when he stood in front of a lorry, for at most nine minutes, in order peacefully to persuade the driver not to deliver his load to a building site where an industrial dispute was in progress. According to the Lords, pickets may signal drivers to stop but have no right to compel them to do so!'
>
> Source: Picketing A Trade Unionists' Guide, Labour Research Department, 1976

In spite of many people's wishes for the police to have more power to deal with those on the picket lines, they do in fact have a good deal of power already when it comes to picketing and the criminal law. Police can arrest pickets for obstructing a policeman while doing his duty, assaulting a policeman, damaging property and so on. If we take one of these, obstructing a policeman while he is doing his duty, it is here that the human element, the personal ideas and attitudes of the police start to show through. If a policeman thinks that the pickets are about to break the law he has the power to do what he sees fit in order to stop anyone breaking the law. It is, incidentally, not enough for a policeman to *believe* that the law is about to be broken, he must have *reasonable grounds* for that belief and obviously that is where the feelings and emotions of the policeman involved become very important and it is at that point that the 'formal' law really bumps up against the 'informal' law of the individual.

We can see then that it is not so much that the criminal law cannot handle picketing which is violent or attended by a large number of people. The police have the legal powers to handle this. Their problem is how to carry out and enforce

> *It's not so much that government has become more interventionist in industrial relations through *law*, it is that laws have been made which have enabled trade unions both collectively and trade unionists individually to use the law more on their behalf. There has been a vast increase in individual rights and an increase in trade union immunities through using the law.'*
>
> Source: courtesy   Alan Swinden, CBI

that law in the difficult situation of the picket line with its unpredictable human beings!

If workers picket they are protected from the civil law. They have 'immunity' (protection) from the law. There is, in fact, no legal right to picket, but peaceful picketing has for a long time been recognized as being acceptable; lawful if not legal. It is a *Civil Wrong* to try to persuade someone to break their employment contract between worker and employer. But the law makes an exception of those people involved in a dispute with their employer providing that they keep within the following:

(a) the pickets are standing outside their own place of work (secondary picketing by flying pickets is in fact breaking the law);

Section 16 Employment Act 1980

(b) the picketing is for the purpose of communicating information or for trying to persuade someone peacefully to work or not to work;

(c) it is carried out with the idea of a dispute between management and workers in mind or in support of one already in progress.

If workers do *not* keep to these guidelines, the immunities we were talking about disappear.

For example, you are picketing outside your own factory when the lorry of one of your firm's suppliers brings in some equipment. You tell the driver that there is an official strike on and that the union members would be pleased if the driver does not deliver those supplies. He agrees and returns to his depot. Since you have encouraged a break in the contract between that supplier and your employer you have in fact committed a wrong (or in legal terms you have brought about a *Tort*). However since you have only done this because of the dispute between yourselves (the workers), and your employer you are given immunity from the law.

However, if you picket the *supplier's* depot, this is *secondary picketing* and does not have immunity. The pickets would then be liable and the supplier could take those pickets to the civil court to try to obtain an injunction to stop the unlawful picketing. The 1980 Act makes pickets more liable under the civil law.

The 1980 Act also deals with the thorny issue of the 'closed shop'. The Donovan Report (1968) said that a 'closed shop' is:

Closed shops are a somewhat controversial fact of British industrial life. Since this is the case there must be good reasons why they have become established and it might be useful to see what the 'pros and cons' are of the 'closed shop' arrangement. Not all the reasons given here are what you can call straight 'industrial relations' reasons. As we have already seen many different subjects have to be taken into account when we try to make sense of what goes on at the workplace and the closed shop is one of the areas

a situation in which employees come to realize that a particular job is only to be obtained *and* retained *if they* become and remain *members of one of a specified number of trade unions.*

Source: The Closed Shop in Britain, W. E. J. McCarthy, 1964

In some cases a person may have to be a member of a trade union before he can obtain the job he seeks. This is a 'pre-entry' closed shop. In other cases he may be obliged to join a trade union within a short time of beginning the job he has secured. This is a 'post-entry' closed shop.

Source: The Donovan Report, HMSO, 1968

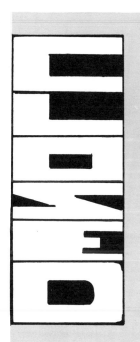
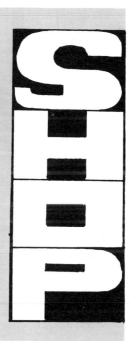

In Britain we value very highly the idea that everyone should enjoy as much individual freedom as possible. We believe that people should be able to 'do their own thing' as long as they don't hurt anyone else in the process. Some people believe that making an individual join a union before or after they take up a job goes clear against the idea of personal freedom. Besides aren't trade unions voluntary groups that people may or may not join?

Secondly, the closed shop can mean that individuals who do not join the closed shop get 'picked on' by union members and can be put under pressure by members to join.

Because the 'closed shop' set up says who can, and who cannot join a firm, critics of it say that it does not give management a fair chance to employ the people *it* thinks are best suited for the job.

where we have to make use of different subjects such as politics and philosophy.

Taking the case *against* the 'closed shop', first of all, let us see some of the arguments that have been put forward to attack them (above).

One point about closed shops that can be seen as 'good' or 'bad' depending on which side you see it from (management or union) is that the closed shop increases the power of the trade unions when they are having negotiations with the management. It also means that if and when the union takes some kind of industrial action (work to rule, strike, etc.) that action will prob-

ably be more effective.

If we now go on to look at the case for having a closed shop, we find these reasons to *support* it:

From the employer's viewpoint the closed shop has the advantage that it allows him to select the union(s) that he wishes to work with and to shut out those unions he does not want.

It also helps to give more stable collective relationships at work because the union has security at the place of work, for example, its membership is more secure. It should not feel threatened and because of this may not need to be aggressive. It does not need to prove to its

'*It's a voluntary organization (POEU). We have some 130 000 members, none of whom is compelled to be a member of the organization. Clearly workplace pressures . . . do bring pressure to bear on people to belong to the union, but there's absolutely no evidence at all that people are actually bullied into the situation . . . besides they are articulate, critical and independent. They are not the kind of people you can bully and they pay £32 a year (April 1981) voluntarily towards the maintenance of the union's organization. They expect service from it and a very high level of service too.*

'*It's not just a matter of pay bargaining, or straightforward conditions of service, it's a comprehensive insurance policy. They know that if they get into trouble (for example, with discipline, or they have an accident at work) that the union is in a position then to defend and protect them effectively.*'

Source: courtesy Peter Shaw, Post Office Engineering Union

members that it can do its job. Besides, if a union feels secure about its membership it may think more about the firm's needs in the more distant future rather than become over worried about short-term problems.

A closed shop means that the union represents all the workers (whether they like it or not!) and so this means that other unions won't be so keen to come in and fight for members.

Again, (depending on your viewpoint), the next point can have good or bad implications. The closed shop does give the union real power over its members. Union officers and shop stewards can make sure that people in the union do keep agreements. It *may* also mean that you as an individual lose some of your individual free-dom to the needs of the majority of the workers and members of the union.

We've already seen how the closed shop covers all the workers in agreed procedures at the workplace and so it overcomes a common objection that many unionists have to those people at the workplace who are not in the union. Union members often say that only union members should get the benefits that unions give. So that if a union gets its members a 10% pay rise non-members are, in fact, not entitled to that pay rise. The closed shop overcomes all that. Everyone is in the union so everyone is entitled to the benefits!

Under the *1980 Employment Act* changes have taken place regarding the closed shop. For example, the Act strengthened the position of the worker who does not want to go on strike. It's also given that person the right to claim that he has been unreasonably expelled from the union if he does not, in fact, go on strike. The Act does not declare the closed shop unlawful as such but it does allow claims of compensation for unfair dismissal where a person *is* dismissed for not belonging to a specific trade union.

However, things move very fast indeed in industrial relations' law and in the autumn of *1982 a new Employment Act* went on to the statute books. This has brought about a further tightening up of the law relating to the closed shop and other key issues. Under the 1982 Act union funds (and not just union officials) are liable to damages in unlawful strikes. The definition of an industrial dispute has been cut back to confine union immunities to strikes that are concerned with the pay and conditions of workers. Among other things, it has made it much more difficult to set up and maintain the closed shops that we were just talking about. For the main points of the 1982 Act *see* p. 114.

As this book goes to press there is the likelihood of more industrial relations' law in that the government has just published (January 1983) a *Green Paper* which explores some of the ideas that we looked at in Chapter 6. Called '*Democracy in Trade Unions*', the Green Paper, a discussion paper, suggests that there are three areas in which new law is necessary. These three areas are as follows:

(*a*) there should be secret ballots for elections in trade unions;
(*b*) there should be secret ballots before strikes; and
(*c*) there should be changes in the 1913 Trade Union Act, one of the major changes being that of replacing 'contracting out' with 'contracting in'

All of these measures would, of course, be controversial while the third measure would weaken. the Labour Party quite considerably since the Party gets most of its money from the political funds provided by the unions.

As students of industrial relations all of these changes remind us that:

(*a*) the law is very complex indeed;
(*b*) that it is changing all the time and that it will continue to adapt and change in the future; and
(*c*) that it can be interpreted very differently by different individuals and different groups.

How much impact the 1982 Act and the 1983 Green Paper will have on everyday industrial life is difficult to say at this early stage, but one thing that you, the reader, must continue to do is to watch the changes that are taking place in the law. Only in this way can you possibly hope to keep some kind of track of the key role that the law has to play in industrial relations.

'*We don't need a closed shop, we can attain a level of organization well up in the ninety per cent area without a closed shop simply through voluntary methods of persuasion plus the deductions at source scheme where the employer actually collects the subscriptions for us. There isn't any need for us to have either a 'pre-entry' or 'post-entry' closed shop; none whatsoever. We would expect other unions to judge their own position in exactly the same way.*

'*The National Union of Seamen has a closed shop arrangement with the British Shipping Federation and it clearly needs one; the union could not organize itself effectively without a closed shop; the same goes for the printing industry . . . it's straightforward pragmatism.*'

Source: courtesy Peter Shaw, Post Office Engineering Union

The 1982 Employment Act

. . . trade unions liable up to £250 000 for unlawful actions through injunctions and damages. . . .

. . . strikers to be dismissed fairly for refusing to return to work after a brief set period. . . .

. . . state cash for secret ballots on wage offers. . . .

. . . closed shops that are now in existence to be subjected to periodic ballots. . . .

. . . increased compensation for unfairly dismissed non-trade union members. Stiffer provisions for re-instatement. . . .

. . . union-only contracts to be outlawed. . . .

Trade dispute definition to be tightened up to exclude from immunity industrial action motivated by political or personal considerations. . . .

. . . those unfairly dismissed in a closed shop because of union pressure should be able to seek compensation directly from that trade union. . . .

. . . trade union only members as a condition for (work) contracts to be illegal. . . .

Assignment 7.2

Green for Go?

In 1981 the Conservative Government published a 'Green Paper', that looked at *Trade Union Immunities*. In one part of the paper it made the following points:

> *Good industrial relations cannot simply be legislated into existence.[1] Reform must also come from within: from trade unions and employers adapting their situations and practices to the social and economic pressures for change.[2]*

With reference to point 1 the question I want you to think about is 'why cannot good industrial relations simply be legislated into existence?' What other pressures are there, apart from the law, that determines the way people behave in their relationships with one another at work?

Using the chapters you have already read, make a list of those points that you think help to make up 'good' industrial relations.

With reference to point 2 why do we *need* to change the ways in which we work? Make a list of some of the reasons that you think are important when we are talking about changing ways at work.

THE LAW

'*The European Court of Human Rights ruled by eighteen votes to three that the dismissal in 1976 of Noel James, aged 52, Ian Young, aged 27, and Roger Webster, aged 67, was an infringement of Article II of the European Convention of Human Rights, which guarantees everyone "freedom of association with others, including the right to form and to join trade unions for the protection of one's interests."*

They lost their jobs for refusing to join a union after their employer, British Railways, had reached an agreement with the three rail unions under legislation brought in by the previous Labour Government that all their employees would have to be union members.

The judgement emphasized that it was confining itself to the cases and particular circumstances of the three individuals and was not a review of the closed shop system as such. At one point it said: "Compulsion to join a particular trade union may not always be contrary to the convention."

Source: courtesy The Guardian, *14 August, 1981*

Recommended reading for Chapter 7

There are very many books on industrial relations' law. Those I would recommend as useful reference books to your own legal rights at work are:
Rights at Work by J. McMullen (Pluto Press, 1979)
The Worker and the Law by K. W. Wedderburn (Penguin, 1971)

Books that you have read and found useful should be added below

Chapter 8
What we need here is a change of attitude

'*It's a slowly, slowly attitude change business and attitude change in industrial relations is the hardest thing of all.*

'*There are basically three areas when you're dealing with industrial relations reform and change:*

> '*you've got to get the bargaining institutions right;*
> '*you've got to get what I call the "remuneration package" right (pay, conditions, pensions, etc.);*
> '*the third thing is that you've got to get employee and managerial attitudes right.*

> '*It's the third one that takes the time and it's the third one to which probably the least attention is given.*'

Source: courtesy Pat Lowry, formerly Director of Personnel and External Affairs, BL Limited, currently Chairman ACAS

Objectives

At the end of this chapter you should be able to:

1 say what an attitude is and list reasons why attitudes are important in industrial relations;
2 list and discuss attitudes held by people to industrial relations matters such as the power of the unions, the closed shop and picketing using information from opinion polls and other sources;
3 outline and discuss some of the attitudes and beliefs held by the main political parties in Britain (namely, the Conservative, Labour and Liberal/Social Democratic Parties) and understand how these tie in with industrial relations.

THIS CHAPTER COVERS the following topics:

1 attitudes: what are they and why do we need them?
2 attitudes in industrial relations: what are they and who holds them?
3 attitudes and the political parties: which party holds what views and what attitudes and how

do these affect industrial relations?

In this chapter I want to look at the attitudes that people have. You can be sure that most people have fairly strong views one way or another about industrial relations and trade unions. In the next few pages we are going to see some of the evidence for those opinions: opinions that are held by the public at large, by management, by unionists and by individuals involved in day-to-day industrial relations.

Let's start our investigation into attitudes by looking at what an attitude actually is. I think we would all agree that attitudes are very important to us in the way in which we live our everyday lives. When you ask a person about trade unions, or the economy or the way that the government is handling some of the problems that Britain has these days, you are really asking about that person's beliefs. You are saying what do you believe about industrial relations? You are asking for that person's feelings towards the trade unions and management. You are waiting to see how (s)he answers your question because knowing what (s)he believes and feels about workers, unionists and all the other people involved in our industrial life will tell you a great deal about that person and his/her attitudes to life.

One important reason that we need to know what other people think and feel about the world in which they live is that by knowing that we are able to predict what they are going to do to a much greater extent. Our world becomes a little safer, a little more secure when we know how other people are going to react to us when we ask them for an opinion. This, in turn, leads us on to ask; what then, is an *attitude*? Briefly, the way we treat people in the world is very much determined by what we think of them, what we believe and feel about them. If we take someone we know very well and ask ourselves questions about them such as 'do we like them?'; 'do we worry about them?' and 'do they mean something special to us?'; we are on the way to discovering what we think about them and what our attitudes are towards them. In simple terms, an attitude is the way a person thinks and feels about another person or a subject or issue in society. Knowing a person's attitudes is very important to determining how we react to and treat that person when we meet and talk with them. An attitude is a way of thinking about a person, an object or a situation and it makes us ready to respond and react to that person, situation, etc. in a predetermined way. For example, if we *trust* someone, say a friend, that attitude of trust will allow us to respond to that friend if (s)he offers us help. We are prepared for their help and glad to let them help because we trust that they will not let us down.

Some of the other reasons that attitudes are important are as follows. First, we feel really good in saying what we actually think and feel. It allows us to 'blow off' steam a little. It makes us feel better when we can strengthen the pictures we have of ourselves as people. For example, a shop steward fighting for the rights of his workers feels useful and feels that what he is doing is worthwhile, valuable and is helping others, and that in turn makes him feel good. Managers who have organized work and have succeeded in getting the order out on time also feel useful. Their self picture gets a boost. Their beliefs are reinforced. Also, it's important to remember that we use our attitudes to protect ourselves when we are attacked by others, for example, in an argument. When someone says something about us that we do not like we can come back, through our attitudes, with counter arguments. 'You may not like the orange jeans that I've bought but I think they suit me!' It's because of reasons like these that attitudes in industry are so hard to change. People will feel threatened if you try to change their attitudes forcefully. You can only put across another view to which in time they may decide to change.

Obviously we have attitudes to all kinds of things. We have attitudes towards certain individuals, and towards groups of people such as men, women, teachers, students, trade unionists, management, etc., etc. We also have attitudes towards issues such as the 'best' colour for GPO telephone boxes or the 'best' (British) car on the market or the 'best' political party on the

'*The small employer, generally speaking, regards the closed shop as an evil. The big employers take a rather different view; a more pragmatic* view, (or cowardly depending on how you look at it). . . . You get those sorts of differences of attitudes about trade union power.*'

Source: courtesy   Alan Swinden, CBI

'*I think that you've got to work on the shop floor at the point of production. You've got to be involved in its activities and take a part in the role of shop steward; and that is the only way you can gain experience and understand the problems one gets in industry.*'

Source: courtesy E. Bone, National Officer, TGWU

* practical

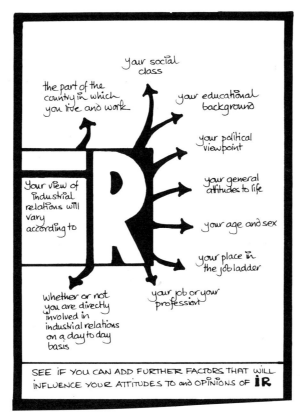

British political scene. As we grow up we develop attitudes to more and more people, issues, questions, etc., and gradually our attitudes fit together to form sets or systems that help us to make sense of the world. Your attitudes will lock and interlock together, so, for example, if you have a sympathetic point of view towards the poor of this world it might be fairly

safe to predict that your attitude towards other less well-off groups such as the physically or mentally handicapped will also be sympathetic. One can, perhaps assume that if you care for 'under-dogs' in general, you will care for 'under-dogs' in particular, whether they are poorly paid workers in a 'Third World' country, an unemployed school leaver in this country who is being used as 'cheap labour' or a man in his late fifties who has been made redundant, has very little money and has even less chance of getting another job.

Having talked about attitudes in general, let us now have a look at some of the *attitude surveys* that have been done in the specific area of industrial relations. The first study I want to mention was carried out during early 1976 by MORI (Market and Opinion Research International) when they researched attitudes and understandings of workers in industry to the *market economy* on behalf of the CBI. The research included an opinion poll of over 1 000 employees in the manufacturing, construction and mining industries, while a parallel survey was also carried out on a sample of 231 managers.

The results showed an overwhelming amount of support for the free enterprise system that we talked about in Chapter 1 when we discussed the role of the CBI. The survey also showed that employees believed that firms needed to make profits that could be then reinvested in the company to keep it healthy and to make it stronger. There was also general agreement on the need for good communications.

Taking each of these points in turn, the

survey, in an attempt to investigate workers' attitudes and views thoroughly about such things as profits and the quality of British management, asked employees how far they agreed or disagreed with the statements opposite.

In addition, the CBI was very keen to discover how effective communications are between workers, unions and management. The MORI survey looked at this subject in some detail. It examined, for example, how well people felt that their boss, shop steward, management and Member of Parliament looked after their interests. The results came out as shown on p. 120.

It's interesting to note too that the survey showed considerable degree of good feeling towards both the worker's immediate boss and shop steward, highlighting, perhaps, the importance of the work group to industrial relations' attitudes. The survey went on to say that these two particular people are obviously good *potential* channels through which to communicate to the top management of both the firm and the union.

The survey concluded that it believed that its

findings show that the majority of workers were reasonably keen on the present economic set-up and they wanted to hear from their management about the way that the economy worked. This was especially true if the information were related to their own place of work, such as the achievement of a new order for a firm or cut backs in staffing in a firm due to a lack of

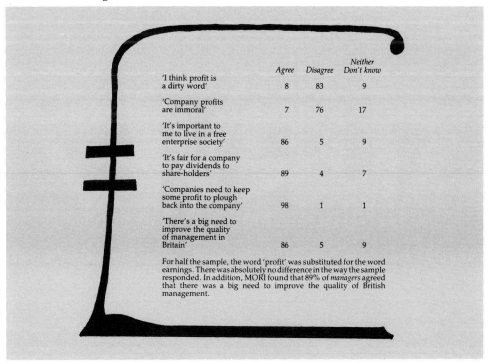

	Agree	Disagree	Neither Don't know
'I think profit is a dirty word'	8	83	9
'Company profits are immoral'	7	76	17
'It's important to me to live in a free enterprise society'	86	5	9
'It's fair for a company to pay dividends to share-holders'	89	4	7
'Companies need to keep some profit to plough back into the company'	98	1	1
'There's a big need to improve the quality of management in Britain'	86	5	9

For half the sample, the word 'profit' was substituted for the word earnings. There was absolutely no difference in the way the sample responded. In addition, MORI found that 89% of *managers* agreed that there was a big need to improve the quality of British management.

orders. The survey also added that it believed that the workers need to know more about exactly what a 'manager' does, and that managers themselves need more information

In answer to the question 'How sure are you that your interests are being well looked after by. . . ?'.

	Very/fairly sure	Not very sure/ Not sure at all	Not applicable/ Don't know
Your immediate boss	64	32	4
Top management	51	42	7
Your shop steward	50	18	32
Your union's national executive	42	29	29
Your local MP	28	58	14
The government (then a Labour Government)	30	63	7

In a study of London dockers and their attitudes, a sociologist Stephen Hill, discovered the following opinions and attitudes about trade unions and their roles and responsibilities.

Trade unions ought to get unions a say in management:

Agree	81%
Disagree	14%
Neither	5%

Trade unions have too much power in this country:

Agree	40%

and training if they are going to communicate more easily and more clearly to the workers.

A most interesting report of the attitudes and opinions of trade union officials was carried out by MORI in the autumn of 1979. This report contained the results of two surveys, one carried out among *General Secretaries* of trade unions affiliated to the TUC, the other of *delegates* to that year's Trades Union Congress annual conference, held at Blackpool. The report began by listing the main problems the officials said their unions were facing at that moment. Predominant in their answers were, not surprisingly, matters that were of particular interest to their own unions. However, apart from these, one in three General Secretaries and Conference delegates mentioned the traditional issues of *pay levels and unemployment.*

> *Operating in a labour-intensive industry you need to get the right pay for members while making certain it doesn't do anyone out of a job.*

General Secretary

> *Action to maintain the living standards of our members; action to maintain the level of employment. To associate with the TUC in fighting the adverse policies of the Tory government.*

Conference Delegate

In addition, a significant number of individuals referred to the impact of new technology and the effects of the cuts in public expenditure in such areas as education, health, transport, etc.

Around a third of both the General Secretaries and the Delegates mentioned the *possible reduction in the number of trade unions* in this country. One General Secretary who wanted to see a reduction in the number of unions come about, was quoted on this as shown here.

The trade union officials surveyed were far from happy with the Conservative government and their policies and, of course, this difficult relationship with the government still continues at the present time. In an interview with Ray Buckton of ASLEF (in December 1980) he made the comments (opposite) that reiterated difficulties encountered within the then current union–government relationship.

However, we will say more about the trade unions' relationships with the various political parties later in the chapter so, now, let's move on.

The MORI survey then turned its attention to two crucial and interrelated aspects of the employee–employer relationship. The first of these was *how a firm treated its employees*. This was regarded by over half the trade union officials as one of the main factors that they take into account when they are rating an individual company. In addition, the attitude of manage-

Disagree	49%
Neither	11%

Trade unions ought not to support the Labour Party:

Agree	61%
Disagree	32%
Neither	7%

Trade unions are no longer so necessary as they used to be:

Agree	16%
Disagree	82%
Neither	2%

Source: The Dockers: class and tradition in London, *Stephen Hill, Heinemann, 1976*

ment towards its workforce and its willingness to include them in decision making was a common theme running throughout the answers given as shown in the quotes on p. 122.

Poor communications in general, the second important aspect of the employer–employee relationship mentioned, was brought up by over half the General Secretaries and around a third of the Conference Delegates. This implied criticism of both management *and* unions, incidentally. A third of both the delegates and the general secretaries mentioned the *failure of management to consult the workforce.*

In summary, it was obvious, the survey concluded, that trade union officials regard communications as the key to the satisfactory running of industry. When they go wrong, then the problems really start.

> *If you want a blunt answer, I think the Movement will alter very little unless changes are made somewhere else (I mean the government) which will force the trade union movement to change, for example, the trade union movement is made up of a considerable number of unions in the same industries and as a result a great deal of conflict takes place between unions. There is an obvious need for the combination of unions but because of the conservative* attitude of unions and the self-protective attitude they have, this development is most unlikely.*

General Secretary

* here means: 'unwilling to change'

'My union is like every other union in the country, the government doesn't want to know us officially. We realize what the government's doing, so we pressurize and endeavour to let the public of this country know what is happening to the trans port system* – an essential national asset.'

Source: courtesy Ray Buckton, General Secretary, ASLEF

* British Rail

'You Get a Nice Class of People at our Place!'

Social Class and Attitudes in Industrial Relations

'I believe that the industrial relations' system which operates in any country is, to a certain extent, a reflection of the social class system generally. If you have a divisive society generally then probably you are going to have an industrial relations' system which is divisive and it's the good management which is able to reduce the divisiveness; but the basic divisiveness is there

and we are, I'm afraid, a country which is basically divided: a country that has different sets of social objectives, social priorities, a status-ridden bloody country, a class-ridden country and I think that that feeling of divisiveness is not hung up with the old overcoat in the corner when people come to work. It's still there at the place of work and it's a good management which can contain it; it's a bad management . . . when it gets exaggerated and it becomes worse, but you just cannot take an industrial environment and expect it to be ideal when you've got an outside environment which is divided.

'If you take Russia at one end, the USA at the other, I do not believe that the social divisiveness . . . is as great as it is in this country.'

Source: courtesy Pat Lowry, formerly Director of Personnel and External Affairs BL Limited, currently Chairman ACAS

'Its attitude and relationship to the employees: a company that will deal with its employees' representatives is likely to make progress.'

General Secretary

'Awareness of people as individuals. Ability of middle management to know their employees. . . . Mutual respect between management and workers.'

Conference Delegate

'Communications and lack of communications. This covers a multitude of sins.'

Conference Delegate

'Prejudice on both sides. A management that treats workers like serfs and a union that treats management as robber barons. You start with unfavourable premises.'

Conference delegate

'Reactionary management. . . . General lack of information supplied to shop stewards, lack of consultation, letting people know what is going on. 'Press notice redundancies.' You find out that you're losing your job by reading the Daily Express.'

General Secretary

'Management. There are two different types – the top management, the executive, etc., whom I always find are gentlemen, willing to listen to any point of view and do their utmost to satisfy the requirements of the workers on the shop floor and offices, that's my opinion of the top people; then you have the departmental management, whom I find are arrogant and have no knowledge and understanding of the needs of the staff on the shop floor or staff workers on their chairs.'

Conference Delegate

What do members think of the unions?

	Union members		Non-members	
	Agree	Disagree	Agree	Disagree
Trade unions are essential to protect workers' interests	90	6	65	20
The police should have the power to stop mass picketing	61	31	81	12
The trade union 'closed shop' is a threat to individual liberty	59	31	73	13
Trade unions have too much power in Britain today	58	31	77	14
Bad management is more to blame than trade unions for Britain's economic problems	57	23	38	35
Most trade unions today are controlled by a few extremists and militants	55	35	76	14
Trade unions help to improve the efficiency of British industry	49	33	29	51
The Labour Party should not be so closely linked to the trade unions	46	39	64	19
In the long term the government's policies will improve the economy	36	55	51	37
Everyone who works should have to belong to a trade union	36	58	15	74

'It is known that they (trade unionists) make up about half Britain's work force, and that three-quarters of union members are men; but after that, information is remarkably scant. Myths and sterotypes* abound – that trade union members are mindlessly militant, or contrarily that they are fundamentally conservative (with a small 'c') – but the evidence to measure their validity has been elusive – until now.'

Source: courtesy The Sunday Times 31 August 1980

* Let's leave the mythst and stereotypes and see what information the opinion poll came up with.

† A 'myth' is a widespread but *false* belief while stereotypes are *simplified* beliefs about a particular group of people. A stereotype is a belief that everyone in that group is roughly the same ('*All* workers are . . . ; *all* women are . . . , all students are . . . ').

Assignment 8.1

Pick out what you think are the key figures and key conclusions from this table. Keep the information up-to-date by using new polls and surveys as they are carried out.

Before we investigate political attitudes and industrial relations, I want to take one more glimpse into the industrial relations reality that opinion polls can provide. This most interesting and revealing poll was carried out on the eve of

THE TRUTH AND TRADE UNIONISTS

You may think the truth is like this..

..but, in fact, it's like this...

TRADE UNIONISTS

OF TRADE UNIONISTS

are left wing*

only 51% of union members support Labour

are unskilled manual workers

72% are white collar or skilled manual

live in council houses

56% are owner occupiers

blindly follow their union leadership

31% are dissatisfied with their union's national leadership

are firmly committed to the closed shop

59% are opposed to the closed shop

go on strike at the drop of a hat

84% think strikes should only be called after a postal ballot

Source: courtesy The Sunday Times, *31 August, 1981 MORI*

* *see* the next section of this chapter for further information on this.

the 1980 Trades Union Congress held at Brighton and in the case of this particular poll I want to present you just with the basic findings (*see* opposite).

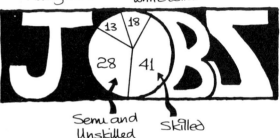

UNIONISTS'

UNIONISTS'

Source: MORI

When you explore attitudes in the office, over the negotiating table or on the shop floor, one very important thing to remember is that there are very *real* differences of opinion in the industrial relations field. We can and do talk about union representatives and management sitting around a table trying to reach some kind of compromise solution. It all sounds friendly and supportive. However, there are very deep divisions in the attitudes held by the various groups in industrial relations, the relationship between the present Conservative (1983) Government and the TUC being a very good example of this.

Over the last few pages we have seen some of the views and attitudes of people who are directly working in the industrial relations arena. I would now like to broaden the area under discussion and look at some of the political attitudes that have an impact on what goes on in the industrial field, by taking a brief look at some of the attitudes held by members of the various political persuasions.

The three main political parties are the Conservative, Labour and Liberal Parties. In the future, the Social Democratic Party (the SDP) may also grow and develop. Rather than pick out party policies in detail, I want to look at the various attitudes that lie behind those policies. Let's look at some of these beliefs and attitudes starting (in alphabetical order) with those held by Conservatives.

1 JOBS

	White Collar	Skilled	Semi Skilled
TGWU	10	48	42
AUEW	16	56	28
NUPE	21	41	38
NALGO	69	16	15
GMWU	11	37	52
All TU members	31	41	28

3 SEX

	Men	Women
TGWU	84	16
AUEW	87	13
NUPE	34	66
NALGO	54	46
GMWU	66	34
All TU members	76	24

2 POLITICS

	Cons.	Lab.	Lib.
TGWU	18	64	14
AUEW	24	61	12
NUPE	26	57	15
NALGO	34	41	22
GMWU	24	67	5
All TU members	26	58	13

FEELINGS TOWARDS OWN LEADER 4

	Satisfied	Dissatisfied	Don't Know
TGWU	55	36	8
AUEW	61	32	6
NUPE	51	32	18
NALGO	51	33	16
GMWU	49	36	15
All TU members	56	31	14

All figures are percentages

Source: courtesy MORI

POLLS, PROFILES, POLITICS and PEOPLE

ATTITUDES CAN KILL !

'In mortality rates alone, sea-faring is twice as dangerous as mining and many times more dangerous than other shore occupations. So it is no exaggeration to say that those who ignore safety precautions are pressing their luck. In some cases, it is safer to play Russian roulette.

'Attitudes are all important. But unfortunately they vary — from officers who try hard to see safety precautions strictly observed, to those who are still in the press gang days and consider the man who wants safety standards strictly observed to be a trouble maker.

'As for ratings, too many of them are their worst own enemy where safety is concerned. The older hands are often blasé about danger and forget that with their experience a job might be safe, whereas to the less experienced man it would be dangerous.

'The union is currently bringing great pressure to bear on owners, not only to improve the way they deal with safety, but to re-think from scratch their own attitude and efforts to provide

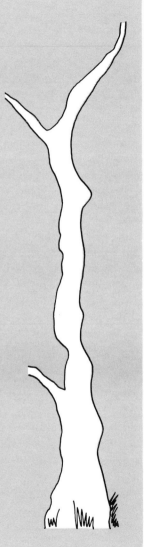

Conservatives are especially interested in:

the idea that society is a living growing tree. It loses some of its branches and grows other new ones. Changes take place but they take place slowly and gradually; society is the same: it wants slow and gradual change.

the idea that the country is one nation united in trying to achieve good industrial relations, good social relations, rich with poor, black and white, etc. In 1845, the then Tory leader *Disraeli* took up this idea. He saw the country as being divided into two nations:

'Two nations between whom there is no intercourse and no sympathy; who are as ignorant of each others' habits, thoughts and feelings as if they were dwellers in different zones, or inhabitants of different breeding, are fed by a different food, are ordered by different manners and are not governed by the same laws. . . . The rich and the poor.'

(It might be interesting, incidentally, to ask whether the statement is true today. Are we still two nations?)

law and order in any group or society. Keeping to the law and maintaining order are very important to the Tories. The state must keep order and it has the armed forces and the police at its fingertips to do just that, if it needs to. However, as a country develops and becomes more and more settled in its ways it does not need armed force and violence, as other more unstable and unsettled countries do, because people learn to respect the law.

That is why the law is important in industrial relations for the Conservatives: it provides, they say, authority and structure; a way in which order can be kept.

One of the reasons for the law being so important is that they believe that there has been a decline in discipline. 'People do just as they please today. . .'. 'Young people have no respect for their parents anymore. . .'. In industry it's the same picture. 'Unions tell management what to do. . . . You cannot sack a man anymore. . .'. The unions must be forced by the law to come back into line and not have so much say in the running of industry otherwise they will take over. It's managements' right to manage. All these statements show just how important it is, say the Tories, to bring back discipline.

Individual freedom, which at first seems a contradiction when you read what the Conservatives have to say about law and order and the importance of discipline. Although the Party stands for law and order, it believes that it is understanding enough to let individual people within the Party have their own opinions.

The idea of society as a 'hierachy' or ladder, where those at the top have reached the top by hard work and ability. The 'elite' at the top lead, the rest of society follows. If you reward people and they get a good education and work hard, they can move up the hierarchy and according to the Conservatives indi-

proper and adequate safety precautions.

Source: article by NUS Legal Officer George Senior in The Seaman, *June, 1980*

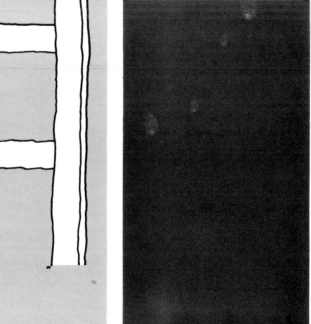

POLITICAL STANDPOINTS

1

LEFT   CENTRE   RIGHT

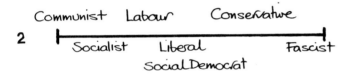

2

Communist Labour   Conservative

Socialist   Liberal   Fascist
         Social Democrat

3

LEFT WING   RIGHT WING

LABOUR

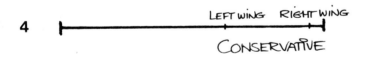

4

LEFT WING   RIGHT WING

CONSERVATIVE

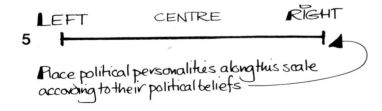

5

LEFT   CENTRE   RIGHT

Place political personalities along this scale according to their political beliefs

viduals should be given every incentive to do this.

The ideas which are connected with free enterprise capitalism, where a person raises capital and starts up a small business on his or her own. Indeed, the words 'free enterprise capitalism' really sum up the approach in that the Conservatives will say 'free enterprise' (enterprise and initiative on the part of an individual to set up their own firms using borrowed capital from friends, or from a bank) provides competition and this in turn encourages individuals to be efficient and make the greatest profit possible.

Using the scale opposite of political attitudes let us move across to the left-hand end of the scale and look at some of the beliefs and political attitudes held to be important in the Labour Party. This particular political party covers a very wide range of beliefs and political attitudes ranging from the (political) 'centre' through to the extreme 'far left'. However, the two main groups of beliefs that we need to look at which have influenced the growth of the Labour party

Any political party is a collection of individuals who agree on the majority of ideas that the party holds but they may well disagree on certain other issues. Some Conservatives are more convinced that the law should be rigidly applied to trade unions than others. Some want hanging brought back; others would say that hanging is never the answer. The same applies to the Labour Party where there is a collection of ideas and attitudes with which most people agree. This forms the basis of the Party. However, there are marked differences within the Party on, for example, something like nationalization where some Labour MP's believe we have enough, some would like a little more; still others would like to see a lot more.

are those of 'socialism' and 'Marxism'. As we saw in Chapter 3 Marx was very concerned with the following: (*a*) economic; (*b*) social; and (*c*) philosophical problems* and he believed that:

B
O
S
S

there are two major classes (or groups) of people in society, the workers and the bosses. The workers were in competition with one another for jobs while the bosses were in competition to make profit. The capitalist system required people to compete and not co-operate. The products made by the workers were sold by the bosses at a price well above that of production and so a large profit was made. However, that profit does not benefit the workers; it only benefits the boss who puts the profit into his own pocket. Of course, Marx said that since there was a 'back up' army of unemployed that if the workers disagreed with the boss then it would be easy for them to get new workers;

W
O
R
K
E
R

For Marx the real problem was the class war between the workers ('*proletariat*') and the bosses (the '*bourgeoisie*');

* N.B. (*a*) economics: the making and spending of money
(*b*) sociology: the ways people behave in groups, for example, how they work together and how they spend the money they have made
(*c*) philosophy: what kind of world people feel they should have; and the kinds of thoughts people have on the 'right' and 'wrong' way of running our society.

Marx predicted that the proletariat would, in time, get so tired of being 'used' that they would revolt and overthrow the capitalist system. This would be replaced by 'socialism' a form of government where the power was held by the people and not by some small 'elite' group in power.

We have already said that within the Labour Party there is a wide spectrum of political attitude, through from the centre (social democrats and liberals) to the extreme left wing as exemplified by the Marxists and communists. Between these two groups are the 'socialists'.
They believe that:

capitalism makes people live and behave as if they were animals in the jungle and that society works by the 'law of the jungle' whereby the rich get richer, the poor get poorer and eventually the poor 'go to the wall' unable to survive the competition;
because of this 'law of the jungle' attitude that capitalism breeds into people, it is vital that human beings are interested not only in the economic aspect of life but also, and most importantly, in the *quality* of human life. Socialists are concerned not just with the 'elite' group within a society but with the well-being of *all* members of that society;
the hierarchy that the Conservatives talk about is

W O R K E R

all wrong and that as human beings we are all equal. We all have something that we can contribute to the groups and to the society to which we belong;

if the society of which we are a part is unequal and unfair then we must change it. The way to do this is to collect together in groups (for example, in trade unions or in a workers' party like the Labour Party) and to stick solidly together in the face of any opposition. The way to bring about the changes that are wanted is through *co-operation and mutual help*;

industry should be in the hands of the workers. There should be worker control of industry. In this way the profits that those industries make could be ploughed back into those industries rather than going into the pockets of private capitalists. (If we look back into the history of the British trade union movement we have already seen in Chapter 4 how 'syndicalism' was an important force in Britain in the period just before the First World War when the miners and other workers tried to get control of the industries in which they were working);

industries of key importance for example, the banks, the coal, electricity, gas and nuclear power industries, should be under the control of the State so that these plans can be made for these industries in the long term. In this way these major industries can be worked in the most efficient way possible;

the State (this being made up of the government at Westminster, the civil service, the armed

S T A T E

forces, the police, local government, etc.) has a key part to play in the running of the economy. The State should provide free education, free health facilities, etc. so that there is no need for people to have to buy these services. They are a natural right and people should have the benefits of a *'welfare state'*.

The views of the Labour and Conservative Parties move together in the middle of the political rainbow to meet the views of the Liberals and Social Democrats. In the centre of the political spectrum there is a lot of overlap with the views and attitudes of the other two parties. It's just not possible to say that, up to and as far as that belief, you are a Conservative, after that you are a Liberal, and then past this point here you become a Socialist. The different views merge quietly together. The views of the political parties overlay and overlap one another. If we look at the views, beliefs and attitudes of the Liberals and Social Democrats (since their views *closely* overlap I want to discuss them together) we can see by the very name 'Democrat' that these (centrist) parties are particularly concerned with the idea of 'democracy' that we have already looked at in Chapter 6.

F
R
E
E
D
O
M

The Liberals and Social Democrats believe that:

the way to run a society or a country is by agreement. Every (wo)man has certain basic human rights. These include the right to live in the way (s)he wants (providing no-one else gets hurt because, others have the right to live the way they choose), to be free and to own their own property;

the role of the State is not to dominate the life of the individual as they believe happens when the Socialists come into power. For the Liberals, the State is there to protect those basic individual rights that we talked about in the last paragraph;

the Government should not be authoritarian but 'human' and caring and based on the agreement of the people being governed;

agreement, equality and freedom are all important basic individual rights to be guarded and encouraged. Liberals believe that a solution to problems can be found by being both reasonable and moderate. Only those who are unreasonable and extreme and who break the law should have action taken against them.

Other parties worth noting on the British political scene are the Marxist left wing and the right wing, National Front. The Communist party, formed in 1919 after the Russian Revolution, has declined enormously in strength. In the 1945 election it won over 100 000 votes. In 1979 it got just 16 000. Other far left parties include the Trotskyites and the Socialist Workers' Party, the International Marxist Group and the Workers' Revolutionary Party. The main party on the far right is the racist National Front. This was formed in 1966. Although it has had some success, its support at the ballot box is very small.

From left to right: an overall view

Generally speaking the right wing of the Labour Party and the moderates (or centre) of the Conservative Party make policy when their respective party is in power. It has to be added, however, that the current Thatcher government is very much a *right wing* government and is therefore somewhat unusual in modern British politics.

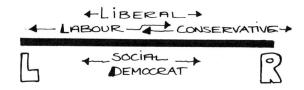

Let us now see how these beliefs and attitudes affect what goes on at the workplace. It is as well to remember that these ideas, beliefs and attitudes are not held just by Members of Parliament. They are general thoughts, feelings and attitudes that we all have. We all have attitudes about the kind of animal man is. We all have strong views about what is wrong with the country and with industrial relations although many people are still totally apathetic when it comes to discussing politics. However, we all vote and so we need to see how our attitudes match up with those held by the various political parties outlined here.

What I want to do is to get you to imagine that there has just been a general election in order to show what policies and views the various parties (and the so called 'wings' of those parties), would probably take if they were elected to power. The Labour Left (although it could be argued that it rarely gets that close to political decision making) believes very strongly in socialist planning and industrial efficiency. It would encourage high investment in industry and would want to foster powerful worker involvement. It would encourage workers to participate in the management of firms; the encouragement and involvement being introduced through the channels of the trade unions.

The Labour Right, the group who are normally in charge of policy-making when the Party is in office, would want to encourage and develop close understandings with trade union leaders and it would build on these understandings to help to keep the country stable and strong economically. The right does not like shop floor workers to be militant because this will upset the stability that they are trying to encourage for the country. The right would, to a certain extent, be prepared to intervene in the workings of the market place to get economic growth. For example, they would encourage the building of

houses, the electrification of British Rail and the rebuilding of Britain's antique sewerage system to get money moving in the economy again and also to provide jobs in times of high unemployment.

In many ways some of the views of the Labour Right are quite close to those of the Tory Left. However, one important difference to remember is that the Labour Right will link naturally with the *unions* while the Tories will be more concerned about free competition and *market forces*; in other words, those pressures, such as supply of and demand for products and the price at which they sell.

Having mentioned the Conservatives let us now examine the views that moderates in that party take when they are in power. In general terms, the unions will be invited to join the moderate Conservatives in discussions about running the economy. Like the Labour Right they will also intervene to a certain extent in the way the economy is handled. There will be three-way discussions (unions, management, government) and moves to encourage informal understandings and agreements in such issues as industrial relations. These discussions, along with measures such as incomes policies (that is, agreement between management, unions and government to keep pay rises and levels of incomes down so that inflation does not get out of hand) are used to make sure that unemployment does not reach levels that people feel are unacceptably high.

As you move further to the Right of the Conservative Party you will find them less keen to get involved in the running of the market place. Let the market be free with businesses able to compete with one another without the interference of government in business dealings. It's believed that industrial relations problems are taken care of by the level of unemployment with, perhaps, some legal back-up that will make strike action more difficult. In this kind of climate the unions have to be content with a *non-political* role of industrial bargaining. They are not encouraged into the political arena. If disputes in industry get very difficult then the government may intervene although this is not encouraged.

No control is made over workers' incomes; each group being in competition with one another to get the best pay rise possible. Unfortunately, many of the measures outlined above (particularly, for example, high unemployment) tend to give increased conflict within society in general; and so because of this the Government *has* to step in, as happened for example, in the summer riots of 1981 in Britain. With these higher levels of tension right-wing Conservatives then tend to use even more tough-minded measures such as trying to stir up public hostility against 'deviant' groups such as strikers. They also rely more heavily on the police and (occasionally) the armed forces to break up strikes.

We have already seen that conflict does exist in industrial relations. Some of it may be due to a certain amount of bloody mindedness on the part of certain individuals. However, much, much more is due to the very different beliefs that different groups engaged in industrial

relations' work really do have. These beliefs are strongly held and are fought over when someone (or some other group) attacks the person's particular viewpoint or attitude. As we saw in Chapter 6 those members of our society who believe in a Marxist or conflict view of the way society is built will, by definition, believe in the view that industrial relations is a battleground between the workers and the capitalists.

One thing all this does show is the importance of peoples' attitudes in both everyday and industrial relations life. They affect the ways in which we think, feel and react and explain, to a certain extent, the differing points of view put across by employees, employers and government: a lot depends on the attitudes!

Assignment 8.2

Try to place the writer's own political view on the left to right scale given in the chapter. What evidence do you have for deciding where the writer stands politically?

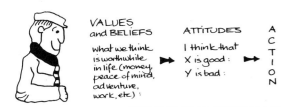

ATTITUDES and ACTION

VALUES and BELIEFS — What we think is worthwhile in life (money, peace of mind, adventure, work, etc):

ATTITUDES — I think that X is good: Y is bad:

ACTION

I have my own personality — I am ME

I want to study industrial relations

I have certain VALUES

because I think it's important

and these in turn give me certain ATTITUDES

and because I have a positive attitude to industrial relations

which make me BEHAVE in certain ways

I am going to read, study and become involved in I.R.

Assignment 8.3

Check the dictionary definition of the word 'attitude'.

List those factors that go to make up a 'positive' attitude to life and give a list of reasons why a positive attitude is important both at work *and* in your everyday life generally.

Assignment 8.4

This chapter uses information taken from opinion polls and surveys about attitudes in industrial relations. Keep this information *up-to-date* by using the results of current attitude and opinion polls as they are given in newspapers and on the television. See if attitudes to certain topics, such as union democracy, union power, the closed shop, etc. change over a period of time (or do not change, as the case may be) and make a list of any attitude changes that you *have* seen take place.

Recommended reading for Chapter 8

One very good introduction to the study of attitudes is:

Values, attitudes and behaviour change by B. Reich and C. Adcock (Methuen, 1981)

Books that you have read and found useful should be added below

Section Three

Chapter 9
We've always had a special relationship

Objectives

At the end of this chapter you should be able to:

1 very briefly describe the development of the British Labour Party;
2 to list and outline the various relationships between the unions, the TUC and the Labour Party;
3 to define, describe and give examples from the industrial and political fields of pressure groups;
4 to simply outline the political role of British unions as compared to their American and European counterparts.

THIS CHAPTER COVERS the following subjects/topics:

1 the early progress of the Labour Party;
2 the 'special relationships' that exist between the Labour Party and the Unions in Britain;
3 pressure groups of the 'interest' or 'sectional' type;

4 the unions' political role in Britain as compared to that of American and European unions.

IN CHAPTER 3 we have already seen how the Chartists, in the 1830s and 1840s formed a very early working class movement. During the 1860s, 1870s and 1880s more and more people became entitled to vote and this helped clear the way for the growth of the first working class *political party*, the Labour Party. After the success of the strikes in the late 1880s, the ideas of socialism became stronger in the unions* until in 1892, three independent Labour MPs were elected. One of these MPs, the now legendary Keir Hardie, was central in setting up the Independent Labour Party at the 1893 Bradford Conference. The ILP was very much a socialist party. It wanted a whole range of social reforms to take place.

---

* N.B. Socialist ideas were also spread at this time by the Fabian Society, a group of middle class intellectuals, such as the writers, H. G. Wells, George Bernard Shaw and the Webbs.

'As far as the activities of trade unions are concerned we can't help but become involved in politics.'

Source: courtesy Sidney Weighell, formerly General Secretary, NUR

'. . . Union activists tend to be political activists as well. There is a fairly high degree of correlation . . . and most of them will have been brought up in an environment where they started canvassing at the age of twelve. . . !

'There is a very deep level of loyalty to the traditional Labour Party machine.'

Source (both quotes): courtesy Peter Shaw POEU

'One of the troubles, in my book, with the trade union leadership is

that it is far too interested in politics and not interested enough in industry.

'There is too much involvement in day-to-day politics. [We have to] get [them] more involved in day-to-day industry.'

Source (both quotes): courtesy Cliff Rose, Board Member, British Railways Board

---

' Socialism is an attitude towards life which recognizes that the freedom and development of the individual personality can be secured only by harmonious co-operation with others in a society based on equality and fraternity. In the economic sphere this necessarily leads to a belief in the conscious organization of the material resources of the world in the interests of all.'*

Source: Clement Attlee quoted in Labour Party documents

'The CSEU is a trade union organization: very much so. We

work for trade unionism. . . . The trade unionism that we preach envisages a much fairer and a much more just society. We believe that despite tremendous changes that have taken place in our society, there are still tremendous gaps between the "haves" and the "have nots". There is still a grossly unequal distribution of the nation's wealth.

'Having said that we are therefore no different from the trade union Movement . . . that in 1898 decided that, in a democratic parliamentary society, in order to achieve some of their aspirations, some of their desires for workpeople in general, it was necessary to have a voice in the Parliament which made the decisions and it was from that type of philosophy that the Labour Party was formed in 1900.

'The Labour Party was formed by the Trade Unions in order to process their policies and their desires in a democratic way and therefore the Labour Party is the child of the Trade Union Movement in this country . . . and there is nothing that is going to break up that family. Therefore our relationships politically are very obviously biased, and rightly

so, towards the Labour Party and we will do everything in our power to ensure that the Labour Party is strong, is healthy and is successful and success in parliamentary terms means the achievement of power through the ballot box.'

Source: courtesy Alex Ferry, General Secretary, CSEU

The only thing that South Wales manufactures now is history[1]

Down Fabian Way

'The first iron and steel town in South Wales was Merthyr Tydfil. In 1831 it was by far the largest town in Wales, four times the size of Cardiff. In that same year, during the general election after the first reform bill, there was an insurrection in Merthyr, when local workers held out for four days against the Argyll and Sutherlands. One of the rebels, Richard Lewis, was hanged. A miner, aged 23, he has since become the folk hero known as Dick Penderyn. Two weeks after the uprising, the first trade union lodges were formed in South

Wales. In 1900, Merthyr had the first Labour MP in Britain, Keir Hardie.'

The only thing that South Wales manufactures now is history[2]

'Everything used to happen here: coal and chapel, steel and socialism, cheese and choirs. You can only understand South Wales, the way people talk about it, by knowing what used to exist. It doesn't make sense the way it is now, the way museums don't make sense unless you know where all the stuff inside them all came from.'

Source (both quotes): courtesy New Society article by Ian Walker, 20 November, 1980

'If we wish to influence the way in which the State manages the organization, then we have to have access to the government machine, and that means a political attitude of one kind or another. The basic reasons why we're affiliated to the Labour

The 1893 Independent Labour Party had a good deal of support among trade union leaders, but interestingly it did not convert the TUC of those late nineteenth century days to socialism. This in itself had important implications for the development of the Labour Party then (and now). The socialist ILP had two real alternatives facing it. It could remain truly socialist and go its own way without the support of the TUC and the unions. Alternatively, it could decide to have less radical policies and join with the unions. They would help get the Party on its way and would, in addition, give financial help. The second alternative was the one that was taken up. In 1900 a special Conference of co-operative, trade union, socialist and working class groups set up the Labour Representation Committee. The Labour Party as we know it today had been formed, although the LRC did not officially adopt the title until 1906.

With the unions' help the Labour Party became established in the first twenty years of this century and, in 1924, it formed its first government. Today the Party still has very close links with the unions. They still provide the Labour Party with around three-quarters of its funds, while the Party's individual membership (around 700 000) shoots up to over six million when you add into the equation the fact that members of unions belonging to the TUC are automatically linked to the Party.

The threads of today's complex special relationship between Labour Party and unions that I want to look at are as follows:
The large number of trade union representatives

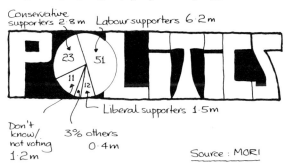

U N I O N I S T S'
POLITICS

Conservative supporters 2·8m   Labour supporters 6·2m

23 51
11 12

Liberal supporters 1·5m

Don't know / not voting 1·2m   3% others 0·4m

Source : MORI

on the National Executive (NEC) of the Labour Party*
The political levy which allows the trade unions to pay affiliation fees to the Labour Party
The influence of the unions on the Labour MPs in the House of Commons (the Parliamentary Labour Party or PLP) and also sponsorship of MPs by trade unions
The TUC/Labour Party Liason Committee (or TUC/LPLC).

Under the Labour Party's constitution (the set of rules governing the way that the Party is run) there are two categories of membership. The first of these is the *individual member* (that is the ordinary person who has decided to join their local Labour Party branch because that is the political party with which they want to be actively involved) and the second category that of *affiliated member*.

* N.B. Like the national executives of the unions themselves, the NEC of the Labour Party manages the administration of the Party between the annual conferences held by the Party. It is elected annually at each conference.

Party are partly ideological[1] but primarily pragmatic[2]. Our members look at the policies of the two parties[3] and decide for themselves which one of them is more likely to take account of what we have to say about the organization of the public sector and the telecoms business in particular.

[1] Concerning ideas underlying some economic or political system;
[2] Or 'practical';
[3] It may be interesting to watch the SDP/Liberal Alliance here.

Source: courtesy Peter Shaw, POEU

NEC LEVY PLP TUC/LPLC

The affiliated members are mainly trade unionists who are Labour Party members through their *unions'* association with the Labour Party. To give some idea of the figures involved, if we look at the 1979 membership figures for the Labour Party, we find that total membership in that year was just over 7 235 000. Of that total 666 000 members held individual membership while 6½ *million* were affiliated members. In other words 90% of the Party's membership on paper were affiliated members through the trade unions.

In addition to providing the mass of the membership, the affiliated unions also provide most of the Labour Party's finances, while at the times of general elections, the unions are again the main contributors to the special appeals, which the Party makes.

It is important to remember that the contact and connections between the unions and the Labour Party are made by the individual unions themselves. Union members decide (through balloting) whether or not to affiliate to the Labour Party. It is quite possible for a union to be affiliated to the TUC* and not to the Labour Party. Indeed, currently (1983), NALGO is in that particular position. It's quite interesting to think that the two major unions in local government (NALGO and NUPE) behave very

* N.B. The TUC itself is *not* affiliated to the Labour Party. It has no vote that it can use at the Labour Party's annual conference. Although informal links with the Party are strong, formally no trade unionist is a member of both the TUC General Council and the Labour Party National Executive Committee.

differently here. NUPE affiliates enthusiastically to both the TUC and the Labour Party, while NALGO has not, as yet, affiliated to the Labour Party, although it has to the TUC.

Because of the strength of trade unionists in the Labour Party's membership, the unions have a large representation at the Party's annual conference. Attendance here is on the basis of *one* delegate for every *five thousand* members (of the union). Voting on most issues is carried out

The "SPECIAL" RELATIONSHIP

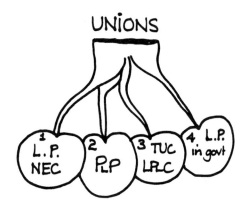

UNIONS

1 Trade union representatives on the National Executive Council of the Labour Party

2 Influence of unions on the Parliamentary Labour Party

3 Contact through the TUC/Labour Party Liaison Committee

4 The "special relationship" with the Labour Government when in office

by a 'card vote' (one vote for every thousand of their members). By this method the leaders of the largest unions can make or break policies at the Party conference. The same, of course, happens at the annual TUC (*see* Chapter 2) where the leaders of those largest unions fill seats on the TUC's General Council. Here then is a very strong link, worker with Party.

As we saw in Chapter 7 the legal right of British trade unions to become involved in political activities was guaranteed by the 1913 Trade Union Act which allows unions to spend money on achieving *political* goals and in *assisting candidates to become Members of Parliament.* However, there are certain conditions that have to be met:

1 Any cash that is to be spent for *political purposes* must come from a special political fund and this fund must be kept separate from the union's general fund.

2 Any member who objects to the political fund (even where the majority of the members of the branch are in favour of it) may '*contract out*' of these 'political' payments. At the same time the law guarantees that they are not deprived of any of the other membership rights simply because they have decided not to pay into the political fund.*

*In fact, what usually happens is that many unionists do not know that, when they join the union, they are contributing to the Labour Party. 'Contracting out' may not always make the person who does it the most popular person on the shop floor, especially in a firm that is strongly unionized. William Rodgers, a former (union-sponsored) Labour MP, and now a member of the SDP/Liberal Alliance, had this to say in a speech given in Billingham in the Spring of 1981:
'*The plain fact is that many trade unionists are paying a subscription to a political party they no longer support. It is nonsense that the law should sustain such a distortion.*'

Where the power lies . . .

The seventy-ninth Annual Conference of the Labour Party opened at the Winter Gardens, Blackpool, on Monday 29 September, 1980, the number of organizations and voting power represented being as follows:

Organizations	Delegates	Number of organizations	Votes
Trade Unions	610	52	6 450 000
Constituency Labour Parties	595	588	689 000
Socialist Societies	10	8	38 000
Co-operative Organizations	7	2	29 000
	1 222	650	7 206 000

Source: courtesy Report/Labour Party, 1980

Where the money is . . .

Affiliation fees and contributions   1979

Trade Unions	£1 842 383
Labour Parties	208 182
Parliamentary Grant	42 333
Socialist and Co-operative Societies	12 973
Parliamentary Labour Party	6 710
Overseas Members	249

Source: as above

The Unions and the Labour Party: literally living in one another's pockets

'On 15 May 1928 another of Bevin's dreams came true. In a simple, but moving, ceremony, Transport House was declared open. The leaders of the TUC, the Labour Party and the T & G were all present. Bevin was presented with a golden key. Two plaques were unveiled: one to the Executive Council which had decided to build the offices; and the other to the workers who had constructed it.

'Work had begun on the building less than two years after the creation of the union in 1922. Well before drawing up its final plans, Bevin had captured the TUC and the Labour Party as tenants.* In the summer of 1926 the Union itself had moved into the first section finished. Now its tenants, the two key arms of the Labour Movement, had come to join their landlord.

'All that Bevin stood for was represented in that symbol. It was

* N.B. Today Transport House is used exclusively by the Transport and General Workers' Union.

If a union-sponsored, Labour Party candidate is successful at the ballot box, then (s)he will join colleagues in the House of Commons. They become part of the Parliamentary Labour Party (or PLP) and these MPs will form a union group within the Labour Party represented in the House of Commons. This is yet another way in which the trade unions can influence (sometimes

quite markedly) the way in which the Labour Party works, thinks and votes.

A fourth way in which we can see yet another of the threads in the special relationship is that of the TUC/Labour Party Liaison Committee. This committee is made up of members from the TUC's General Council, the Labour Party's NEC and the PLP. It was set up in the early 1970s and is concerned to build up a joint approach between the TUC and the Labour Party on such key matters as industrial relations and economic policy.

Having seen something of the special relationship between the unions and the Labour Party we must remember that however close this relationship may be, there will be other governments in power as well as those that are socialist. It is, of course, true that in the last Labour Government the unions enjoyed a special relationship with the government in the form of the 'social contract' where, in return for pay restraint on the part of the unions, the Labour politicians agreed to listen and watch out for trade union interests. With the present Conservative administration (1983), the relationship is more difficult and so it might be a good idea to look at the more general ways in which the unions can act as a set of 'pressure groups' on the government of the day.

First of all, what is a 'pressure group'? In simple terms, they are organizations which try to influence what government does both at national and local level. They are not the same as the political parties. Political parties want not only to try and influence governments, they actually want to form them. Pressure groups work with whatever government is in power but, as we have just seen, some groups have much closer links with one party than the other (the links between the unions and the Labour Party and the other well-known link between big industry and the Conservative Party; *see* pp. 144 and 145).

In their attempts to try and influence the ways in which governments have behaved, the unions have used various methods. They have used parliamentary pressure through their special links with the Labour Party. They have some-times used direct action, the best example of which was the 1926 General Strike. They also use pressure on Whitehall, the Treasury, etc. to get their views across to the country's decision makers. Let's have a look at each of these methods in turn and see what the situation is today.

Up until the Second World War the first method, parliamentary pressure, was the most important. The unions didn't have the informal contacts in government circles and so any influence they had was through friendly Labour MPs in the House of Commons. Direct action was never very popular. It was even less so after the failure of the General Strike. During and after the Second World War things changed. Leading trade unionists such as Ernest Bevin entered the government. The unions were in on the decision making. Trade unionists were appointed to committees whose job it was to advise govern-ment. Again the unions were in on the decision making. Since the war, unions have become

more and more part of the process of negotiation and consultation with the making of government (both Labour and Conservative) policy. They are now part of the 'Establishment'.

However, two things are worth mentioning at this point. The first is that although it is important that these formal committees exist, there are many *informal* contacts that unionists have made within the world of Whitehall. They have built up friendships and close contacts that allow the process of consultation to go on more positively and more usefully. Secondly, it is again important to remember that formal and informal links through groups such as 'Neddy' (the NEDC) also allow industry, unions and government to get together.

Another key pressure group is, of course, the TUC. Most manual unions and a growing number of white collar unions all come under the 'umbrella' of the TUC which has built up a good set of contacts with successive governments. Obviously central government finds it easier to deal with a small number of groups when talking about industrial relations and pressure groups like the TUC and CBI make the whole process more manageable. In addition, the TUC has become even more important because govern-ments of late have wanted the TUC's help with incomes policy. They have wanted the TUC to keep union pay claims down as low as possible and have also wanted a reduction in the number of strikes. Unfortunately, the TUC has not been able to guarantee either of these.

Leading on from what we said about the TUC in Chapter 2 it is easy to see why. We saw how

---

the biggest union headquarters. It was the closest to the corridors of power; within a stone's throw of the Houses of Parliament and Whitehall. . . .

Source: courtesy: A Portrait of Ernest Bevin 1881–1951, by Mark Stephens, TGWU

The 'Special relationship': not always sweetness and light!

Labour's cash crisis led to a special meeting in Blackpool last night of union leaders and party officials. Joe Gormley, the (then) miners' leader, said that the party was in for a shock. Scoffing at claims that the party will go broke without extra funds, he went on; "It's their bloody pigeon, isn't it? They'll be coming to us again, and if they expect us just to take it lying down and not question some of the things on which money is being spent, I think they're in for a rude awakening. We'll keep the cheques in our bloody bank."

Source: The Sunday Times, 28 September, 1980, 'Labour cash row with unions grows'

'*Unions belonging to the TUC should not have to affiliate to any political party, a union leader said yesterday. John Lyons, of the engineers and manager association, said that unions should be independent of the Labour Party.*'

Source: Daily Mirror, 6 September, 1980

'*The weakness of our movement is that you have 112 General Secretaries, the General Council of the TUC has about 40 on it. . . . It cannot always deliver on what it says it's going to deliver on economic strategy because we have so many unions who continue to act in line with the Rules and Constitutions of their own organizations.*'

Source: courtesy Sidney Weighell, *formerly General Secretary NUR*

the TUC can *suggest* to unions the kinds of things they should do. It cannot tell and so, if a member union refuses to make or accept a bargain the TUC makes with the government of the day, then there is little that the TUC can do about it.

One other point about the power of the TUC that is significant when we are thinking about power relationships between the unions and the TUC, is that, as we have seen in our historical look at the unions, there has been a change in emphasis in where collective bargaining is carried out. When the unions started to be involved in Whitehall discussions about the economy (after World War Two) most pay bargaining was done at national level. Agreements were industry wide. However, through the book we have seen how the local level has become more and more important of late. The workplace and the local shop steward are much more important in the negotiations for wage levels. In other words, the *national* union leaders and the TUC at *national* level, are less able to make bargains with governments about pay, etc. because the negotiations on these are dealt, more and more so, at a local level.

In the last few paragraphs we have broadened the special relationship between the unions and the Labour Party into a more general chat about the relationships between the unions, the TUC and governments in general. Let's finish the chapter off by looking even more broadly at the unions' political role, not only in Britain but in America and Europe. It's obviously a very broad area to look at but the figure below will give you some idea of the similarities and difference

between the three types. As you can see one of the key points to note about the British unions is that the unions founded the Labour Party and not the other way round. The special relationship is important even on international scale!

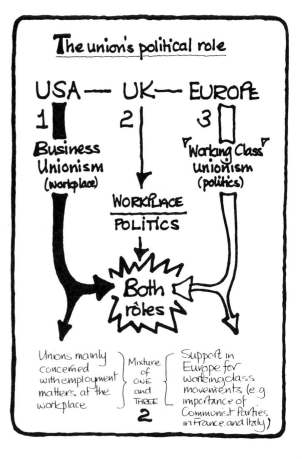

The Conservative Party: where it gets its money from

The Labour Party's Research Department in its annual survey (August 1979–August 1980) of political donations discovered that over two and three quarter million pounds was given by 470 private companies and that of this over 70% of this money went directly into the Tory Party's funds.

Total donations to the Tory Party and other political organizations 1979–80

Organization	Number of companies making donations	Amount £
Tory Party	370	1 936 660
British united Industrialists	46	444 254
Industrialist Councils	59	185 330
Economic League	84	117 386
Aims	35	36 494
Centre for Policy Studies	21	26 500
Others	36	16 189
	470	2 762 813

Source: courtesy Labour Party Research Department Paper, September 1980, 'Company Donations to the Tory Party and other Political Organizations'

In the same paper the following are some of the companies that gave large amounts of cash (£10 000 and over) to the Conservative Party between August 1979 and August 1980:

Beecham Group PLC
The Bowater Corporation PLC
Cadbury Schweppes PLC
The General Electric Co. PLC
Mothercare

The Plessey Company PLC
Ranks Hovis McDougall PLC
Sun Alliance Insurance Group
Unigate PLC
George Wimpey PLC

Recommended reading for Chapter 9

1 *The Politics of Industrial Relations* by C. Crouch (Fontana, 1979)
2 *Understanding Politics in Modern Britain* by J. S. Sutton (Harrap, 1977)

Books that you have read and found useful should be added below

Chapter 10
Money to make money to spend

Getting the balance right!

'We have learned the lesson that a job lost in the public sector means a job lost in the private sector. The private sector does not want weak and dispirited public services but strong viable services for itself and its workers.'

Source: courtesy A Fisher, formerly General Secretary NUPE at the TUC Conference September 1981

Objectives

At the end of this chapter you should be able to:

1 list and describe industries and services that are part of the private and public sectors of the economy;
2 think about and discuss the role of the trade unions in the public sector;
3 identify some of the problems faced by those involved in industrial relations within the public sector.

THIS CHAPTER COVERS the following subjects/topics:

1 what do we mean by the 'public sector'?
2 what groups and unions are to be found within the public sector?
3 industrial relations problems and possibilities within the public sector;
4 the future of the public sector and some of the changes that could come about there.

THIS CHAPTER IS all about the public and private sectors of the economy and the relationship between the two. In the next few pages I want to try and get across the concept of a society where the private sector (private industry and commerce, for example) produces profits. Private firms pay taxes and rates and the money is then spent in the public sector (health, education, housing, social services, etc.) to provide services. The public sector in turn provides a market for private sector firms. For example, the housing required by the various councils requires materials and these are provided by the private sector, who pays taxes to provide services and so on.

Public money (that is money from taxes and rates, for example) is also used to provide and support really large-scale firms, organizations and services (British Rail, National Coal Board, the National Health Service, etc.) which would be difficult to finance privately, exactly because they are so large and require so much money for research and support. In our economy some organizations make money, others spend it. The two parts need to be kept in balance. This balance will be determined by the government in power. The Conservatives are strong supporters of the private sector. The Labour Party are strong supporters of the public sector. When in office, the two parties have different emphases and so the different groups in society (such as those in the private sector and those in the public sector) will get differing degrees of support depending on which political party is in power. Whatever happens however, the public and private sectors have to be balanced one with the other. Achieving that balance is the task of the government in a 'mixed economy' and no matter what firm, business, shop, etc. that you look at, all of them 'fit into' this mixed economy. All have a part to play within it.

Very basically, we can say that:

the private sector generates profit and pays taxes

(However, it has to be remembered that some of the public sector nationalized industries make profits and they also have to pay taxes.)

the public sector spends taxes on providing society with certain services, such as health and education

(However, it has to be remembered that some of the public sector industries and services provide a market for firms in the private sector.)

public funds are used to support industries and services (for example, telecommunications, railways, health and education services) that private industry might find difficult financially to provide and support

(However, increasingly within the private sector firms are getting larger and more powerful all the time (for example, some of the multinationals in the oil and chemical industries) and often these firms do have the money and the resources to run large railway or health networks as in the United States.)

Having looked at the overall part the public and private sectors have in the British economy let us now see the actual 'nuts and bolts' workings of the public sector by seeing exactly what the public sector is and how it affects all of us on a day-to-day basis. The first point that I think has to be made is that the public sector is a very important employer. It employs something around 30% of the civilian labour force. In round numbers this means that about 7 million people work directly for the government. If we try to see who is actually involved we find that about

3 million people work in **local government**

JOTTINGS!

PUBLIC SECTOR	**PRIVATE SECTOR**
Main motive : SERVICE	Main motive : PROFIT
involves : national government	involves : hotels and
local government	catering
education	entertainment
health and social	betting/gambling
services	media services
the post office	insurance, banking
telecommunications	and finance
air transport	distribution
railways	business services
sea transport	legal services
port and inland	professional
water transport	services
gas	hairdressing
electricity	laundries
coal mining	dry cleaning
water	boot and shoe
steel	motor repairers
British Leyland	road transport
	sea transport
	construction
	mining
	chemicals

Public   *Private*

about 2 million work in **central government** (including the National Health Service)*

while another 2 million work in the **nationalized industries** (such as British Gas, British Rail, British Leyland, etc.)

These industries are obviously very big business and are very often large and complex organizations.

Assignment 10.1

Below are listed the abbreviations of various unions, all of whom have members in the public sector of industry. Check their full titles with the list of unions on pp. 20–23. In addition, make another list showing those unions that are essentially *white collar unions* (that is, those unions with members who are involved with professional, administrative, clerical and secretarial work).

NALGO	NUT
NUPE	TGWU
COHSE	GMBATU

*N.B. The National Health Service on its own employs round about 1 million staff in such jobs as doctors, nurses, white collar administrative and clerical staff, ambulancemen, etc.

Assignment 10.2

Within your family what *local* government services do you use? Remember to cover *all* members of the immediate family.

Assignment 10.3

Are any members of your family workers in the public sector? If so, get them to describe their job to you. Do they belong to a public sector union? If so, which one and why?

Assignment 10.4

In your street what services are provided by the local authority? For example, a hole is dug in the road by the Gas Board: who else in the public sector could be involved?

We have already said that an important part of the public sector is the various *nationalized* industries. True nationalization means that the State takes over firms and companies that were formerly in the hands of private individuals. A good deal of nationalization took place in the early years after the Second World War when the Labour Party was returned to power with a large majority in the House of Commons. They nationalized the coal industry in 1946, the rail-

What is it?	Who runs it?	What does it do?
The public sector includes: the civil service the NHS the education service the nationalized and power industries	**The government**	It provides a wide variety of goods and services such as: steel coal ships health social services education

What is it?	Who runs it?	What does it do?
Local government is in the hands of the various County and District Councils, etc.	The **local government** authorities	Some of the services it gives are as follows: police fire education social services housing rubbish collection

ways in 1947, electricity was also nationalized in the same year, while gas and iron and steel industries were nationalized in 1948 and 1949 respectively. The *nationalized* industries, as the name suggests, are owned by the nation and any profit that these industries make returns to the government. In the same way, if an industry makes a thumping good loss, the government has to find the money to cover that loss!

The public corporations that have been set up to control the nationalized industries have a Chairman, a Deputy Chairman and a Board of Management. All of these are appointed by the government minister who is responsible for the field in which the industry's activity belongs. For example, the British Rail Board is responsible, not surprisingly, to the Department of Transport and the minister responsible for transport. The Chairman and his colleagues are responsible to Parliament (through the minister) for the way that British Rail is run but they are responsible for the day-to-day running of the business. The other nationalized concerns all work in the same way.

As we can see, from the list of industries and organizations on p. 148, the public sector is a real rag bag. One of the real problems is to say exactly where it starts and where it finishes. For example, parts of Rolls Royce are private sector (the car-making division, for example) while the aero-engine division went bankrupt and was bought by and for the nation. However, one thing is very clear: the government is very heavily involved in the public sector as 'boss' (for example, the civil service, the armed forces, the

health service, etc.); as 'bank' (for example, when it provides loans and subsidies to the nationalized industries).

It is, of course, through pay that the government can strongly influence the level of pay in

> *'We're a public sector organization first of all (but I wouldn't make too much of a distinction between that and the position of*

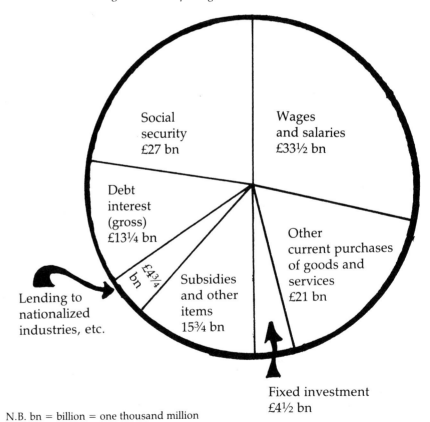

Where the cash goes in the public sector – central and local government sepnding 1981–2

Social security £27 bn

Wages and salaries £33½ bn

Debt interest (gross) £13¼ bn

£4¾ bn

Subsidies and other items 15¾ bn

Other current purchases of goods and services £21 bn

Lending to nationalized industries, etc.

Fixed investment £4½ bn

N.B. bn = billion = one thousand million

any private sector organization) but the fact is that the Government is our banker and it controls, to a very considerable extent, the way in which the telecoms business operates.

Source: courtesy Peter Shaw, POEU

the public sector since it has hold of so many workers' wages (for example, those of the police, the fire services, the armed forces, civil servants (both local and national), teachers and lecturers, doctors, dentists, nurses, midwives, etc.).

In the private sector the main constraint on pay is how profitable a firm is. If it makes a large profit the chances of the workers getting a large pay rise to match are much better than when the firm just 'breaks even'. But in the public sector industries that provide a service (such as the social services, health and education) there is no question of there being a profit. They are there simply to provide a service. The profit motive is obviously out of place. This will mean that the main factor controlling the size of workers' pay rises in these jobs will depend on how keen the government is to put cash on the table.

It also means that any industrial dispute in the public sector will automatically become 'political' because the government itself is the 'boss'. Obviously, there will be governments who will look kindly upon the needs of its workers and, as has happened in the past to groups like teachers and nurses, will provide fairly large pay increases on the basis that these groups have 'slipped behind' in the pay stakes. Other governments apply fairly stiff incomes policies to their workers because the economic going has got rough. This may be very different from firms in the private sector who can get away with a certain percentage increase. Indeed, one of the very real problems of pay in the private sector is how do you compare levels of pay in the public and private sector? In the private sector greater productivity can mean better levels of pay for the worker. In the public sector it seems that there are very real problems of increasing worker productivity (except perhaps in the possible areas of electricity supply and in telecommunications, for example).

Having mentioned workers in the public sector do they have common features about which we ought to know? One point worthy of comment is that most public sector groups are usually large and highly unionized. Indeed,

Who works for the Council?

Education		Social services	Construction	Libraries Parks, etc.	Refuse Collection	Rest
Teachers	Other staff					
29	20	10	7	6	2·5	25

All nationalized concerns work to the following:

1 The minister appoints (and can of course dismiss!) the Chairman and the members of the Board.

2 The minister has power as to the general direction in which the nationalized industry ought to be run but he leaves the 'nitty-gritty' day-to-day running of the organization to the managers of the industry.

3 The Board supplies the minister with any facts and figures, schemes and statistics that he requires.

4 The Board is expected at the end of each financial year to, at least, 'break even'. In other words, the money coming in should be sufficient to balance the money that has to go out.

5 If the industry makes a profit, the minister, along with his colleagues in the Treasury, decides how that money is to be spent.

6 If the industry wants to set up new projects, for example, British Rail wants to go ahead with a large scale electrification of its main routes, it can finance these projects with money from the private sector banks, if it cannot afford to spend any money of its own.

7 The minister can set up councils to look after the interests of the public using the service provided by the nationalized industry.

8 The annual reports and the finances of the nationalized industries are discussed every year in Parliament.

9 Whatever plans the government of the day has for the nationalized industries, these plans must have the approval of Parliament before they can be put into action.

about half of all Britain's trade unionists are in the public sector. In addition, employer/employee negotiations are usually always highly centralized at *national level*. In the past, one very attractive feature of the public sector was that it was generally a safe job for life (for more on this see the discussions with the NALGO union representative later in this chapter). Today this is less true. Of course, some public sector workers still have fairly safe employment (top civil servants, for example) but many jobs within the public sector are far from safe. You only have to think about the recent cutbacks in British Steel, British Leyland and in the National Coal Board to see how precarious working in certain sections of the public sector can be!

Looking at the public sector from the unions' viewpoint the years following the Second World War have seen a considerable growth in the number of workers in the public sector as you would expect from the nationalization programmes and the growth of the health, social service and education sectors in the 1960s and 1970s. This growth, tied in with the growth of white collar jobs and the number of women being employed generally, has benefited the membership of white collar and professional unions very considerably, especially when you consider the loss of union membership in basic industries like iron and steel, coal mining, the railways and the docks.

Mention of the local branch in the last quote gives us an excuse and opportunity to return to the workplace and see some of the things happening there in the public sector. I recently talked to a NALGO shop steward in one of the water authorities about what happens at shop-floor level in his union.* Roger, the union representative and branch secretary concerned, discussed his everyday union and working life under the following three headings: branch matters; negotiation with management; and case study material, to show the kinds of problems with which he regularly deals.

Roger told me that in the past one of the most commonly heard comments from local government workers was that 'I'm employed in local government so I'm OK for life'. However, the economic recession has changed all that. The job was no longer safe and this fact had helped union membership over the previous year. There was talk of jobs going, voluntary redundancies, a reduction in staffing levels and all these had helped membership and branch attendance. Indeed, Roger told me that there was good branch attendance while the last AGM of the union had had an excellent attendance. He reckoned that although the union's newsletter helped the recruitment cause, the best method, without any doubt, was word of mouth. This was the most important way of recruiting members. There were other unions at the workplace, of course, and these included NUPE, MATSA and the Association of Water Scientists.

* N.B. In local government the union situation is, roughly speaking fairly simple, with two large unions making up the bulk of the bargaining power. The two unions concerned are NALGO, with (1981) 782 343 members and NUPE for the manual workers, with (1981) 699 156 members.

Apathy was still a problem, however. Many workers (and members) simply do not realize what unions are doing. They think that good working conditions and the existence of the tea lady in the morning and afternoon simply have always 'been there'. They forget that many aspects of good working conditions have had to be bargained over and fought for. People often thought that the union's Branch Secretary was paid to do the work. Indeed, he reckoned that something like 50% of the membership if asked why had they joined would probably not know. They had done it because most people did. Once they had joined many members simply saw the union's role as getting pay rises and perks, such as cheap holidays, etc.

There were encouraging changes taking place however. For example, people on all sides were realizing the importance of being increasingly adaptable and flexible. If one job disappears and another is offered the person has to take the new job and adapt him or herself to it. Roger said that he personally found change stimulating and he gave an example to make his point. A chemist working for the water authority was told that, due to reorganization, his job would disappear. However, he was offered computer work for three months to see how he would adapt. Although the chemist was unhappy about the situation, Roger told him to 'give it a chance' and see how things went. After one month it had been a total success. The chemist was happy and Roger felt that the 'softly, softly' approach that he had used had been completely successful.

Other hopeful changes that had taken place

'*Being involved, as my union is, in the public sector (British Rail, British Rail Engineering, London Transport, National Bus Company, British Rail Transport Docks Board): all these are accountable to Parliament, and so there is a very heavy political involvement in the background. So I spend a lot of my time talking to ministers (for example, the Minister of Transport) and, of course . . . as we develop in the sort of society my union visualizes in the future, we visualize more involvement with government, not less, for example in economic planning . . . I can see no reduction in the political activities of my union or the movement generally. In fact, I see the absolute reverse of that.*'

Source: courtesy Sidney Weighell former General Secretary of the NUR

NUPE's view   1

'*Wages in the public services* are negotiated nationally. If the government has economic problems, then there is considerable pressure for low pay settlements.*

As cutbacks in public spending begin to bite, there is even the possibility of redundancies in some areas.

'*The Union can fight tooth and nail against redundancies and cutbacks. But unless we can argue an alternative economic strategy and persuade the labour movement to support us then our effort to save jobs and services will be seriously weakened. Trade unions have to involve themselves in politics, and our relationship with the Labour Party is thus a very important one.*'

* It is important to see and understand the difference between public *sector* and public *service*. On p. 148 there is a fairly comprehensive list of all the firms and services within the *public sector*. However not all of those organizations provide *services*. Some provide *products* (such as British Steel and British National Oil Corporation). *Public service* organizations include local and national levels of the civil service, education, health and social services.

Source: NUPE documents

included a greater involvement in the running of the branch on the part of women members. In 1980 there were five women on the branch executive whereas in the previous year there had only been one.

When asked about running the branch Roger said that his own style was 'open' in nature. He believed in 'open government' whereby the members knew exactly what he was doing and where they were encouraged to be involved. 'It's an ability to listen intently to the members that counts' he told me. They often told him that they 'couldn't stand up in a branch meeting and make a point because they were afraid of making a fool of themselves'. He told them not to worry because everyone felt like that at some time and the important thing was to say what they felt. Roger reckoned that by removing tension and introducing humour into both branch meetings and negotiations was a good way of encouraging communication. Being seen to be human was an important quality. After all, we all have feelings and we all make mistakes.

When I asked Roger about the qualities needed to make a good negotiator he told me that he didn't really know what these were. I felt that this was probably due to the fact that he was a skilled person in that area and skilled people often do not know what makes them skilled. All they possibly know is that they do their job well and in a skilled way. He did, however, admit that negotiators need to have an 'open mind'. They should be prepared to hear both sides of the argument. In addition, he believed that an *informal* chat with management often solves problems in industrial relations very quickly. 'Solve problems before they become problems' he told me.

In negotiation, he believes, that it has to be true that 'the more I go in for, the more chance I've got of coming out with something'. He has found that very often management understands the difficulty of his position and he, in turn, has been able to appreciate how difficult situations can be for them. There must always be a 'way out' or a 'sweetener' in the discussions. 'It's not a good move to back anyone into a corner' he said. They must have a face-saving, 'way out'. In this particular water authority, industrial relations had a good record. For example, good access to information was given to unions by management. As always a strike was an 'admission of failure'. Commitment was important, as was the building up of a good trust relationship between management and unions. Service to the public came before all other things; that was the name of the game for both unions and management.

Finally, to round off our conversation Roger gave me this example to illustrate the fairly typical problem that he has to deal with on behalf of his members.

Two of his members, Mrs H and Miss C, were employed by the water authority as clerk/typists. In the spring of 1980 the water authority introduced word processors in the office where these two ladies were working and it fell upon Mrs H and Miss C to set up the systems. However, according to the 'blue book', which was the agreed union rule book, their jobs consisted of 'routine clerical, typing, machine operating and technical services'. So the union on behalf of the ladies put forward the case that setting up the systems fo these word processors was beyond the job definition. So the union asked that the ladies concerned should be given some (monetary) reward for the extra effort and work that Mrs H and Miss C had put in.

No formal training was given. All that happened was that the two women were given the instruction manual for the equipment and were expected to produce results. This the union reckoned they had done.

It must be said at this point that the individuals, the union and the management had discussed this matter informally, management had rejected the application, the union had taken the matter up and had then started the formal 'grievance procedure'.

The management made three points after further discussion as shown.

1 They could find no claim in respect of the work that had been done in learning the new techniques (no luck on this count!).
2 They could see no difference between using, in a generally routine way, the electronic typewriter of the (word processing) terminal (no joy on this one either!).
3 However, management did agree that, during

the period in question, the two ladies were being asked to do innovative work for part of their day. They had to act on their own initiative in setting up a completely new process. (Hit the jackpot here!)

NUPE's view   2

*'Public employees have to deal with a variety of individuals or groups, all representing 'management'. The wages of some 1 100 000 local authority manual workers are decided by the National Joint Council (NJC) for local authorities' services. For 1 400 000 white-collar workers in local government, wages, etc., are decided by the National Joint Council for local authorities' administrative, professional, technical and clerical services. A similar negotiating machinery operates in the health service, which employs 800 000 people, consisting of ten Whitley Councils.**

* Notice how highly centralized (that is all taking place in one place, at one [national] level). This, incidentally, makes it easier for a government to enforce a pay policy.

Management agreed that the last point was outside the guidelines laid down for the job and that a small fee should be given to both ladies concerned (£50 each). A typical, and unspectacular case, but obviously a very important case to the people involved.

We have seen some specific problems faced by workers, unions and management at *local* level, let us for the final section of the chapter look at some general problems at *national* level that the public sector may have to tackle in the future.

Writing in *The Sunday Times* on 4 December, 1977 Mr Basnett suggested that because of incomes policies in the public services there ought to be a whole new way of tackling pay in the public service sector. He suggested the following themes and ideas:

'It would first involve establishing a more comprehensive trade union machinery which would bring together unions in local government and the health service, and the industrial and non-industrial civil services, to form a new TUC Public Services Committee.* (This was set up in 1979.)

Leading on from this Mr Basnett suggested:

(a) *a direct relationship between the Committee mentioned above and the government who is paying the wages. The new Committee would build up even more regular contact with government ministers;*

(b) *that there should be moves towards getting a standard time of the year when pay rises are negotiated and agreed upon.*

For example, here are a list of public sector groups and the months of the year in which their pay round is fixed:

1 *January: 220 000 Post Office workers*
2 *February: 30 000 electricity workers*
3 *March: 230 000 miners*
4 *April: 500 000 civil servants*
5 *May: 50 000 electricity supply staff*
6 *June: none*
7 *July: 320 000 local government workers*
8 *August: 26 000 staff in BSC*
9 *September: 116 000 policemen*
10 *October: 35 000 university teachers*
11 *November: 1 063 000 local government workers*
12 *December: 238 000 workers in the NHS*

(c) *permanent review bodies that would compare pay levels in the public and private sectors and that would also deal with 'special cases' such as the police and the firemen;*

(d) *that the wages set-up would need to be reviewed at least once every three years to sort out any special problems that the public sector may have;*

(e) *that there should be a look at the present negotiating machinery to ensure that as many local problems as possible can be solved at local level.*

All of these are ideas worth watching for the future. The public sector is a crucial part of the economy. One in four of those workers employed in manufacturing industries, for example, are on the State payroll: in 1980 over 100 000 workers became unemployed from State companies. This was around 6% of the workforce. *Watch the trends and see what happens.* Do the last two assignments in the chapters to keep up-to-date as to ownership of companies and also to see what jobs can be usefully created within the public sector to help the country or, as critics of the public sector would say, to hinder the private sector getting back on its feet!

Assignment 10.5

There are roughly twenty or so unions in the public service sector. It may well be the case that because of more government cuts in the amount of cash available to the public service sector some of these unions may join others so that they can face the cuts more effectively by becoming more powerful. It could even mean that there are two or three really large unions with over a million members each.

Your assignment is to follow the progress of one of the public sector unions (for example, NUPE, NALGO) and see what changes take place in that union over the next two or three years. Make it a long-term project and try to study one particular aspect of the union that interests you (for example, the role of women within the union, political affiliation; will NALGO affiliate to the Labour Party?).

Assignment 10.6

The present Conservative Government (1983) is selling off (or 'hiving off') parts of the public sector. These industries and firms are going back into the private sector. Below I have given a list of those public sector organizations that have been sold off already, those that make *losses* and those that are *profitable*. Keep an eye on the list and see which of the profit makers are sold off into private enterprise in the future.

Sold Off Already

	Number of Workers
British Aerospace Limited	73 000
Cable and Wireless	10 000
National Freight	26 000

Loss Makers

National Coal Board	294 000
British Steel Corporation	109 600
British Railways Board	227 000

'All these councils consist of a management side and a staff side representing the employers and the workers. The two sides have their own meetings between the regular council meetings to draw up claims on the staff side, and responses to claims on the management side. NUPE is well represented on the staff side of all the most important councils.

'At local level, the Branch may settle local problems with employers, sometimes in direct talks between Union Stewards, Branch Officers and the management, sometimes in a local joint committee of the Union and the management.'

Source: NUPE documents

'*A five year £24 billion programme of public investment will provide jobs throughout the economy. First in the building and civil engineering industries, then in the building materials and mechanical engineering industries, and so on as extra orders and spending power work their way through the economy.*

'*These 500 000 jobs are not artificial. They are not the result of make-work schemes or extravagant 'white elephant' projects. These jobs will help meet real needs.*

'*The housing waiting list is growing.*

'*The energy crisis demands better insulation and investment in new forms of energy.*

'*The cracks in our motorways and the delays they cause are well-known to all those who travel by road, as are British Rail's old-fashioned and dilapidated rolling stock to rail passengers. Britain's sewerage system – the legacy of investment in the Victorian era – is breaking up.*

'*The high technology end of the public sector needs funds too, for example British Telecom desperately needs extra funds to modernize the telecommunications system.*

British Airways	51 000
British Shipbuilders	67 500
British Leyland	104 000
Rolls-Royce	55 000
British Waterways Board	3 283
Central Electricity Gen. Board	59 729

Profit Makers

Electricity Council	154 910
Post Office	185 000
British Gas	106 000
British National Oil Corp.	2 000
South of Scotland Elec. Board	13 500
National Bus Company	58 399
N Scotland Hydro-Electric Board	4 115
British Airports Authority	7 459
British Transport Docks Board	10 950
British Nuclear Fuels	16 000
British Telecom	248 538

Figures: courtesy The Sunday Times *25 October, 1981*

Assignment 10.7

With high levels of unemployment it is often suggested that useful work could be created by putting public money into important projects in the public sector such as those outlined in the extract above.

Using the headings given below suggest some of the advantages and disadvantages of putting more public money into the public sector:

employment, service to the *public, cash borrowed by the public sector, political viewpoints* and a *caring society.*

'So the public sector needs in-vestment to survive, that is the crucial, but not the only argument.
'All of the private sector will benefit from this investment. This will come from extra orders, and also through a boost to private sector efficiency, for example, through improved transport and com-munications networks.
'One thing and one thing only is holding up the introduction of this programme. It is not finance. The savings are there to finance investment. What is lacking is the political will and 'the imagination to put these savings to work for the benefit of the British people.'

Source: The Reconstruction of Britain, TUC February, 1981

Recommended reading for Chapter 10

There are relevant sections on the public sector and its unions in:

1 *Unions and Change since 1945* by C. Baker and P. Caldwell (Pan, 1981)
2 *Trade Union Directory* by J. Eaton and C. Gill (Pluto Press, 1983)
3 If you want a much more detailed study of a white collar, public sector union, try: *The Dynamics of White Collar Unionism* by N. Nicholson, G. Ursell and P. Blyton. It's detailed and somewhat difficult to read but it's very interesting.

A good deal of useful information for this section was collected from an excel-lent NALGO publication entitled *Pay Policy*, 1978.

Books that you have read and found useful should be added below

Chapter 11
Women don't understand industrial relations anyway

Objectives

At the end of this chapter you should be able to:

1 list and describe the kinds of work women are involved in;
2 show, by giving examples, some of the problems faced by women in trying to combine responsibilities at *work* with responsibilities at *home*;
3 describe women's role within the trade unions;
4 think about some of the changes that have already taken place in the role of women within our society and to consider some of the changes that may take place in the future.

THIS CHAPTER COVERS the following subjects/topics:

1 women at work;
2 women in the Unions;
3 women in Law;
4 women in the future.

OVER THE LAST thirty years the number of working women has increased drastically.

Married women have contributed most to the increase. Women now make up over 40% of the total workforce. In general terms they earn considerably less than men, even once you've taken the facts that they work shorter hours and do less overtime than men, into account. Women are still, in many cases, a cheap form of labour.

They also work in a much narrower range of jobs than men. They do not get the same

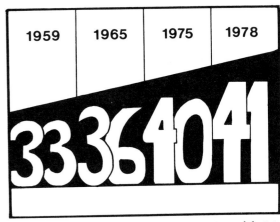

Employees in employment: women as percentage of the total workforce

education or training chances as men and they are less likely to get into management or professional jobs. Women do much more part-time work than men, indeed the part-time workforce is, in the main, made up of women. In addition, you must remember that women are still reckoned to be in charge of a large amount of unpaid work in the form of cooking, cleaning and care of the family.

Women are spread very unevenly throughout the workforce. The jobs that they do are usually the low paid ones. In 1978 nearly 60% of all women worked in just three service industries. These were the professional and scientific services (typists, secretaries, technicians, teachers and nurses), the distributive trades (shops, supermarkets, mail order warehouses, etc.) and a mixture of other services such as laundries, catering jobs and hairdressing. Indeed, in clothing and footwear manufacture, professional and scientific services, the distributive trades and banking, insurance and finance women outnumber men quite markedly.

We have also said that women still (in spite of changes in attitude) take the main responsibility for the home and children. One survey discovered that women could spend anything from around 50 hours to over 100 hours a week on housework. The average time was around 80 hours. In spite of this, a large and increasing number of women go out to work as well. (By 1978 50% of married women went out to work.) Quite often the strain of doing two jobs is very high, but, so is the strain of not going out to work and recent research has shown that women who are confined all day to the home are very likely to suffer from depression.

In research recently carried out by the University of Lancaster*, and concerned with the pressures faced by women doing factory work, the research workers found (among other very interesting things) that most of the women interviewed received very little help with housework from their husbands or from the older children in the family. The pressure of both housework and factory work led to considerable stress.

There are some people who would say that it doesn't really matter if women earn less than men because the money that women earn is really only 'pin money' that they spend on luxuries rather than on necessities. The evidence does, in fact, suggest that this is not the case. Often women's earnings are a vital part of many families' incomes. Roughly one in nine of all families are one parent families and here the one parent is almost certainly a woman. For one out of six families the women's earnings are the main source of income while the DHSS estimates that three times as many families would be below the poverty line if women stopped working.

We have already talked a little about the low paid jobs that the majority of women are employed in, now let us have a look at the small minority of women who get into managerial and

* Original research carried out by Shimmin, McNally and Liff University of Lancaster

'Why do we talk about the "underachievement" of women in public life outside the home, rather than about the "underachievement" of men in the home, with children and also in personal relationships?'

Source: courtesy 'The Failure of the Movement for Women's Equality' by Ann Oakley in Work: A New Society Social Studies Reader (3rd edition)

WOMEN'S

'There's no place like home for working women. Nothing can rival it for worry, stress and sheer hard work.
'Many of them start their household chores before dawn and finish them well after dusk, according to a survey published by the Department of Employment.
'They get little help from their husbands or children.
'They also spend hours each day in a factory doing a job that most men would consider to be a good day's work.

'The report is a sad comment on a country which has women as Head of State and Prime Minister and boasts laws for equal pay and opportunity.

'Many wives live under a stress that is bad for them, terrible for their children and often disastrous for their marriages.

'When they complain, they are usually told that they should not go out to work.

'But many get a job to provide comforts that their husbands cannot. Others need the money just to make ends meet.

'Fifteen years after the birth of the Women's Lib movement, life for many women is still as hard as it was for their grandmothers.

'They need more than tea and sympathy.

'They need equality at work and equal partnerships at home.

Source: courtesy Daily Mirror, *Friday 28 August, 1981*

professional jobs. According to an article in *Labour Research* (January 1979) shown on p. 163 there is only a tiny proportion of women in the professions. For example, less than 1% of bank managers are women while 2% of chartered accountants and university professors are women. Architecture is obviously very liberated with its 5% of female architects!

Even in those professions with a high proportion of women (teaching and nursing, for example) they do not get the *top* jobs. In 1975, 27% of doctors were women but only 12% of consultants were female. Three-quarters of all primary school teachers are women but only 10% of them is ever likely to become a head or a deputy head. The boards of the nationalized industries are virtually all male dominated. In industry less than 10% of all managers are female and even when women succeed in taking on managerial responsibility domestic problems can often arise.

One thing that these figures and comments do show is that if women are determined enough they can succeed. Indeed, a minority of women have, in spite of all the obstacles, succeeded. Those women who have had access to higher education, those who have no children (or who can afford to have their children looked after by another woman who is paid to do the job) and those who have good jobs and good job prospects can and have succeeded. What it takes in personal terms is still however very demanding on the woman concerned.

To give you an example of how difficult things still can be for women in industry I would like to look at women in the engineering industry.* Here, as in other professional and managerial posts women are still grossly underrepresented. In September 1980 just over 40% of workers in all industries were women. In manufacturing industry only one-quarter of the total workforce were female. Women are employed in three main types of work in engineering. These are office jobs, low skilled operator jobs and unskilled 'other' jobs. Why is this? Well, there are obviously a variety of reasons: the first of which is that, in Britain, engineering has been reckoned to be a second rate career for any young person, male or female. The Finniston Committee reports a survey asking 'How would you rate professional engineering as a career for a young person?'. It was considered to be a very good career for a man (60% of the survey thought this) while only 25% thought it would make a good career for a woman.

On top of this there are other problems that girls have to face if they want to do well in engineering. Women are still not seen by people as 'engineers' and many people believe that engineering is not 'quite right' for women to be in. ('They're not strong enough' and 'Engineering is a man's career' are the kind of comments frequently heard.) Girls are often encouraged at school to take subjects that are more 'feminine' while research shows that girls with the same qualifications as boys often have lower expectations as to what they can do with those quali-

---

* I acknowledge the information and approach taken by Walsh and Isherwood in an excellent article (*Labour Research*, April 1981) that examines the role of *'Women in Engineering'*

fications than do the boys.

Many firms are still prejudiced against women as skilled craft workers. ('They'll only get pregnant and leave the firm' is still sometimes given as a reason for not giving a job to a woman.) It would seem much more likely that women would be able and willing to stay on in a job if better child care facilities were provided. It would also seem to be the case that if more women are to go into engineering there has to be changes in:

(a) how much we value engineering as an industry in Britain;
(b) the prejudice that exists against women being in engineering; and
(c) the stereotyping (see Chapter 8) that exists when girls select subjects at school.

We've said a little about women at work, let us now look at the position of women in the trade union movement.

In the unions it is without a doubt true that there are more women in positions of responsibility and power than there were in the past. However, they are still consistently under-represented as lay (i.e. shop stewards) and full-time officials. By 1976, nearly 29% of all unionists were women yet there is still not a single woman General Secretary, even in the

Women's membership as a percentage of total TUC membership (rounded figures)

1939 1958 1968 1978

11 16 20 28

unions that have a large majority of women members. The general picture has hardly changed since the beginning of this century. Unions are still dominated by men at both local and national level. *It is the men who decide the policies and priorities* and it is this last point that needs emphasis in any discussion relating to women's role not only in the unions but in the wider society as well.

It is the lack of women's representation in many of society's key positions (such as on the Boards of Directors of large and influential firms and businesses) that is a vital factor in the direct (and very important relationship) between those particular issues that are of especial concern to women and the failure of these issues being taken up because the women's perspective is still not being put across. In all too many cases, the women's view is not being fought for simply because there are few, or no, women in that area

'I think basically it is working full time and then going home and you see things that haven't been done and have got to be done, and meals to be cooked. It's a bit of a drudgery you know, doing two jobs. You can't sort of say, "oh, I'm going out for the night". I suppose you could, you know, but, like your husband will say, "my mates asked me to go for a drink", and he's gone. He's had his dinner and he's gone. Whereas you think, oh, I've a pile of ironing to do there; if I don't do it perhaps it won't get done, or something like that. I suppose you can make yourself a martyr and you shouldn't do really, should you, you know. But I think this all builds up inside till you explode.
Source: courtesy Employment Gazette, August 1981

'Women do not generally get to the top. They are extremely under-represented on influential bodies, and even when they do manage to enter the professions, they rarely rise to the higher positions. For example, there are no women amongst the 288 directors on the board of the 20 largest companies in Britain, and only 27 of the 635 Members of Parliament are women.
Source: Labour Research, January 1979

Problems can also arise when the women overtakes her husband in terms of salary and status. A top female executive, divorced and in her early fifties, describes her experience:

"*Earning more than my husband has been a problem, that was a problem in my first marriage, that he felt inferior. I climbed the ladder much quicker than he did, and I left him behind completely . . . wonderful marriage, but he had this enormous inferiority complex. . . . I will marry again very soon. The person is higher status than me and earns more, and that was a very important factor in my decision to remarry. I don't think men will ever accept women earning more than them in a relationship. You see, the women don't only leave them behind financially, they leave them behind mentally.*"

"*I am always conscious, like anyone else, that there is prejudice about. . . . It's there, you've got to fight it. You can only overcome it by being better at your job than the man.*"

"*The change that I would like to see come about in our society is that organizations and people react to people simply as people.*"

The TUC Charter

The TUC Charter on Equality for Women within Trade Unions, which owes its origin to the work of the Women's TUC, was approved by Congress in 1979. These are the points that it makes, each one building up (hopefully) to a stronger, more united and more just trade union movement.

1 The National Executive Committee of the union should publicly declare to all its members the commitment of the union to involving women members in the activities of the union at all levels.

2 The structure of the union should be examined to see whether it prevents women from reaching the decision-making bodies.

3 Where there are large women's memberships but no women on the decision-making bodies special provision should be made to ensure that women's views are represented, either through the creation of additional seats or by co-option.

4 The National Executive Committee of each union should consider the desirability of setting up advisory committees within its constitutional machinery to ensure that the special interests of its women members are protected.

5 Similar committees at regional, divisional, and district level could also assist by encouraging the active involvement of women in the general activities of the union.

6 Efforts should be made to include in collective agreements provision for time off without loss of pay to attend branch meetings during working hours where that is practicable.

7 Where it is not practicable to hold meetings during working hours every effort should be made to provide child-care facilities for use by either parent.

Not as male people and female people.

Source: (all extracts) 'What Women Managers Face' by M. Davidson in Management Today, *February, 1981*

8 Child-care facilities, for use by either parent, should be provided at all district, divisional and regional meetings and particularly at the union's annual conference, and for training courses organized by the union.

9 Although it may be open to any members of either sex to go to union training courses, special encouragement should be given to women to attend.

10 The content of journals and other union publications should be presented in non-sexist terms.

of business, industry, commerce or government to put that view across. What is still happening in our society and in our unions today is a repeat performance of what happened in those early unions mentioned in Chapter 3: womens' perspectives and problems were, to a large extent, ignored by a *male dominated union movement*. However, it *must* be said that this ignorance exists today not only in unions, it's 'across the board' in many firms and businesses. The key decision-makers in our society are still, in the main, *men*.

We have talked about women serving in unions. It is, of course, equally important to ask, do the unions serve their women members in a satisfactory way? There are often problems on the shop floor where male shop stewards may not understand or regard as important problems specific to their women members. Male union reps may see the problem not to be the problem that the women bring up for discussion but they

The Workplace, Trade Unions and Women

Between 1968 and 1978 female membership of unions went up by 60%. Male membership went up by only 19%. The greatest increase in women's membership took place in the following five unions:

National Union of Public Employees (NUPE)
National and Local Government Officers' Association (NALGO)
Confederation of Health Service Employees (COHSE)
Association of Professional, Executive, Clerical and Computer Staff (APEX)
Association of Scientific, Technical and Managerial Staffs (ASTMS)

However, for those women reading this book, be warned! There are still a lot of problems for women to overcome if they want to succeed and make the fullest use of unions and their resources. There are a good number of practical problems to

BLACK

WHITE

FEMALE

overcome and generally speaking the unions are still heavily male-dominated.

In a survey carried out at the University of Hull Industrial Studies Unit (May 1980) the following facts emerged about those women who do play an active part in unions. They:

tended to be over forty and most of their children were over eighteen;
had a father or husband active in his union;
worked because the money was essential to meet the family's needs.

Of the women in the survey who were not active in the union, half of them wanted union meetings to be held in working hours while nearly half of them wanted to know more about the ways in which the union worked. Over a third of the sample gave *'lack of confidence'* as the reason why they were not actively involved. The problems of entering what was seen to be *'a man's world'* were also quoted by many in the study.

Assignment 11.1

Think about and list some of the reasons why women should have '*lack of confidence*' about joining unions and say what you think is meant by the expression '*a man's world*'. Can you give any evidence to suggest whether or not it is, in fact, '*a man's world*'.

may see the woman herself as the 'problem'. Things are not all black, however. Improvements have taken place and attempts are being made to change things even more. In many unions special seats are being reserved for women on the national executive and greater involvement on the part of women is being more actively encouraged. But there is still a lot of resistance particularly in the older, more traditional craft unions.

' . . . it is misleading to see the "problem" as women, the problem might more correctly be identified as some of the traditions and preoccupations of the male-dominated trade unions. It is not just a question of "educating" women (like some colonized race about to be enfranchised by the colonizer) in the ways of trade unionism. It is a question of examining how the principles and practices of Trade Unionism can work against the interests and involvement of women, and exploring means of overcoming and changing this situation.'

Source: courtesy Ruth Elliot, TUSJ, Autumn, 1980

Women are not the only targets for prejudice

'A call for the Government to give a lead against racialism came from the chairman of the TUC's Equal Rights Committee, Mr Ken Gill.

'Mr Gill wanted the Government to give a public lead against racialism but the unions, he said, had to look at themselves, too. "If in your industry or occupation there are no blacks, why?", he asked. "If there are no black lay or full-time officials, why? If there are no black activists, why?" As part of its "black workers' charter" the TUC would keep on asking unions what they were doing, because a failure to respond would breed cynicism.

'Turning to discrimination against women, Mr Gill said that the unions, again, were not above reproach and that they must promote positive action through collective bargaining. In his own industry only 2% of engineering technicians were women, and less than half a per cent of craft workers.'

Source: The Guardian, 9 September, 1981

'There had always been some active women in the union but speaking generally, the average woman member did not take much interest in her trade union.

She would attend meetings, but being usually in a minority, she rarely expressed her views or took much interest in the business, except to pay contributions.

A familiar and unremarkable enough comment on the involvement of women in unions. What is perhaps more interesting is that this comment, from a member of the National Union of Shop Assistants, was made 70 years ago.'

Source: courtesy 'Women in Unions: The Contribution of Trade Union Education' by Ruth Elliot, TUSJ, Autumn 1980 ·

'Women do play a part and a number hold very senior positions in the Movement, both in the voluntary field and as full-time trade union officers. But women generally could do much more if given greater encouragement and if more attention was given by the individual unions as well as by the Movement to those problems which hinder even dedicated women from seeking to play a fuller part in trade union life.'

'One in every 11 900 trade unionists could be a delegate to the 1978 Congress but the ratio for men was 1:7 800 whereas for women it was 1:38 800.'

Source (both extracts): Report/Women's TUC, 1979

It's still a (white) man's world

'A better deal for women and black workers was demanded by Ken Gill, chairman of the TUC's equal rights committee.

'He told delegates: "Many women, like ethnic minorities, are trapped at the bottom of the pay scale in jobs where the risks of redundancy are high and prospects are nil."*

*Assignment 11.2

What sorts of jobs is the Daily Mirror talking about?

'Mr Gill called on the Government to give a lead against racism and said failure to deal

with the problem had appalling social and political consequences.†

†Assignment 11.3

What kinds of consequences do you think these could be? Give some examples if you can.

'Congress must tell Mrs Thatcher that racialism was socially unacceptable. "It would not be tolerated," he said.'

Source: Daily Mirror, Wednesday 9 September 1981

Assignment 11.4

Give a list of reasons why women do not reach the top and discuss ways in which these obstacles can be overcome.

If we look at the effect the law has had on equality for women we again find disappointing results. It would seem that recent changes in the law have barely scratched the surface when it comes to the ways in which women are actually treated. The main laws relating to equality are the Equal Pay Act (1970) which came into force in 1975, the Employment Protection Act (1975) and the Sex Discrimination Act (1975). All of these seem to have had a very small effect on women's status at work and in society at large. However, they have made people much more aware of the unfair ways in which women are treated at work and, hopefully, this will encourage people to overcome some of these inequalities. Even the setting up of the Equal Opportunities Commission to look after women's rights seems to have had very little impact upon people's attitudes.

'*The gap between women's and men's earnings has widened despite the Equal Pay Act and is unlikely to improve, the Equal Opportunities Commission says in its annual report to the Home Secretary, published yesterday.*

'*During the early and mid-1970s women's pay increased steadily to a peak of 75.5% of male earnings in 1975. By 1979 it fell back to 73%.*

'*Average gross hourly earnings for women were now £1.65 compared with £2.26 for men.*

'*One of the main reasons for women's low pay is their concentration in low paid female occupations, but that does not explain it all. Women teachers earn less on average than their male colleagues because they are employed on lower scales.*

'*The report complains that the number of women appointed to public bodies by ministers is increasing extremely slowly and that no government department has more than a third of women on the quangos* for which it is responsible.*

'*The Commission mounted four new formal investigations last year. One was into the appointment and promotion of teachers at the Sidney Stringer School and Community College at Coventry; the second was into the appointment and promotion of staff in the Business Studies Department of North Gwent College of Further Education. The third was into membership conditions of a print union, the Society of Graphical and Allied Trades; and the fourth into employment practices at the Leeds Permanent Building Society.*'

* Quangos are organizations which are partly government and partly independently run.

Source: The Times, *10 July, 1980*

We have seen some of the problems women face. Let us now see if we can be somewhat more positive for the future. A report entitled *The Female Boss – A report on the pros and cons of working for women* and produced by the Alfred Marks Bureau in January 1980, had this to say about the role of women in the secretarial sector.

'*The end of the 1970s sees more women working for other women than at any time in the past. Gradaully the numbers of female managers are increasing, as are those of women in the professions and, at a slower rate, senior women in industry. Legislation to end sex discrimination at work has given more women the confidence to aim for equal opportunity, as well as making employers offer the same promotion and job options to both sexes.*

'*But real change is the result of a shift in attitudes, not law. And although employers now have laws to guide and direct them, it is clear from the results of this research that attitudes among employees to women bosses still have a long way to go. Many people – men and women – instinctively prefer to work for a man and some are not prepared to work for a woman at all. At the same time, it is evident that some female bosses who, it might be claimed, have to try harder to establish and maintain their positions, do not help their own cause at work. The group recorded in the survey who are unable to communicate clearly on tasks and roles with their staff, for example, are making rods for their own backs. After all, employees are always quick to criticize any boss for inadequacies in management skills and female bosses will inevitably be more vulnerable to such criticism while they are in such a minority.*

Source: courtesy Alfred Marks Statistical Services Division January 1980

The future for women at work will, undeniably, give women new opportunities for equality. The possibilities are there: but so are very real problems. For example, new technology in the office may well create new jobs where the flow of information is great. The technology will also mean, however, that many jobs traditionally done by women, will almost certainly disappear. Shop work may give way to fully automated warehouses where increased demand for goods can be met by fewer and fewer (skilled) individuals. The TGWU has this to say about the future relationship between new technology and women's work:

New Technology and Women's work

'A vital point to make is that women will be most seriously affected by the technological changes ahead.

'In just about every sector of industry, the kind of jobs women do are the most vulnerable to microelectronic innovations.

'In factories, the repetitive assembly jobs, and packing and filling jobs are at risk.

'In offices, the situation is probably even more serious, as women easily outnumber men. All the jobs the women usually do are threatened: typists, secretaries, filing clerks, billing clerks, cashiers, accounts clerks, bank and insurance employees – all are in danger.

'There has been a dramatic increase in the last few decades in the number of women going to work. But the new technology could have the consequence of forcing women back into the home. Unemployment may well be most widespread amongst women, many of whom already form the "hidden" unemployed who do not register and so are not counted. This is a further problem that negotiators will have seriously to take to heart.*

Source: Microelectronics: New technology, old problems, new opportunities, TGWU, 1978

It's all stacked against women . . . still

'Looking at causes of inequality in Britain, the report shows that prejudice against women doing non-traditional jobs or part-time work still persists; career counselling is still inadequate; and unemployment generally is considered a more pressing problem than the particular employment problems of women.

'Another factor limiting choice of occupation is that many women have to look for jobs or training close to home, with hours compatible with family responsibilities. And the attitudes of women themselves sometimes add to their disadvantages; women may lack the confidence or ambition to apply for jobs traditionally done by men.*

Source: Employment News, November 1980

Women's pay becomes more unequal

'There is all too much reason to fear that the next few years may see an even greater deterioration in the relative position of women in the labour market. This is partly because women, often not strongly unionized, fail to compete successfully when wage-bargaining grows tough. A more important factor is that a high proportion of women are still employed in declining industries like clothing, footwear and textiles, and very few in industries with better ultimate prospects, like chemicals, mechanical engineering and instrument engineering. Further into the future, the spread of microchip technology is likely especially to affect the kind of clerical employment where the number of women is high. The proportion of women in work is in fact higher in Britain than in other West European countries, but it is made up to a far larger extent by part-time workers, with limited prospects for promotion and limited job protection.'

Source: The Times, 10 July, 1980

A hard road ahead?

Sue Slipman, a full-time trade union official and member of the SDP has this to say about women's role in the future:

'So we can either accept the rules and twist ourselves in knots to try to gain access to positions of power – or we can try to change the rules. For women to play a proper role in trade unions will take more than a bit of positive discrimination, or the occasional women's seat. It requires a completely different approach to work – for men as well as women.

'The unions must accept that women are still struggling to combine domestic responsibilities with paid jobs. They must fight for the right to hold meetings in work time without loss of pay, and for the wider recognition of part-time members as full union members. But that can only be a halfway house. Ultimately, we have to change the way work is organized, to structure it around our whole life as human beings, including our need to care for children.

'Until that happens we are salmon swimming upstream. The urge to do so is great, but the going is tough.'

Source: The Guardian, 29 May, 1981

Recommended reading for Chapter 11

1 *Women at Work* by C. Aldred (Pan, 1981)
2 *Women at War* by A. Marwick (Fontana, 1977)

Books that you have read and found useful should be added below

Chapter 12
It's the way they tell it

In Chapters 1 and 5 we looked at those groups who are involved in industrial relations at both national and local level. I want to take up where Chapter 6 finished and show some of the communication problems and possibilities that can occur at workplace level for unions, workers, management, etc. Incidentally, by 'communication' I mean the 'imparting or passing on of messages and information: an exchange of ideas or information with others: a being in touch with, or having access to or being connected with other people'. Let's start, then, with management and look at the way firms are 'organized' and 'structured' and see what strengths and weaknesses there are, all the time bearing in mind just how well people need to communicate with one another in the organizational set-up and, of course, in life generally.

Any firm, office, college, school, no matter what the size, must be well organized. But what exactly does the word 'organized' mean? For me

'Think like a wise man but communicate in the language of the people.'

Source: courtesy Masimba Mele, OND student, 1979/80

'Nothing is opened more often by mistake than the mouth.'

Anonymous

'When we drop a hammer on our toe we say "Damn" or "Blast" merely to relieve our feelings. Our exclamation does no good and may not even be heard by anyone else. We curse when we are alone. We complain about the cussedness of things – the door that jams, the tool that breaks, the

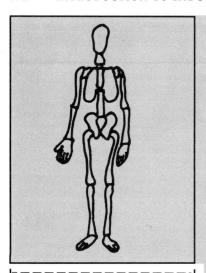

screw that is lost, the light that fuses. The first thing to realize, therefore, is most people want to talk but few of them have anything to say. Anyone who doubts this should watch someone in a glass-sided telephone kiosk. Note the gestures and expressions, the pointing finger, the clutched fist, the smile, the frown, the tapping foot. All these signs are wasted on the telephone. We realize, in fact, that they are not seriously meant to convey anything to anybody. They are means of self-expression and that is all.

Source: courtesy Communicate by C. Northcote Parkinson and Nigel Rowe, Pan 1979

JUST AS THE human body needs a firm, strong structure in order for the legs, arms, etc., to work, so, all firms and companies need to be given a strong structure to which to work. This structure we call 'organization'. Groups of workers, unions, companies all need to be organized before they can produce goods and services, and, in order for an organization to work well, there must be good communication between people working at the same level in the hierarchy and those working at higher and lower levels in the same hierarchy. As we shall see, the *structure* of an organization can be put down on paper in the form of an aptly named *organization chart*. However, it is as well to remember that what happens on paper doesn't always happen in practice!

it brings the following ideas to mind. It implies arrangements that have been deliberately made to involve, as effectively as possible, all the workers in the firm so that they can work together and co-ordinate their efforts to produce the goods and/or services that the firm is in business to supply. Organization also means the framework (or skeleton *see* above) or structure which shows 'who does what' in the firm at which we are looking. Thirdly, if a firm is organized it has formal (i.e. 'official') lines of authority and responsibility. An organized structure (like a firm or union) should also have clearly marked out lines along which people can

communicate with one another. These lines of communication should build up and maintain relationships between people and between departments within the firm, union, college, etc.

To see how these ideas work in practice let us have a look at the ways in which small, medium and large firms can be organized. All the time bear in mind the importance of communication within the firm concerned and try to see how easy (or difficult) it is for effective communication to take place.

1 Small Firm

It's easy to see why this form of formal organization is so popular among small units. Its advantages are that it:

(a) is simple to understand and operate;
(b) has one source of authority and responsibility;
(c) has clear, direct personal lines of communication.

'This is the page of the train'

'Communications are a terrific problem*. . . . We're spread from Land's End to John O'Groats and yet we haven't got the advantage that many national and multi-national companies have of having a series of individual production units. We are linked together. . . . The performance at Euston this afternoon depends on the performance at Preston this afternoon or Glasgow this afternoon. . . . We're an integrated whole.'

* that is, communications within a geographically well-spread out organization like British Rail.

Source: courtesy Cliff Rose, Board Member, British Railways Board

On the other hand:

(a) it can be rigid and inflexible;
(b) it lacks specialist skills;
(c) the owner's absence can cause problems.

As the business flourishes and grows (providing of course that it does!) the need to expand becomes obvious and so the organization has to change to meet the changing circumstances. The firm might now look something like this:

2 Medium-sized Firm

The advantages with this set-up are that:

(a) the owner now has the time to concentrate on deciding much more clearly which way the firm is going and on the best ways of doing this;
(b) if the owner is ill, or away on a business trip, the firm can keep going in his absence.

Of course, there are snags with this set-up. These are that:

(a) the foremen might make very bad decisions when the boss is away, and that's a risk (s)he has to take;
(b) there may be arguments *between* the fore-

men themselves as to what should be done and how it should be done;
(c) the lines of communication are starting to get longer and the boss is becoming more 'cut off' from his/her workers.

Once a firm becomes very large, a completely different skeleton or structure has to be devised. There is an example of an organization chart for a very large firm on p. 175.

Quite often, particularly in firms where the unions are very strong, workers see the union representative as the main source of information about what is going on in the firm. As we have seen, union representatives talk to members about the various matters that go to make up their industrial relations' work, like keeping them up-to-date about such things as wage negotiations, etc. In these firms the union view may well be the only view of things that the worker gets, particularly if management is weak and is poor when it comes to communicating with its workforce.

Assignment 12·1

List some of the advantages and disadvantages of organization charts in showing *realistically* the way an organization works.

(*See* p. 176 for some suggested answers.)

'I wouldn't survive 20 minutes in Sir Peter Parker's position . . . and he wouldn't survive 20 minutes in mine . . . different organizations, different backgrounds, different styles. . . . I've got to persuade not only the members of my National Executive but my Annual conference as well. I've got to argue and persuade them.'

Source: courtesy Sidney Weighell, formerly General Secretary, NUR

'I don't want to know about that . . .'

'The overall position is quite clear. The information which employees find least interesting, but to which companies devote most time and resources, is on company performance. At the same time, less attention is paid to the information which employees find most interesting — that is, things which affect them personally. Some surprising differences between company information and employees' needs were found.'

'The grapevine, even though it is often the most usual source of information, is actually the source that employees least prefer. The most preferred source is the immediate supervisor, who usually holds a much more important place in employees' working lives than most of them imagine. Interestingly, factory employees prefer the benevolent autocrat as a supervisor, rather than the more democratic participative type which is liked better by clerical and administrative staff. The preferred characteristics in general were said to be decisiveness, technical proficiency, trustworthiness, openness, fairness, firmness, and being a good disciplinarian.'

Source (both extracts): courtesy 'The Communications Gap' by Graham Cole in Management Today, November 1980

The steward as a communicator

'As a union steward you are in direct contact with the members and management at the workplace; your role as a communicator is extremely important and

unless you can cope with this task you will find your job much more difficult than it need be. It is therefore in your own interest, as well as that of your members and the union as a whole, that you equip yourself with basic skills of communication. This does not mean that you should treat communications as something separate from your day to day work as a union steward. Whenever you talk or write as a union steward you are a communicator. Your aim must be to express yourself in clear language which leaves no room for misunderstanding.'

Source: Union   Stewards Handbook, NUPE

'Trade   unions   are   different things in different circumstances. If you've got a factory with 3 000 workers in the union, then the structure and how you use it, are of vital importance to the people who want to be part of the union. If you've got a small geographic branch, in North Wales for example, it's more likely to be Tom Jones' branch than it is the General and Municipal: but the fact is that the major trade union

branches are in large places of work and therefore it is essential that members know something about the structure.'

Source: courtesy   David Basnett, General Secretary GMBATU

COMMUNICATIONS

'The TUC leaders are selectively bred as communicators. . . . The General Secretary of a trade union cannot become General Secretary unless he has been through a process all his official life of talking to groups of people in public; getting their support, making speeches. . . . These are the "tools of his trade". That's how he becomes a great trade union leader. The great ones are demigods* and many other things as well. You are really selected and bred by the union and, those people, any one of them can get up at Congress and make a resounding speech and they can appear on the television and do it.

Employers are really in a different category. Of course,

* demigod: someone   who   is worshipped

As we have already seen in Chapter 6 one of the most important areas of work that shop stewards and union representatives are involved in in their everyday union work is that of negotiating – whether they are negotiating with their members, with other union officials (lay or full-time) or with the management. As we saw with Roger, our NALGO union representative in the last chapter, one of the most difficult things for an experienced shop steward to do is to say exactly what skills go to make up a good negotiator. Often the very good ones will say that the negotiating skills that they have are due to particular personality characteristics ('I don't really know what it is really, it's something you can just do' was the one way one union steward put it) rather than special training. Usually in the workplace negotiators come up through the shop stewards' committee.

As various people have stressed throughout the book one of the most important aspects of communicating when negotiating is that there has to be mutual trust and respect on both sides, bearing in mind, of course, that unions and management are trying to achieve different as well as common aims. Both sides have to decide upon targets that are realistic and that are able to be achieved. It's no good at all going for something that's really 'pie-in-the-sky'. Decide what you are going for; stick to it, if possible, but decide before you go in that if you can't get exactly what you want (and you rarely ever will) then you must know at what position you will stick.

Both sides have to research their case well.

3 Large Firm

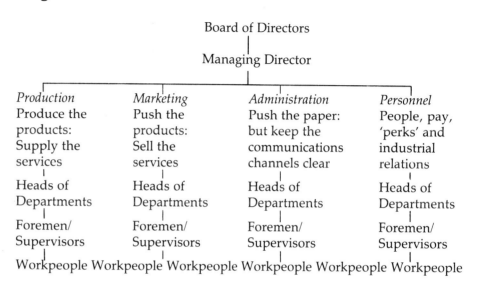

Board of Directors

Managing Director

Production	*Marketing*	*Administration*	*Personnel*
Produce the products: Supply the services	Push the products: Sell the services	Push the paper: but keep the communications channels clear	People, pay, 'perks' and industrial relations
Heads of Departments	Heads of Departments	Heads of Departments	Heads of Departments
Foremen/ Supervisors	Foremen/ Supervisors	Foremen/ Supervisors	Foremen/ Supervisors

Workpeople Workpeople Workpeople Workpeople Workpeople Workpeople

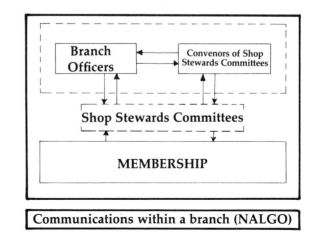

Communications within a branch (NALGO)

You have to know what arguments you are going to use and, in addition, you need to think out the kinds of arguments the other side will use to present their case. The union representative, once (s)he has prepared the case will have to tell the workforce what kind of figure (s)he has in mind and will obviously have to gain their support. The union representative must gain the solidarity and agreement of the workers. Any improvements that they suggest will be added into the case to be put forward. Workers and union representatives need to present a united front throughout the negotiations and so good communication is absolutely essential.

Answer to Assignment 12·1

Most large companies tend to use organization charts these days. They show the company in diagrammatic form and help to point out possible problem areas such as:

(a) overlap of responsibilities;
(b) span of control problems;
(c) possible communication problems.

All organization charts, however, have two basic weaknesses. These are:

(a) It's a structure on *paper* only. It shows management what *should* be happening, not necessarily what *is* happening.
(b) It takes no account of human personalities. It shows the formal organization not the informal organization and that, is often where the real power lies.

For both management and unions, there needs to be opportunities for face saving. Both sides need to be flexible and prepared to reach some kind of agreement. If the negotiations are successful the final proposed agreement has to be put to the workforce by the shop stewards. This may be done on a department by department basis (within a firm) or at a mass meeting. This is where the ability to communicate by word of mouth is absolutely vital. It is in these situations that the stewards' leadership qualities and spoken words (the 'gift of the gab') come to the fore. Experienced shop stewards will have a 'gut feeling' as to whether or not the members will accept the agreement. If they miscalculate and the workers reject the agreement, then it's back to the negotiating table.

From all the things that we have said until now it is obvious just how important good communication has to be in firms in order that people know what's going on, what they are expected to do and, perhaps, most important of all, to feel that if the organization communicates fully with them as workers, it must mean that the organization values them as *people* as well. Mike Bett (Board Member for Personnel and Industrial Relations at British Telecom) made the following comment in an interview with *Personnel Management* in August 1981.

'We continually lose sight of the fact that people need to feel needed and heeded . . . that they get upset if they think they are not being

employers can or should communicate with their people; many of them do it very well. They certainly have to communicate with their Board Room colleagues but that kind of power and persuasion and communication is a totally different one.

'I have known men who were marvellous at persuading a group of people around a Board Room table and who were dismal failures on a public platform, and would have been horrible on television.'

Source: courtesy   Alan Swinden, CBI

'Well, of course, the phrase "industrial democracy" is a problem in itself. . . . I wish someone would definitively explain to me exactly what it means. It certainly indicates a desire by workers, all workers, very often senior management as well as the lads on the shop floor, that they should be involved more than they are at the present time in the organization in which they work. . . .

'I have never been a great believer in the idea that by elect-

*listened to and that what they are
doing is not appreciated.*

He goes on to say that he thinks that the number of people who actually want full-bloodied industrial democracy in decision making is very small but

*. . . legions say it's not bloody
right how managers arbitrarily
change things.*

Having mentioned industrial democracy let's have a very brief look at the ways in which it could improve communications and worker involvement in industry and commerce.

The problems connected with industrial democracy lead us on rather well to the question of how we can get information, attitudes, new ways of looking at the world over to a large (mass) audience.

'MEDIA'* is the general word that we use to describe the various ways in which we communicate with a mass of people.

These include the television, radio, books, newspapers and so on. They have one essential thing in common. Usually the communication is one way. There are some exceptions to this rule, for example, a telephone, in which the conversation is a two way process and a radio

* A 'medium' (the singular of media) is simply a means by which something is communicated.

phone-in say, but even here calls are selected which means that the access is never direct. There is someone else involved who selects the calls which are to be put out over the radio. Someone plays what the sociologists call the 'gatekeeper' role.†

In reporting the news, because human attitudes are involved, 'bias' will inevitably occur. For example, it is fairly easy to spot the political colour of the various national newspapers. The range is clear to see from the left wing *Morning Star* through to the right wing *Sun*.

Answer to Assignment 12.2

Using the Left to Right scale found on p. 128 in Chapter 8, classify the following newspapers in terms of Political viewpoint:

Daily Mirror
News of the World
The Guardian
The Morning Star
The Daily Telegraph
The Times

A suggested answer (which in itself may provoke argument) is to be found on p. 179)

---

† A 'gatekeeper' is a person who decides which information will be sent out via the media (for example, a newspaper editor, an editor in a TV newsroom, even a teacher has a 'gatekeeper' role). We are also 'gatekeepers' to ourselves in that we receive much information into our bodies which we select out. This often happens when we receive information and attitudes with which we disagree. We 'hear what we want to hear', for example.

ing a couple of people from the shop floor to the Board of Directors that you solve all your problems in industry – I don't think it's as simple as that but I do believe that the more managements and employers take the workers into their confidence, not in a paternalistic way, but in a very positive way explaining exactly what the company is trying to do: explaining what the company and the shareholders are hoping to get out of it and what they are getting out of it in total *terms . . . explaining to the work people what they've got to do in order to make the company a prosperous one: what their rewards will be and providing that trade union representatives can then see there is a fairness operating and there is a real desire by the company and the management to utilize the tremendous skills and knowledge of the workers in shaping the future of the company . . . then that's what I mean by industrial relations.*

Source: courtesy Alex Ferry, General Secretary, CSEU

The ship of 'Industrial Democracy': which rock will it hit first?

Rock 1: Exactly what is industrial democracy? (*See* Alex Ferry's extract on pp. 176 and 177 for more on this one.)
Rock 2: Why bother with it say many of the workers? After all it's management's job to manage and make decisions.
Rock 3: The employers don't want it either. After all many managers feel strongly that it's *their* job to manage and make decisions.
Rock 4: Where do the unions and the Labour Party stand on industrial democracy. They're not too sure about it either.

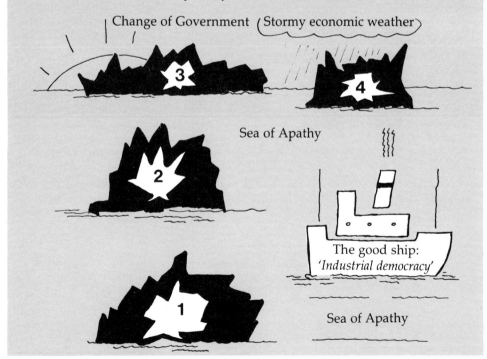

Change of Government   (Stormy economic weather)

3

4

Sea of Apathy

2

The good ship:
'Industrial democracy'

1

Sea of Apathy

As we can see, it is quite clear that newspapers tend to reflect a certain way of political thinking when it comes to the presentation of news. You can see newspapers which are broadly Left, Centre or Right. This does not mean, incidentally, that a Right wing newspaper will not express any disagreements it may have with the Conservative Party, it simply means that the disagreement is perhaps, 'played down' and kept very much 'within the family'.

If we look at the newspapers and the broadcasting organizations in Britain one of the biggest differences between them is that broadcasters are bound by the law to be 'impartial' while newspapers are not. So there's no real surprise that newspapers select the news that they regard as important and present it in a way that reflects the thinking of the people who own and work for that newspaper.

With TV and radio it is supposed to be a different matter: broadcasters are expected and required to show 'due impartiality'. However, human beings are, almost by definition, 'subjective'. As we saw in the chapters on ideas and attitudes in industrial relations their values and beliefs are always important. So it is in the broadcasting media where (some researchers believe), that while broadcasting people may think they are, in fact, being impartial and unbiased, they are not.

The media often claim that they are giving a wide and impartial view of the way things are in the world. Since there is more news around than the media can handle, it is obvious that some kind of sifting will inevitably take place. This will in turn mean that they cannot possibly cover all opinions in our society and so will select some opinions and reject others. So, in fact, although the media would claim that they are presenting a wide picture it is often the case that they are really giving only a small part of the total picture, and a biased part at that.

Some sociologists have said that the media 'set the agenda' for people in society by including certain items in the news and by leaving out others. Some issues get a lot of airing in the media while others get very little. For example, in industrial relations Britain clearly suffers from a large (often over-large) amount of reporting on strikes. Britain does not in fact have an exceptionally high strike record but if you keep close watch on the media this does not come across at all clearly. For example, we do not hear often enough of the workplaces where industrial relations are good, where strikes are unknown and where new technology has been introduced in a sensible and painless way. These are not sensational items and they do not sell newspapers, for example.

Answer to Assignment 12.2

LEFT		RIGHT
Morning Star	Observer The Times	Daily Telegraph Sun
Daily Mirror	Guardian The Sunday Times Daily Express	Daily Mail

Source: courtesy Society Today, 25 January, 1979

Assignment 12·4

What are some of the barriers to good communication in (a) your family; (b) your college; (c) your place of work; (d) your union; (e) your group of friends?

Assignment 12·5

In what ways and at what times do the mass media affect and influence your daily life?

Assignment 12·6

Which political party does your particular paper(s) support? How can you tell? List evidence of your view.

Assignment 12·3

Judging by the facts, opinions, extracts, etc. that I have included in this chapter, what do you think are my own personal views on the role of the media in industrial relations. Please quote evidence to support your case.

Assignment 12·7

Take extracts from different newspapers concerning the same news item about an issue in industrial relations and see in what ways the extracts are similar and different.

'Very little of what we know of the social realities of the world are found out first hand. Most of the "pictures in our heads" we have gained from the media – even to the point where we often do not believe what we see before us until we read about it in the paper or hear about it on the radio. The media not only gives us information; they guide our very experience. Our standards of credulity‡ our standards of reality, tend to be set by these media rather than by our own fragmentary experience.

‡ that is, what we believe.

Source: courtesy The Power Elite, C. W. Mills

It Really is 'The Way They Tell It'

Trade Unions and the Media

'Many trade unionists distrust journalists. This is an understandable reaction. The editorial policy of the vast majority of the press, if not hostile to trade unions as such, is certainly opposed to the ideals of the trade union Movement.

'Most editors and journalists are not deliberately instructed to disseminate a particular view of the trade union and labour Movement. However, past – and recent – experience has shown that stories which support the editorial policy are likely to be given greater prominence than those contrary to the paper's policy.

'As far as radio and television are concerned, both the BBC and the Independent Broadcasting Authority, which controls both commercial radio and television, make great play of their impartiality. However it is clear that many of the attitudes and terminology of broadcasting are borrowed direct from the press. Their 'impartiality'* is within very limited boundaries. Activities which fall outside those boundaries, including many trade union activities such as strikes, picketing and demonstrations, tend to become labelled with such value-laden terms as "extremist" or "militant".

'But this does not mean that trade unionists should ignore press, radio and television. If they do, their views may go by default. In fact, unions should try to use*

* N.B. 'impartial': not prejudiced, fair, just, disinterested.

the media to their own advantage.

'If trade unionists fail to put over their point of view in the media then other people unsympathetic to trade unions will get their views across unopposed. For all these reasons the media is a nettle you must grasp – before it stings you.*

Source: courtesy How to Handle the Media: A Guide for Trade Unionists, TUC, 1979

'Most of the best deals that are done never reach the newspapers; it's the failures that reach the newspapers. If the railwaymen's union, for example, fails to persuade the government through the normal methods of influence (through Secretaries of State, etc.) that they ought to invest £100 million in the electrification of the system, then you get a lot of noise in the press about it. . . . It's usually an indication that they're on the point of failure. We didn't want this Bill that's gone through the House of Commons breaking down the monopoly. The fact that it's become a public issue is because our normal methods of influencing government have failed.

Source: courtesy Peter Shaw, POEU*

'It's difficult sometimes to be able to persuade people that things are not as bad as they appear to be in the Press.

Source: courtesy E. Bone, National Officer, GWU

RIGHT WING VICTORY AT T U C *

TUC POLITICAL COUP LEAVES LEFT REELING†

* This headline was taken from *The Daily Telegraph* for 8 September, 1981.
† This headline, relating to the same event, was taken from *The Guardian* of the same date.

Same issue, different newspapers, different viewpoints

'The TUC carthorse loosened its reins yesterday and cantered briskly towards the creation of a new power structure which strikes directly against the Left and the old craft unions.

'In the battle between Left and Right, the growing white collar and public sector unions emerged as the beneficiaries. During one of the most important debates on internal politics for many years delegates during the first day of the Trades Union Congress at Blackpool decided in principle to give automatic representation to unions on the TUC with more than 100 000 members.

'The implications are wide-ranging. For the first time in recent history the TUC Right wing has organized a coup and succeeded.

'The proposal still has to be considered by the TUC General Council in the next twelve months but it could mean the disappearance of well-known smaller unions, like the train drivers, led by Mr Ray Buckton, the cine technicians, led by Mr Alan Sapper, and the agricultural workers, led by Mr Jack Boddy. Even the power of the miners could be cut by half, with the NUM losing one of its two seats.

Source†: The Guardian, 8 September, 1981

Tied in with 'agenda setting' is the idea of 'norm setting'. This simply says that even if items do occur in the media, certain items will be given greater emphasis than others. A simple example here can be given by two sets of figures and a question. There are roughly 150 murders a year in the UK. The annual death toll from accidents in industry is around 3 000. Which of the two issues do you hear most about in the media?

Assignment 12·8

Tape-record news items from both BBC and ITN news and list:

(a) what was selected;

(b) major items of news not selected; and

(c) discuss the order in which the various news items were given.

Recommended reading for Chapter 12

1 *Social Skills and Work* Edited by M. Argyle (Methuen, 1981)

2 *Person to Person* M. Argyle & P. Trower (Harper & Row, 1979)

3 *People and Communication* G. R. Wainwright (M & E Books, 1979)

Books that you have read and found useful should be added below.

Chapter 13
Nobody seems to work anymore

Objectives

At the end of this chapter you should be able to:

1 list and discuss the various kinds of direct industrial action open for workers to take;
2 differentiate between unofficial and official strikes and list some of the characteristics of British strikes;
3 analyse and discuss the implications of strike statistics;
4 think about and identify some of the causes of strikes;
5 identify and list reasons for the level of unemployment in Britain in the 1980s;
6 pick out those groups in society who are particularly badly affected by unemployment;
7 identify those areas and regions of Britain worst hit by unemployment;
8 identify some of the ways governments, unions and workers are reacting to unemployment;
9 describe the impact upon individual people of being unemployed.

THIS CHAPTER COVERS the following subjects/topics:

1 industrial action including strikes;
2 varieties of strikes;
3 some of the possible causes of strikes in Britain;
4 strike statistics for Britain and for other European, American and Asian countries;
5 major causes of unemployment;
6 casualties of unemployment;
7 crises brought on by unemployment;
8 challenges of unemployment.

THIS CHAPTER COVERS two key, present-day issues; strikes and unemployment. It may seem somewhat strange to put the two together in one chapter; my reasoning is as follows. First of all both of these topics are seen as key industrial issues by many people living in Britain today. Both are interruptions to what is seen to be the 'normal' state of affairs namely, working (*see* Chapter 5 for a recap here). Both topics are often significant events in the lives of individual people. Being unemployed or on strike can have an effect on people's lives and personalities. They can (particularly in the case of unemployment) have a serious effect on a person's identity, while both affect the amount of cash coming into a household.

These are differences, of course. One, for example, is that people decide on a majority basis whether or not to go on strike: very few people, on the other hand, actually want to be unemployed! Both subjects, incidentally, closely relate today in that because of a fear of unemployment, many people are very cautious about going on strike at all. They fear that by striking they may well lose their jobs altogether. Finally, it's important to remember that both issues are areas where there are difficult and different interpretations to be made of statistics.

We have already seen how unions, on behalf of their members, negotiate with management about pay and conditions. Generally speaking, a compromise is reached in most of these discussions. Sometimes, however, industrial action of various kinds is used to bring pressure on management if negotiations break down.

The form of industrial action that comes immediately to most people's minds is the strike (of which I will say more later), but there are various other kinds of direct action that workers can take.

Work-to-rules   1

In the case of a work-to-rule unionists do everything 'by the book'. They keep firmly to all the rules and regulations that control the ways in which they work. They do everything exactly the way it should be done. The 'informal', and often very much quicker ways of doing things are not used. In an industry such as the railways where there are vast collections of regulations, a 'work-to-rule' or a 'go-slow' will both cause chaos very quickly indeed.

Overtime Bans   2

Taking again an industry like the railways where a large amount of overtime is worked simply to keep the 'normal' service going, any overtime ban will obviously severely affect the service provided. Many workers work overtime, it is an accepted part of industrial life, and so any ban on it will soon affect a firm's production.

'Sit-ins'   3

During these difficult days of recession we often hear of workers who are 'sitting-in'. In this case, the workers take over the factory to try and keep it open when management want to close it because it is unprofitable. In order to keep the place going the workers may continue to work for nothing or they may go on to buy up the firm and turn it into a workers' co-operative

Unemployment

'We only seem to be in full work either when there is a war or when we are preparing for a war. . . . But if the nation can organize a great defence programme against war, it can do so against other enemies – unemployment, poverty, malnutrition, disease.'

Source: courtesy A Portrait of Ernest Bevin 1881–1951 *by Mark Stephens, TGWU, 1981*

where they manage, organize and work it themselves.

Still the most powerful bargaining weapon the workers have is the strike weapon, that is the organized withdrawal of labour. It is important to remember that there are various kinds of strike as follows.

As we saw in Chapter 7 peaceful picketing has long been accepted as a measure used by trade unions. Two points that we made in that chapter are worth repeating here: namely that of late there has been a growth in mass and secondary picketing.

Unofficial strikes   1

This is a strike called by a branch, or a number of branches *without* the agreement of the union's executive committee. 95% of all strikes in Britain are unofficial.

The reverse of this is, of course, the official strike where the union backs up the branch(es) out on strike both in spirit and in cash.

In addition, we need to remember there are other activities apart from actually striking, that workers can use when they take direct collective action against employers. Research suggests that

overtime bans are the most popular form of direct action while working to rule and threatening to strike are as important as striking itself.

Sympathetic strikes   2

These occur when one group of trade unionists come out on strike in support of another group who are already on strike (or who are about to strike). If, for example, the miners decide to go out on strike, the railwaymen may refuse to move coal in order to show sympathy and solidarity with them. The coal is 'blacked' (that is, not moved!). One of the best examples of a sympathetic strike was the 1926 General Strike when many of the country's unions came out in sympathy with the miners who were fighting the mine owners' attempts to cut wages.

N.B. Other kinds of strikes worth mentioning are 'token strikes', which are usually one day stoppages to show the workers mean business (this can be very effective if the workers do not say which day the strike will take place) and strikes which are 'unconstitutional'! An unconstitutional strike is one that takes place before all the accepted procedures and processes have been worked through.

1 Strikes are often used by workers as a last resort.
2 Most strikes are unofficial (around 95%).
3 Strikes are mainly about pay.
4 Strikes are over-reported in the mass media.
5 Britain's international strike record is not at all bad.
6 Some industries are more strike prone than others.
7 Illness and accidents at work lose many more working days in a year than do strikes.

Most strikes in Britain are unofficial, that is, they do not have official trade union recognition and backing. Unofficial strikes are becoming more and more common. Partly because of this fact the shop steward has become a central and key figure in managing industrial conflict and compromise. If you remember from Chapter 2,

Assignment 13.1

A firm's negotiating machinery breaks down and after a mass meeting the workers decide they have no other alternative but to go out on strike (the strike has official union support). In what ways will this action affect:

(a) an individual worker from that firm;
(b) the above worker's family;
(c) the firm's management;
(d) the union that brought that group of workers out;
(e) the shopkeepers in the area;
(f) the country in general.

we have seen how the shop steward, the shop-floor representative of the union, the person who collects the subscriptions and who keeps an

Unofficial strikes: Here today, gone tomorrow?

'*In most cases trade unions adopt no official attitude to individual unofficial strikes, since the question seldom arises whether they should be treated as official or not. They commonly take place before any full-time official at district level, let alone at head-quarters, is aware that the problem exists and indeed . . . even senior shop stewards may have no forewarning. . . .*'

Source: The Donovan Report

Strikes: How many are official? (United Kingdom)

Year	Number	of which known Official (%)
1971	2 228	7.2
1972	2 497	6.4
1973	2 873	4.6
1974	2 922	4.3
1975	2 282	6.1
1976	2 016	3.4
1977	2 703	2.9
1978	2 471	3.6
1979	2 080	3.9
1980	1 262	5.0

Source: Employment Gazette, *January, 1981*

eye on conditions in the factory, has now taken on more and more of the workers' negotiations with management at *local* level. This, in turn, reflects the growing importance of agreements on pay and conditions that are being made at the local plant or office. It is because of this growing importance of agreements made at local level that most strikes are unofficial and, not surprisingly, localized.

The present situation on strikes (as given by government statistics) is that strike activity in 1980 was at a record *low* level. The 1980 total of 1 262 stoppages was the lowest* annual number for nearly forty years. It was less than half the *recorded* annual average over the last ten years. There were roughly 11.9 million working days lost in 1980 compared with nearly 29.5 million the year before (and that was a very bad year anyway). This generally compares with an average of 12.8 million over the previous ten years.

As a nation we always seem to want to compare ourselves with other nations to see how well (or how badly) we are doing. Perhaps, we ought to see how the UK's strike performance compares with that of other major countries. Based on figures from the International Labour Office, Britain does, in fact, do fairly well when we look at stoppages in industry. For the 1975–9 period seven countries had a higher rate of

stoppages than Britain, where we lost 990 working days for every 1 000 employees. Australia, Canada, India, the Irish Republic and the USA all had *higher* rates of stoppages.

* N.B. Why do you think that this should be the case? What reasons can you give to suggest why striking should be at a low level at this time? (*See* the second half of this chapter for a possible answer.)

Assignment 13.2

Check the dictionary definition of 'disharmony' and give some reasons why industrial life can be disharmonious.

Assignment 13.3

Check through this chapter and find two sources of 'official statistics'.

Assignment 13.4

Suggest any other forms of industrial pressure.

Returning now to the British industrial scene, one very important point to remember is that strikes do not occur evenly throughout industry. Certain industries are 'strike-prone'. These include the docks, the car industry, shipbuilding, and coal mining. Indeed, if you add the steel industry to the above list, from 1966–76 these five industries, although they had just over one-twentieth of all workers, were responsible for a quarter of all the stoppages and a third of all working days lost.

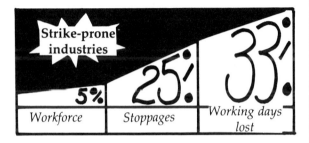

Strike-prone industries

5% — Workforce
25% — Stoppages
33% — Working days lost

Leading on from what we were saying about strike-prone industries, we find that those unions which tend to be most involved in strikes are those that organize *men* in *manual* jobs working in fairly *large* organizations. Few of the unions with less than 10 000 members seem to get involved in strike action. Although, as we have already seen, white collar unions have become increasingly important of late, they do not seem to get nearly as involved in strike activity as their manual worker counterparts.

An international 'Them' and 'Us'

People often compare Britain's strike-prone car industry with the relatively strike-free Japanese and West German car makers. However, this dangerous kind of com-

Causes of Stoppages (United Kingdom)

Principal cause	Beginning in December 1980	Beginning in the twelve months of 1980
Pay	8	607
Length and pattern of hours worked	1	30
Redundancy questions	3	76
Trade union matters	2	69
Working conditions and supervision	4	104
Manning and work allocation	–	220
Dismissal and other disciplinary measures	2	156
All causes	20	1 262

Source: Employment Gazette, *January 1981*

Strikes on European soil : How does the UK compare?

(Working days lost through industrial disputes per 1 000 employees in all industries and services – EEC countries)

Country	Average for 10 years 1970–9
United Kingdom	572
Belgium	269
Denmark	260
France	211
Germany (West)	36
Irish Republic	789
Italy	1 312
Luxembourg	(In Luxembourg the number of strikes is negligible and no figures are available
Netherlands	43

Source: Statistical Office of the European Communities

Driving forward at Datsun

'Kikuji Karahashi, 35, leads a nine-man team checking quality on 200 Datsun Sunny cars every day at Nissan's Zama assembly plant. Many workers leave after about ten years deterred by the nightwork but Karahashi has been there for fifteen, so gets paid well. For his nine hour day, including an hour's overtime, his weekly pre-tax pay with night work allowance is £184. But the annual bonus, around six months salary, can add as much as £4,416 to this. In a year he can make over £13,000. "Perhaps I got promoted faster because I willingly took on responsibilities," he says. "I was active, for instance, in helping to organize things in the bachelors' dormitory". His job is for life, retiring at 60 since union pressure pushed it up from 55, and he has a fair chance of becoming a junior manager. He is cushioned from unemployment by the casual workers, mainly farm labourers from the north coming south after the rice harvest, who are the first to be laid off if there is any dip in car sales.'

Scraping through at Leyland

'Roy Gatehouse, 51 gets £95.90 a week at BL's Cowley plant, with bonus running currently at £8.48. Skilled workers above him in grade one get £104.60 (plus bonus) and sweepers on grade five £48.60 (plus bonus). He has been redundant once and there is no guarantee he will escape the latest cut-backs. With his wife Barbara working full-time and the children off their hands, he counts himself well off. If he had to live on his wage, there certainly wouldn't be the £172 a month mortgage on his house on the outskirts of Oxford. BL doesn't run to Nissan-style paternalism. Barriers between men and management are much more sharply drawn. The canteen Lord Nuffield built at Cowley has five levels of status from executives right down to ordinary workers. Gatehouse has been a shop steward but feels the notion of a fair day's work for a fair day's pay has gone. He doesn't have much praise for the way Cowley was run. "The management used to let us hold paid meetings to organize strikes."'

Source: courtesy The Sunday Times, *29 March, 1981*

parison often gives a very false picture unless you remember the attitude, background and life styles of the car workers in those different countries. They may be doing the same job but in so many other ways they are worlds apart.

For every working day lost in the United Kingdom because of industrial disputes in 1978 forty-three days were lost due to sickness and ill health.

Unemployment

1 Causes of unemployment
2 Casualties of unemployment
3 Crises brought on by unemployment
4 Challenges of unemployment

Since the mid-1970s the number of people out of work has been climbing. The TUC fears that unemployment may rise to 4.5 million by 1990, while the government's 'Think Tank' and the Manpower Services Commission both agree that they expect unemployment to go on rising in the medium term. We seem to be heading for times when those people who have jobs are reckoned to be very fortunate indeed. Instead of asking 'what job do you do?' the question will have to

Cold Comfort for the workers and the country

'In 1970, when striker-days reached a new post-war peak, the total was just over 10 million. By contrast, industrial accidents cost over 20 million working days. An unemployment level near the million mark is the equivalent of well over 200 million working days. And in recent years, loss of time through certified sickness has accounted for over 300 million working days. An effective anti-influenza vaccine – or stricter control over unsafe working conditions – would be likely to save far more working time than the most draconian anti-strike laws.'

Source: courtesy Strikes R. Hyman, 1979

'The report says the figure of 371 million working days lost (peak reached in 1978–9 of days lost to illness in industry) "contrasts sharply" with just over 15 million days lost from industrial injuries and diseases, and 9.4 million days lost through industrial action, in 1978.'

Source: courtesy The Financial Times, August 10, 1981

change perhaps to 'do you work at all?'.

No-one would disagree with the importance, for everyone, of the issue of rising unemployment. The first question we need to ask is why do we have such high levels of unemployment in the 1980s here in Britain? One reason is that there is a world slump in trade at the present time and, like us many other industrialized countries are also suffering from the evils of unemployment. In addition, we in Britain seem to suffer from low growth in our economy. It is not growing as quickly and as strongly as some other economies are. Thirdly, the introduction of new technology based on the 'microchip' is also responsible for some loss of jobs (see the following chapter for more about this.) Lastly, many people would say that the most important reason for the present high levels of unemployment is the policies of the present right-wing Conservative government of Mrs Thatcher. All these reasons plus changes in the kinds of industries Britain has, and the weakness of her manufacturing industry, have helped to keep unemployment levels here high.

'Society Today' on 'unemployment' (New Society, 30 October, 1980) rather graphically describes the process of unemployment in this way:

'The number (of unemployed) quoted each month is merely a snapshot of a constantly moving, and changing, flow of people coming on and off the employment register. As many as four million a year find themselves for

some time on the employment register – nearly one in six of the entire workforce. Until very recently, between 250 000 and 300 000 people a month were registering for work, while an almost equivalent number were leaving at the same time. Now more are flowing on to the register, and the numbers going off have fallen.

'The main reason why unemployment is rising is because the jobless are taking a longer time to find another job, although most of them still manage to do so within a few months. The unemployed resemble, not a pool, but a bath of water, with the taps running, and a plug hole that is becoming increasingly blocked.'

The hardest cut of all?

'The Government should spend more on schools and more on jobs for youngsters, a headmaster told delegates yesterday. "I am glad I am not young any more" said Alan Poole of the National Association of Schoolmasters. "Every morning at assembly I have to look at my pupils and I see the despair in their eyes as they

The union view

Just as we've talked about different kinds of workers, unions, managers and governments so we can discover different reasons for unemployment under capitalism.

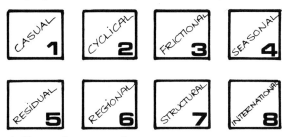

1 Casual unemployment

Some jobs, such as work on building sites, are not permanent. Workers are taken on, on short-term contracts.

2 Cyclical unemployment

Ups and downs in the economies of countries mean that at certain times in history trade has been very high. This has been often true during wars, for example, while at other times, trade levels have been much lower as, for example, during the recession that occurred in the thirties and the one that is occurring now.

Assignment 13.5

As an ongoing assignment keep the figures on the map on p. 191 up-to-date.

3 Frictional unemployment

This kind of unemployment occurs when there is a shortage of workers with a special skill in one part of the country while another part of the same country has workers with those skills and they are unable to get work.

4 Seasonal unemployment

Some work is seasonal, for example, those people who work in factories or at the seaside during the summer holiday season or who work for the GPO at Christmas time. Between these periods of work these same people may well be unemployed.

5 Residual unemployment

There will always be a very tiny minority who do not want or are unable to work. The point does however, need to be made that this minority is very, very small indeed. Most people want to work and be active.

6 Regional unemployment

Some areas of the country have particularly high levels of unemployment (the North West/the North East/Northern Ireland). This is due to the decline of old, long-established industries. As in frictional unemployment workers often do not want to move, arguing that if you are going to be unemployed, it is better to be with friends and

Unemployment in Britain 1982

1 Scotland
13.7

2 North
14.8

3 Northern
Ireland
18.1

4 North West
14.1

5 Yorkshire
12.2

6 Wales
15.0

7 West Midlands
14.3

8 East Midlands
10.4

9 South West
10.3

10 South East
8.7

11 East Anglia
9.7

(All figures in percentages: February 1982)

ACAS Annual Report for 1980

Survival worries lead to a big drop in stoppages.

Frequent causes

Pay and other terms and conditions of employment were again the most frequent causes of disputes dealt with. Trade union recognition continued to be the second largest cause. Redundancy was the cause of disputes in 10% of cases in 1980 compared with only 4% in 1979.

Common features

A number of features were common in many disputes. Among workers affected there was considerable concern about job loss, either as a result of technological change within the industry or as a result of structural decline. Situations were often complicated by apparent conflicts between different groups of workers represented by different unions and a lack of willingness to use or abide by the TUC's own disputes procedure. (See the tables on p. 194 for industries that are growing and are declining.)

Source: courtesy Employment Gazette, *May 1981*

Work and what happens when people are out of work

'A 37 year old electrician who had lost his job five months before said that "apart from getting very bored in the morning," he generally did the housework while his wife was out at work and prepared an evening meal for the children. The children still had adequate clothing and food. However, he would not apply for free school dinners for them: "There's a terrible unemployment situation in Merseyside. I don't think it should have to reflect on the children, that would be begging – it is bad enough that I have to claim, but not to pass it on to the children – I don't agree with it. Children have a wicked nature if they find out. Children take the mickey – I wouldn't like that."'

Unemployment and the Black Economy (A Social Studies Reader) New Society, 1980

'Sometimes the stresses of unemployment threatens the marriage itself. A 28 year old man, married with two children, unemployed for eighteen months, when asked what he did with his

relatives around you for support rather than move to some strange part of the country where you know no-one.

7 Structural unemployment

If changes take place in the structure of the economy, unemployment may well result. If we have an economy where greater use is made of the microchip, for example, in the office, environment, then human beings will be needed much less and more unemployment will be the result.

8 International unemployment

International unemployment, such as that of the 1920s and 1930s occurs when a rich country, such as the United States, has a hard time economically and, because of this, it decides to buy less goods from abroad which in turn hits production in other countries. It's a kind of 'contagious disease' effect where one country's economic collapse (or weakness) spreads to other countries.

Having seen the types of unemployment we need to ask *who* are the unemployed? It seems that a number of groups are particularly badly hit in the unemployment stakes. These groups are:

(a) young people under 20;
(b) men (particularly older men) who have been unemployed for a long time (over a year). These men are often unskilled and work in general labouring jobs;
(c) blacks are also very prone to high levels of unemployment particularly in the decaying areas of inner cities such as Liverpool, Manchester, Bristol and even London in the richer South East of the country has its problem areas as the 1981 Brixton riots showed;
(d) certain areas of the country have been particularly badly hit by the recession and unemployment. These areas are shown on the map on p. 191.

As an assignment keep a check on *Employment Gazette* to see what happens regarding strikes and disputes in the future.

Since 1975, job creation schemes, sponsored by the government, have been provided to try and help unemployed school leavers and young people under 18. There have been a variety of schemes and many of these have now (unfortunately) become an accepted part of British industrial life. One of the best known of these schemes is the Youth Opportunities Programme or YOPs. YOPs give a range of opportunities for unemployed young adults in training courses and work experience. These include courses to help young people prepare for work and work experience schemes of various kinds on employers' premises, in training workshops, on community service and on other special projects.

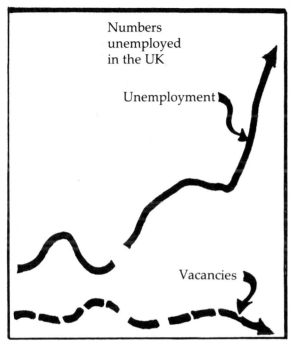

Numbers unemployed in the UK

Unemployment

Vacancies

1970 1972 1974 1976 1978 1980 1981

However, many YOP schemes have not had an easy ride, and there have been criticisms of them in that they do no more, very often, than provide cheap labour. Indeed, YOPs itself is now being replaced in September 1983 by the Youth Training Scheme or YTS.

Among other factors, such as the introduction of new technology, the slump in manufacturing industry in Britain has led to a serious loss of jobs. For example, total employment in British manufacturing industry has dropped by a million in the last two years and by over two million in the last decade. Less than six million people now work in industry.

Some sectors of industry have been worse hit than others. The metal manufacturers have lost over a quarter of their production, while textiles have lost just under a quarter of theirs. Construction has declined another 12% while food and drink, paper and printing have each dropped by 9%.

With growing unemployment *work sharing* could be one answer that could help but there are problems even with this:

"The main trouble is the members", one senior union leader told me. "We ask the negotiators to press the issue, but the lads are not supporting it." The inertia of the unions mirrors the indifference of the rank-and-file. This is most graphically illustrated by the resilience of overtime working at a time of recession for manual workers. Most union leaders agree publicly that overtime is a social and economic evil that should be abolished. In the words of Ken Thomas, of the CPSA, at the 1977 TUC: "We have no moral authority to go to the (then Labour) government and ask them to help us when thousands of our members are working overtime which, if we cancelled it and banned it, would create jobs in this country."

Source: courtesy R. Taylor 'Work Sharing and worklessness,' New Society, 23 November, 1981

time replied, "nothing". He said he just sat in the house and argued all the time with his wife. His wife had actually been to a solicitor about a divorce. He said, "There was nothing to do at home but watch the television, night and day. She doesn't like me sitting there". He used to help in the house but he said you "just get into a rut" and he was not doing anything now. He also said that the children got under his feet and he got bad tempered with them. He said, "Sometimes I'm too hard on them – I play with them and then all of a sudden I get narky".

Unemployment and the Black Economy (*A Social Studies Reader*) New Society, 1980

Who said life was fair anyway. . . ?[1]

Up to 100 000 people may be on the dole because their jobs have been taken by teenagers on the state-funded Youth Opportunities Programme. Trade unions, which have consistently backed YOP, are becoming increasingly concerned about this, especially as young people receive a government allowance of only £23.50 for a 40 hour week. YOP costs an employer nothing, except the time to train youngsters. . . . A supermarket in Merthyr Tydfil (for example) employed a girl on a YOP "work experience" programme filling shelves from 8 a.m. to 6 p.m., Monday to Friday, with alternate Saturdays. Staff leaving were not replaced, so trainees were effectively doing adult work.

Source: courtesy The Sunday Times, *15 March, 1981*

Who said life was fair anyway. . . ?[2]

'An education chief who only a week ago asked school cleaners to take a pay cut is to get a £60 a week rise. Chief education officer in Cambridgeshire, Geoffrey Morris, asked 1 000 cleaners to reduce their working year by four weeks costing some of them £100 in lost wages, to save £50 000. Mr Morris's pay is to go up by £3 000 to £24 000.

Source: courtesy Daily Express, *25 February, 1981*

Industries in which employment will decrease 1978–85

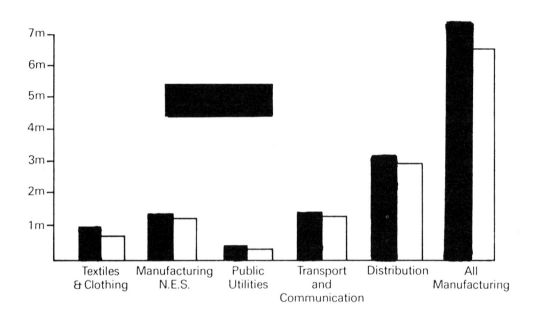

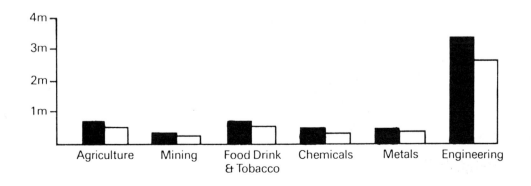

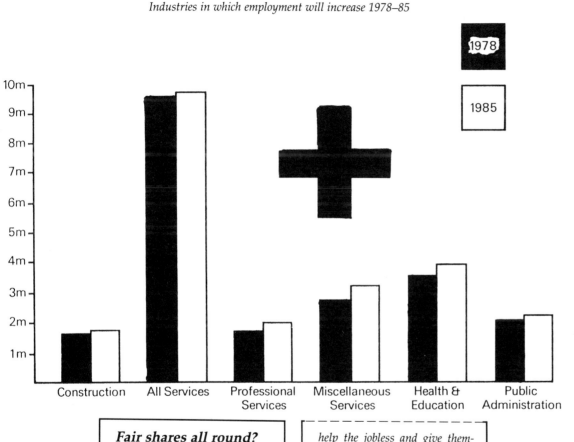

Industries in which employment will increase 1978–85

1978
1985

Construction · All Services · Professional Services · Miscellaneous Services · Health & Education · Public Administration

Fair shares all round?

'Overtime is the "curse of British industrial life", Mr David Basnett chairman of the TUC Economic Committee, told the Congress. He urged all unions to wipe it out wherever possible to help the jobless and give themselves and their families a better deal. Mr Basnett said: "overtime divides worker from worker and workers from their families.",

Source: courtesy Daily Express, *10 September, 1981*

Young people wanting work

'The message from the young people of Britain was loud and clear: "We want a future and we want work", said Carmen Wootton, 23 accepting the annual Congress Award for Youth.

'She said many young people had taken to the streets of inner cities out of frustration and despair in a country which offered them no future.

'Society was geared towards the consumer, and people were educated to believe that at the end of the day, they would have a job and role in life.

'Carmen, a data terminal operator and member of the Amalgamated Union of Engineering Workers' Technical and Supervisory Section (AUEW/TASS) lives at Anstey, Leicestershire. She beat five men finalists to become the fourth woman in 10 years to win the youth award.,

Source: courtesy The Daily Telegraph, *8 September, 1981*

WORK ✔ DOLE ✗

Assignment 13.6

They can't even agree on the figures . . .

Jobless

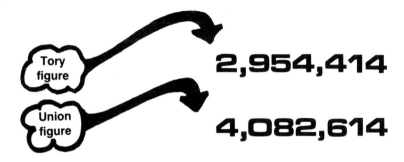

Tory figure   **2,954,414**

Union figure   **4,082,614**

The missing million

'*Top union leaders last night accused the Government of fiddling the jobless figures. They said more than a million unemployed were not included in the official statistics. The Government announced yesterday that there were 2 954 414 in the dole queue – a drop of 34 230 on last month. But the unions poured scorn on this figure, which keeps the total hovering just below the politically sensitive three million mark. They put the number out of work at 4 082 614 and produced figures to prove it.*'

Source: courtesy Daily Mirror, *25 November, 1981*

What other groups could be included in the reckoning to account for the difference in the two sets of figures?
(For some suggested answers please see opposite.)

Recommended reading for Chapter 13

Some interesting articles concerning unemployment training and education of young people can be found in the *Trade Union Studies Journal* published by the W.E.A. (Summer 1982). This is available from:

W.E.A.
9 Upper Berkeley Street
London W1H 8BY

Books that you have read and found useful should be added below

Suggested answers to Assignment 13.6

In the same article as the figures were taken from, the unions claimed that the Government forgot to add in 650 200 *unregistered jobless*, 407 000 kept out of the dole queue by *special Government measures* (such as YOPs etc.), and 71 000 based on days lost by people on *short-time working*.

Chapter 14
People don't like change

Objectives

At the end of this chapter you should be able to:

1 say what 'change' is and give examples of various kinds of change (individual, social, economic, political, etc.);
2 list and discuss the various stages of change that we, as individuals, go through in life;
3 list and discuss some of the economic, political and technological changes that will affect industrial relations during the 1980s;
4 try to identify some of the possible changes that the unions will go through in the 1980s to adapt to the changes outlined above;
5 list some of the difficulties of managing change in industrial relations.

THIS CHAPTER COVERS the following subjects/topics:

1 change: what is it and what kinds of change are there?
2 individual change through life;
3 social, economic, political and technological change and their relationships with industrial relations;
4 the trade unions and change;
5 the problems and possibilities of handling change.

THIS CHAPTER IS all about change; how you and I change and how the world, and particularly the world of industrial relations, around us, changes. In the chapter we will look at all kinds of change. Change at an individual level, for example, change in your own attitudes, and at a social level, for example, what changes people want to see come about in the length of the working week. There are economic, political and technological changes all taking place and many of these changes will affect industrial relations' practices.

However, before we get into those wider questions, let's start with the individual and see how change affects him or her through life. Change is all around us. It affects us all of our lives. We are born to change; what are some of these changes like? If we divide human life up into stages through which we go and change we

All is flux, nothing is stationary.

Heracleitus 513 B.C.

You're up against the big boys. You've got to be efficient. There are no quiet attitudes you can adopt to anything. You're either dynamic or you're dead. People don't like change. It's essentially a dynamic industry.

Source: courtesy Pat Lowry, formerly Director of Personnel and External Affairs, BL Limited, talking about the British car industry

The philosophers have only interpreted the world differently, the point is, to change it.

Karl Marx 1818–83

'The factories of the twenty-first century will be most noticeable for their small size. They will contain far less machinery than today's monster workhouses, and will employ only a fraction of the people. There will be fewer of them as well. Yet by working twenty-four hours a day, for much of this time untended except by maintenance workers, the factories will turn out all the manufactured items that the communities around them require.'

Source: courtesy 'Towards the unmanned factory' by Peter Marsh, New Scientist, 31 July, 1981

'Change: an alteration, variation or replacement of one thing for another; variety; a passing from one condition or state to another, transition; to make a change or modification; to cause to become different; to substitute or adopt one thing for another; to alter the order or nature of a thing or person; to undergo a change, to become different, to be in a state of transition, to pass into a new phase.'

could decide that there are basically five separate stages, each of which brings change down directly upon us. These five stages are as follows:*

1 Childhood;
2 Adolescence;
3 Young adulthood;
4 Adulthood;
5 Old age.

The first of these, childhood, covers the time from birth to our going to secondary school, and it is during this period that our basic personality is laid down. During adolescence, the period from around the age of twelve or thirteen to the early twenties, a large amount of change takes place as we struggle to make the move from school to work and from dependence to independence. It is a period in which we try to find out 'who we are' and a time in which we are working on developing an identity of our own.

The third stage, young adulthood, is closely woven into adolescence in that it too is a transition period. We leave school and go out into the wider world of work, college or university. We may simply move from school to the dole queue. But, whichever of these we move into, we will change aims and identities once more. We become involved in more intimate and more committed relationships at work and at home. We may well marry. The young person begins to

* N.B. The idea of life as a series of five stages is taken from an excellent book on the ways human beings change and develop called *Growing Through Life*. It is written by Rhona and Robert Rapoport and published by Harper and Row.

'settle down'.

In the fourth stage, the 'establishment phase' (roughly between the ages of twenty-five to fifty-five), a person's main intentions are concerned with work, family, friends and enjoying oneself through various leisure activities. Most adults will be married and many will have children. Towards the end of this stage in life the children will leave home and both they, and their parents, will be faced with more change.

In the later years of our lives, the final stage, more changes need to be made as we enter our retirement and old age. We will need to accept that we will eventually die and we will have to prepare for that in our own personal way. Work is now very much less important. We get pleasure in life from other activities such as our hobbies and meeting friends and acquaintances. There is change right to the end.

Briefly these five stages hint at some of the changes we all have to make as individuals. Let's now look at some of the ways that changes in the world generally affect both the individual and people as a whole. First, we can see that many people are affected by many changes happening all at the same time. Change and the effects of change are to be seen everywhere. New laws, new technology, new fashions, new views and values; change is everywhere and affects all of us in some ways, even if it is in changing prices and wages! Change is therefore very important to the individuals and to groups of individuals because we all have to adapt to these changes. One of the most important areas of change is in that of technology and automation with new gadgets and machines being devised and produced all the time. More and more during the 1980s automation is going to become increasingly important. Computers, for example, can control and co-ordinate whole production processes such as those in Fiat's car plants. In the next section we will look at some of the changes that new technology will bring about. More important, we will also look at the ways in which these machines will affect the relationships between people and machines (the 'socio-technical system').

In a familiar setting, such as the office, new office machinery, such as the word processor, will bring about a large amount of change in the office. Some will be good, some will be bad, but change there will be and people will have to respond to those changes.

We've already started to talk generally about microelectronics, let's now have a look at it and its implications in a little more detail. The term 'microelectronics' is the general name given to all electronic parts and circuits that are made to very small sizes. The most common type of 'microchip' at the moment is the silicon 'chip', while the microprocessor is the most widely found

Assignment 14.1

What changes to *social* relationships in the office do you think that new office technology, such as the word processor, will make?

(Some suggestions are outlined on p. 206.)

type of microchip. It is a tiny 'brain' that is used in the central processing part of a computer.

Today we are all familiar with articles with 'chips' in them even if we may be not so sure exactly what they are and how they work. Calculators, digital watches, TV games, all these, and more, are examples of 'chip'-based goods that have appeared for sale in the shops. All the time the goods get more complicated and more sophisticated, yet they keep going down in price. This fact alone is an incredible aspect of the 'chip'. They are getting cheaper to produce as time goes on and, at the same time, they are getting more complicated and more able to do more and more complex things.

'Chips' are cheap to make and, increasingly, use less energy, less floor space and need less maintenance. Microelectronics now give human beings the ability to handle, deal with and remember vast quantities of information, something that is absolutely vital in today's vast, complex, information-hungry society. However, despite all the advantages that microelectronics can give British firms have been slower than most of their overseas competitors to use them. Indeed, both the CBI and the TUC agree that, if British industry does not invest more of its profits in innovation and new technology, industry will continue to decline.

Although the TUC and the CBI may be agreed at national level, much of the real change will have to take place at local level, in the office and on the factory floor. If this is the case then there will have to be a lot of hard negotiating at local level to bring change about. As the Donovan

'Further advances will be required before unmanned factories become a reality. These will incorporate robots that have vision and touch, and which can assemble things with the precision of a human. The "intelligent" robots would feed machine tools with items and decide for themselves when tools become blunt. In such factories, paper would almost certainly be a thing of the past. Draughtsmen would draw new products with a light pen on a computer terminal: and shape and characteristics of the finished design are then transmitted to the central computer in the flexible system, which instructs the machining centres to make the goods. Computers would file and process information that at present takes the form of stock sheets, order forms and so on.

Source: courtesy 'Towards the unmanned factory' by Peter Marsh, New Scientist, 31 July, 1981

'A word processor can speed up the production of documents enormously. Using traditional methods the production of a letter, for example, means a secretary

taking down the dictation of an executive, typing it out, returning the draft for correction and editing, and then often re-typing the whole letter to incorporate the changes. With a word processor, where the words are typed not on to paper, but on to a video screen, words, phrases, even paragraphs, can be altered without having to re-type the whole thing. The machine can also do a lot of routine copy-typing work such as producing standard letters, contracts, and so on. The result is that a typist can do three times as much work as a typist with a typewriter. Or, put another way, an office with a word processor needs only one typist, not three.*

Source: courtesy New Society, 12 May, 1979

'It is social and economic factors, rather than technological factors, which will mainly determine the future development. . . . The formulation of proper social and economic policies . . . is far more important than the formulation of technical policy. . . .*

Source: courtesy 'The future with microelectronics: forecasting the effects of infor-

mation technology' by I. Barron and R. Curnow, Open University Press, 1979

What changes . . . ?

'Facing up to life with microchips.

'The trade unions should seek full agreement on employment levels, any redundancies that are necessary should be through natural wastage. Union members should also see the need for themselves to be flexible. The demarcation lines will have to disappear and retraining will have to take place. It is therefore essential that inter-union relations are sorted out. The adoption of new technology must be seen as a chance to improve job security and increase job opportunities rather than the negative policy of introducing the same output with less people.

'At company level, trade unions should press home to employers the full implications of new technology. The past record of employers concerning their attitudes to, for example, the health and safety* of their employees is appalling. This past

* The author is writing about the farm industry.

record indicates that employers will see new technology as a chance to improve their profits with reduced labour costs and damn the social consequences. It must be made abundantly clear to all employers that what the trade union movement, and indeed the rest of society, expects from new technology is not a 5 million dole queue but increased leisure and a better life.*

Source: Landworker (the NUAAW* journal) August 1980: from an article by poultry process workers and shop steward, Iain McLaren

Change comes slowly . . .

'British management is moving slowly but none too surely towards the adoption of workers' participation schemes, according to a new survey conducted by the British Institute of Management. But it also concludes that there is still a long way to go in implementing the principles of employee participation, due to disagreement on some of the key issues. . . .

. . . But many companies re-

ported that their managers were unwilling to share authority and showed a lack of good leadership skills, while their employees exhibited a high degree of apathy on the subject and unions tended to be suspicious of both Government and company motives.*

Source: The Guardian, 10 June, 1981

. . . and it is not always for the better!

'Stress is becoming a serious occupational hazard for teachers in almost all countries, according to a study prepared by the International Labour Organization, which describes it as a cause for alarm.

'Research in Britain, Sweden and the United States indicates that up to 25% of teachers face enough stress to affect their health. In North America, the incidence of stress among teachers in large urban schools has produced a condition known as "burnout". They compare it with battle fatigue among soldiers.*

Source: courtesy The Times, 3 July, 1981

Report stressed, it is the local, informal norms and traditions that are important in shaping much of what goes on at the workplace. It is at local level that shop stewards and workers have to face new ways of working and/or possible redundancies that have been brought about by the introduction of new technology. The union sees members disappearing, either into another union or out of the firm altogether. The workers, who are told that the new machinery is better for Britain and the firm, will see things very differently if it means possible redundancy for them. The long-term issues are not so important; the important thing is what is happening in the 'here and now'. The handling of these kinds of changes will put a tremendous pressure on what will be the key roles of union representatives and shop floor supervisors.

At the same time, employers will face some very real challenges. They will have to devote more time, money and effort to new ways of doing things. They must learn to handle change well and easily. Many will have to learn how to work with the workers rather than against them.

A positive approach to change

'Successful adaptation to change requires constructive approaches by both employers and union representatives to allay fears about the consequences of change including:

'good communications so that the necessary responses to technological advances and a changing environment can be secured;

'procedures for effective communication, consultation and negotiation that are sufficiently flexible and responsive to handle problems associated with change;

'in the case of major technical changes, full discussion between management, employees and union representatives before decisions are taken, and joint studies on the best ways to achieve changes in working methods;

'the best possible assurances on security of employment, and avoidance of forced redundancies;

'acceptance where necessary of the need for job changes, retraining and redeployment;

'provision for both management and trade union represent-

Employers in the past have often replaced workers by machines in order to push profits up. Microelectronics offer great opportunities to do just that. They are getting cheaper all the time while workers' wages go on rising. Microchips are small and easy to move about, while they learn quickly and do jobs that human beings do not want to do. Finally, they do not go on strike.

Employers, and the country in general, will have to do more about training and retraining. Unions will have to change their attitudes towards apprenticeships, while workers, particularly the highly capable technicians that will be needed to look after the technology, will expect more in the pay packet in return for the new skills they will have learned. One interesting sideline here is that new technology can have two very different effects on skills. Machines, on the one hand, can make a very skilled job very simple and so the now 'de-skilled' job is much more boring for the worker to do. In the other direction, machines may allow a worker to get and keep a better level of product and performance. His or her job becomes 'enriched'. It is more interesting and worthwhile.

We have seen throughout our discussions how the new electronic technology will bring new changes to all. One of the ways in which it will affect union membership is that there will be a move away from skills in mechanical engineer-

atives of any training necessary for the understanding of new techniques;
'joint monitoring of the effects of major changes.'

Source: 'Improving Industrial Relations' *ACAS, July, 1981*

'Employees should be regularly involved in discussions about the organization of their work. This is not just good industrial practice – though it is certainly that; it is a matter of sound business sense. Inspiration and ideas generated by employees in the workplace are simply too valuable to leave untapped.'

Source: courtesy James Prior quoted in 'Changing Attitudes as well as Jobs' by R. Smith (WRU) Education and Training, April 1981

A page out of the health and safety book

'One "social" factor which could seriously slow down the introduction of word processing is trade union concern over the

health and safety aspects of working with visual display units. Last year, the Trade Union Studies Information Unit in Newcastle published a pamphlet (A Worker's Guide to Display Units) which alleged that they cause eye strain, headaches, stress and backache, and emit possibly dangerous levels of radiation. But the truth is that the long-term effects on health are unknown.'

Source: courtesy Tom Forester, The Typist and the 'smart machine', New Society, 11 September 1980

'Conference notes that the growth in the application of microprocessors is likely to cause significant changes in the structure of employment and that many of the jobs which will be affected may be those currently held by women.

'Conference believes that the gain in productivity resulting from the application of microelectronic technology should be used to enhance the quality of life:

(a)in reducing time spent at work by those employed in the sectors undergoing technical change; and

(b)in expanding employment in services such as health, education, welfare, community development and environmental improvement in order to enhance the quality of life for all. Such changes have a particular importance for women because they form a higher proportion of the labour force of these services.'

Source: courtesy Women's TUC Report, 1979

How powerful in the eighties?

'Power is the ability to influence events in the direction that you wish them to go and therefore we're about power and we've got more or less according to the changing political circumstances and changing industrial circumstances.'

Source: courtesy David Basnett, G&MBATU

Watch the members and the money go!

'The trade union movement and the Labour Party are facing their

worst cash crisis since the 1930s.

'Britain's 3 biggest unions have been badly hit by unemployment. Between them they have lost more than a million members since Margaret Thatcher won power in May 1979.

'Because it gets most of its money from the unions Labour is also feeling the pinch. It has an overdraft of £500 000 and a current deficit of £270 000. Biggest victim of unemployment is the mighty Transport and General Workers' Union. It has lost 400 000 members in 2 years. That's £6,000,000 in income.

'Mr David Basnett's General and Municipal Workers' Union has lost 100 000 members in three years and is down to 880 000. This represents an annual drop of £1 500 000 in subscriptions.

'The Amalgamated Union of Engineering Workers, Britain's second biggest union, has slumped from one and a quarter million members to about a million in three years. The drop in subscriptions is costing the AUEW £75 000 a year.'

Source: courtesy Daily Mirror, 31 May, 1982

ing and a move towards electric; and electronic engineering skills. This will mean good news for electrical unions (such as EETPU) but will almost certainly pose problems for some of the traditional engineering unions such as the AUEW. With jobs and members lost because of the world recession and the introduction of new technology, and with problems of a political kind, the 1980s look as if they are going to be difficult years for the unions.

One trend that seems certain to continue is that the workplace and the shopsteward will have more power. If the number of members go down, unions cannot afford to appoint full-time officers and so they will have to rely on the unpaid volunteers. Many of the smaller unions will think about merging since that will be the only way that they can survive. In the eighties 'big will have to be beautiful'. There are over twenty unions in the public service sector (for example, within the health and education services) and some of these may well decide to merge. There are some interesting questions here: who might merge with whom? The 'big boys' of the union movement (TGWU, G&MBU, AUEW and ASTMS) what will happen to them in the next ten years? They will have to change. Their leaders have a key job to do. They will have to change and adapt both themselves and their unions. They will have to decide wisely when it comes to carrying out decisions and exercising power.

In this, the final chapter of the book, we have looked at some of the aspects of change in industrial relations over the next few years. We

Assignment 14.2

Change and the unions

Some unions are quite happy to change: some are less so! At one end of the scale are unions like the Post Office Engineering Union and the Electrical, Electronic, Telecommunication and Plumbing Union (EETPU). They can see advantages for their members and are generally happy to take on developments in microelectronics. Some unions, for example, the Association of Professional, Executive, Clerical and Computer Staff (APEX) and the banking union (BIFU), realize that in their areas of work new technology will give fewer jobs but that to obstruct change would do their members no good at all. At the other end of the scale are traditional craft unions, for example, the printing unions such as the NGA, who feel threatened by new technology. They will fight all the way to make sure that they do not 'lose out' by change.

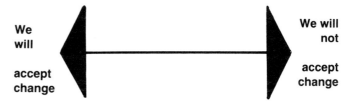

We will accept change ⟵——————⟶ **We will not accept change**

Make a list of other unions and think about (and, where possible, discuss) how keen other unions are to accept change.

Assignment 14.3

We have seen how the patterns of trade union membership are likely to change as some industries become more important while others become less so (see Chapter 13): which unions do you think will become stronger, which weaker, in the next few years? Explain your ideas.

'As the technological revolution develops we will see the gradual elimination of white collar/blue collar differences in conditions of employment. . . . Comparisons between blue collar and white collar workers have narrowed enormously within BL over the last 10–15 years. . . . I think this is something we are going to see more of.

'We'll see changes in working patterns. We're obviously going to see three and four day weeks associated maybe with six day working for plant. I think the great problem will be to reconcile the need to keep expensive capital equipment working with the wishes of people to have more time. I think we've got to work towards five or six day working for plant and three or four day working for people, and new patterns of shift working and so on.'

Source: courtesy Pat Lowry, formerly Director of Personnel and External Affairs, BL Limited, currently Chairman ACAS

Assignment 14.4

A report on the impact that microprocessors will have on French life (the 'Nora Report') suggests that, in the future, there will be the following three major groups in the French economy:

1 Manufacturing industries, once large employers, will decline and die. These industries, such as textiles, will have 'gone under' to the intense competition from 'Third World' countries where the cost of labour is cheap.
2 The second group will be made up of large numbers of people, who are unemployed, but are being given useful jobs to do within the community, along the lines of YOPs and other MSC projects, voluntary and social work, etc.
3 The last group will be made up of small, 'go-ahead' companies in the high technology business. These will be the profit makers, although the competition will be tough.

What jobs will disappear if the Nora Report is* correct; and what jobs will be created? Do you think that what Nora suggests could possibly occur in Britain? Back up your answer with evidence. Make a list of the skills you think people will need to get and hold on to a job in the future.

* For help with this assignment see p. 195 for some further information.

have looked at changes that will affect workers, unions and management. We have seen how new technology will bring marked changes to our industrial, as well as our everyday, life. There are bound to be changes in the law affecting industrial relations. Attitudes will change, some for the good, some for the worse. As we said at the beginning of this chapter 'all is flux, nothing is stationary'. It therefore seems a fitting point in the book to reflect on a more personal change, and that is your own change as you have read your way through the book. Ask yourself, what do I know now that I didn't when I started reading this book? Think about the ways in which your thinking and, hopefully, your actions, have changed now that you have reached this point. Was the journey worthwhile? I hope it was, and I hope even more that it is not the end of your journey into industrial relations; it is simply the beginning of another one.

Assignment 14.5

Read the history of the British Shipbuilding industry on this page and make a list of the technological changes that have taken place in the industry since the sixteenth century.

Assignment 14.6

Add in any more advantages/disadvantages about new technology that you discover.

'On the basis of a moving track where there's a (car) body coming off every 45 seconds, 1 minute, 1½ minutes, or whatever, you can imagine the speed with which an operator has to work in the small operation that he does, putting a wheel on, or two wheels on one side, tightening up bolts all day long . . . the monotony of that particular job is soul destroying in itself.

'People have to understand that this is part of the problem; that is why Volvo of Sweden, for instance . . . have tried to develop a different system of working in that you get group working or you get a much greater operation to perform. In other words you perform a number of tasks, either on the track or off the track where you can get a group of people doing a large proportion of operations and that takes the monotony away from "one every minute or whatever".'

Source: courtesy E. Bone, National Officer, TGWU

Technological changes in the ship-building industry

'Until the sixteenth century Britain was not an outstanding shipbuilding and seafaring nation but during the Tudor period, both began to assume a new importance. In those days, shipbuilding was largely confined to the estuaries of Southern England, where timber supplies were readily available.

'In 1612, James I granted a charter to the Worshipful Company of Shipwrights – an organization still in existence today – and charged it to raise the standard of knowledge and practice among shipbuilders. The industry's growth was accompanied by the founding and development of a number of learned societies (for example, the Royal Institution of Naval Architects, the Institute of Marine Engineers, etc.) to foster the growth of maritime knowledge.

'Shipbuilding as a craft gradually improved itself from hard-won experience but there was little advance in structural methods and scientific principles of ship design until towards the middle of the nineteenth century. This was an all-important period of progress, embracing the transition from **wood** to **iron**, and then **steel**, for **hull construction**, and also the change from **sail** to **steam** propulsion.

'Both the iron and engineering industries were well established in the middle of the last century and the use of iron plates enabled larger ships, with greater carrying capacities, to be built. In 1885, Lloyd's Register of Shipping published its rules for iron shipbuilding and followed, two years later, with rules for steel built ships, allowing a great reduction in weight.

'By the end of the century, **steel** had completely superseded iron in **hull construction**. The introduction of iron, then steel, led to the industry's move *north to the banks of suitable navigable rivers, near the sources of iron ore and coal.*

'The second quarter of this century saw the start of the trend away from **coal** *to* **oil** *as the prime mover in steam ships, and about the same time the beginnings of a parallel trend, which today has seen* **steam** *propulsion largely replaced by the oil-burning marine* **diesel** *engine.*

'Today, the shipbuilding industry is largely concentrated on the North East coast, on Clydeside, and in the North West at Barrow-in-Furness, and on Merseyside. Other ship-yards are located in the East of Scotland, and around the East, South and South West coasts of England.'

Source: courtesy British Shipbuilders

Recommended reading for Chapter 14

1 *Unions and change since 1945* by C. Baker and P. Caldwell (Pan, 1981)

2 The way individuals change is very well described in:

Growing through Life Life by R. Rapoport and R. Rapoport (Harper & Row, 1980)

Books that you have read and found useful should be added below

Here are some suggested answers to Assignment 14.1.
(N.B: Some of the 'pros' and 'cons' are interchangeable. It all depends on your own viewpoint.)

'Pros'

The operator is increasingly likely to have more autonomy over his own movements and work programme and will be less paced by the machine system. (S)he may also spend less time in unpleasant environments.

People normally take a pride in their work and better control systems will mean that higher quality output will be obtained more easily.

With more information more quickly available there will be increased data from which potentially better decisions can be taken with more opportunity to try out alternatives, so increasing the feeling of a job well done.

More variety and responsibility in workers' jobs.

Much more flexibility in organizing the working day, week or year should also become available.

Better communication may reduce the need for travel for meetings or even to attend an office at all.

Increased financial return should be available to fund other improvements.

'Cons'

New technology will cause fear of job security.

Automatic machines may take over work which needed traditional skills. Relatively untrained people will now be able to produce an output of the same standard and as quickly as a highly trained operator once could. With more expensive equipment there will be pressure to get maximum return on the capital expenditure made. This will mean pressure to extend hours of operation into shift working and other 'unsocial' hours of work. (See extract on p. 204.)

More information more easily distributed gives greater opportunity for control of individuals' work by others. This may seem like spying.

With greater emphasis on change it may become general practice for learning and training to become a continuous process throughout the working lives of increasing numbers of workers.

People working at home terminals may feel increased social isolation.

Source: courtesy R. G. Sell, Microelectronics and the Quality of Working Life, WRU, 1980

Reading list

Good, introductory books that you might like to read and buy to develop your interest in industrial relations are as follows:

1 *Ernest Bevin* by Mark Stephens (TGWU, 1981)
2 *Marx for Beginners* and *Capitalism for Beginners* (Writers and Readers Publishing Co-operative, 1981)
3 *National Union Mineworkers (Derbyshire Area) 1880–1980* (NUM Derbyshire, 1980)
4 *The History of the TUC 1868–1968* (TUC, 1968)
   (*a*) (The TUC also publishes a good deal of information for schools and colleges: contact them at Publications Department, Trades Union Congress, Congress House, Great Russell Street, London WC1B 3LS).
   (*b*) The Labour Party at 144–152 Walworth Road, London SE17 1JT also publishes a large amount of useful material.
   (*c*) If you are particularly interested in the history of the Trade Union movement, and the Labour Party contact the National Museum of Labour History who produce some excellent materials. Contact them at NMLH, Limehouse Town Hall, Commercial Road, London E14.
5 *The Story of the TGWU* (TGWU, 1975)
6 *To Build Jerusalem* by John Gorman (Scorpion Publications, 1980)

More difficult books that will deepen your knowledge of industrial relations:

Democracy at Work by Patrick Burns and Mel Doyle (Pan, 1981)
Getting Organised by Alan Cambell and John McIlroy (Pan, 1981)
Health and Safety at Work by Dave Eva and Ron Oswald (Pan, 1981)
Strikes by Richard Hyman (Fontana, 1979)
The Fifth Estate by Robert Taylor (Pan, 1980)
The Politics of Industrial Relations by Colin Crouch (Fontana, 1979)
Trade Unions by Kevin Hawkins (Hutchinson, 1981)
Understanding Industrial Relations by D. Farnham and J. Pimlott (Macmillan, 1983)
Unions and Change Since 1945 by Chris Baker and Peter Caldwell (Pan, 1981)
Women and Work by Chris Aldred (Pan, 1981)
The Politics of the Judiciary by J. A. G. Griffith (Fontana, 1979)

Collective Bargaining by Clive Jenkins & Barrie Sherman (Routledge and Kegan Paul, 1977)
Trade Unions: the logic of collective action C. Crouch (Fontana, 1982)
The Management of Organisations H. G. Hicks (McGraw Hill, 1972)

Index

Names of trade unions are referred to by their abbreviations in the index. There is also a general heading, 'Trade unions'.